IMMIGRANTS
TO THE
MIDDLE COLONIES

A Consolidation of Ship Passenger Lists
and Associated Data
from The New York Genealogical
and Biographical Record

Edited by Michael Tepper

GENEALOGICAL PUBLISHING CO., INC.
BALTIMORE   1978

Excerpted from
selected volumes of
*The New York Genealogical
and Biographical Record,*
1879-1970

Reprinted with a New Introduction and Indexes
Genealogical Publishing Co., Inc.
Baltimore, 1978

Library of Congress Catalogue Card Number 77-15281
International Standard Book Number 0-8063-0792-7

Made in the United States of America

CONTENTS

Appendix

INTRODUCTION

This is the third collection of ship passenger lists to be excerpted from a representative journal, in this case *The New York Genealogical and Biographical Record*. Like the preceding volumes, based respectively upon *The Pennsylvania Magazine of History and Biography* and *The New England Historical and Genealogical Register*, the articles in this collection are founded upon citations in Harold Lancour's *Bibliography of Ship Passenger Lists, 1538-1825* (3rd ed. rev.: N.Y., 1963). Lancour's contribution has been too often acclaimed to warrant an additional chorus, though one is tempted to remark upon the extraordinary reach of his otherwise modest book. It is perhaps sufficient to observe that Lancour's bibliography enables the researcher to ascertain the extent of existing literature on ship passenger lists and to reduce it to requisite proportions. The consolidation and reprinting of articles on ship passenger lists from periodical literature—uniting articles treating a common class of records in a single, convenient volume—is but a means of facilitating access to some of the scarcest and least accessible material designated in the Lancour bibliography.

What first strikes the reader about the passenger lists consolidated from *NYGBR* is that better than half of them are not, properly speaking, ship passenger lists at all, but rather reconstructed, or inferrential, lists of passengers, most of which, to be sure, are founded upon reliable authority, some few even providing evidence linking passengers to specific vessels. These lists approximate ship passenger lists somewhat in the way an early tax list approximates a census of inhabitants, and in lieu of original records, which, in the majority of cases, are no longer extant, we are happy enough to draw sustenance from them. Sensible of the limitations of early ship records, Lancour provides us with citations to a good many published records which cannot by any construction of the term be accounted ship passenger lists and are at best documented lists of early arrivals. The sub-title of his book—*Being a Guide to Published Lists of Early Immigrants to North America*—admits of sufficient latitude to justify the inclusion of lists with no more palpable connection to a ship than the insinuation that all early immigrants perforce submitted to a voyage by sea.

Until Congress in 1819 approved legislation mandating the keeping of customs records—from which developed the customs passenger

lists which until recently were housed in the National Archives[1]—
there was no uniform procedure for dealing with the arrival of immigrants, nor any system of registration. Admittedly, in 1798 an act of
Congress required masters of vessels arriving in United States ports
to file lists of aliens aboard ship with the collectors of customs, who
were then to submit periodic reports to the Department of State, but
these lists have not survived. Only customs lists of aliens for the ports
of Salem and Beverly, Massachusetts, 1798-1800 are known to be
among the records formerly in the National Archives.[2] As early as
1727, however, the Commonwealth of Pennsylvania had enacted
legislation designed to regulate the influx of foreigners (i.e. non-
British subjects—more specifically Germans, broadly and sometimes
mistakenly described as "Palatines"), and the resulting records—
Captains' Lists, and lists deriving from Oaths of Allegiance and Oaths
of Abjuration—constitute the basis of Ralph B. Strassburger and
William J. Hinke's *Pennsylvania German Pioneers*, a seminal work
on German immigration into Pennsylvania, perhaps the most important collection of ship passenger lists ever published.[3] Instances
of this kind are isolated, though, and except for Philadelphia, port
records prior to 1820 are notoriously sketchy.

Some records, to be sure, were kept by the country from which
the passengers emigrated. In England, for example, passenger lists
were maintained for reasons of administration and control, and may
be met with in such diverse and esoteric records as the Bristol
Apprentice Books, the papers of the Custom House (such as remain),
lists of transported rebels and convicts, in Treasury records, and lists
of signers of the Oaths of Allegiance and Supremacy, which established the emigrant's conformance to the discipline of the Church of
England and to the King as temporal head of the Church. Consider-
ing the lamentable destruction in 1814 of the Custom House records,
the indifference and negligence of petty officials, and the cumulative
depredations of time, even these records are imperfect, and we are

[1] I am informed by James Walker of the National Archives that the original
customs passenger lists were transferred in the spring of 1977 to Temple
University in Philadelphia. Microfilm copies of the original lists are, of course,
available at the National Archives. According to Mr. Walker, however, a
number of the original lists were never microfilmed, though in some instances
a transcript or abstract was filmed in lieu of the original.

[2] See Mrs. Georgie A. Hill, "Passenger Arrivals at Salem and Beverly,
Mass., 1798-1800" in *Passengers to America*, ed. Michael Tepper (Baltimore:
Genealogical Publishing Co., Inc., 1977).

[3] Subtitled *A Publication of the Original Lists of Arrivals in the Port of
Philadelphia from 1727 to 1808*, ed. William J. Hinke, 3 vols. (Norristown,
Penna., 1934). Reprinted in two volumes, omitting the volume of facsimile
signatures (Baltimore: Genealogical Publishing Co., Inc., 1975).

frequently obliged to fall back upon immigration records which were compiled at one or two removes from the port.

Chief among these immigration records, perhaps, are those which derive from official sources, i.e. records compiled by appropriate authorities in compliance with various statutes, ordinances, or depart mental directives. These would include records arising from various colonial acts of naturalization (such records crop up in most of the Colonies, and lists deriving from the naturalization records of New Jersey and New York are included in this collection), from oaths of allegiance, from articles of apprenticeship and indenture (again Philadelphia boasts the most complete records), and from affidavits and petitions.

While early immigration records deriving from official sources carry an imprimatur of authority, they are not necessarily definitive, and, like other records, are subject to error, omission, and inconsistency. Moreover, some official records—and here, among others, we might mention those founded upon the various naturalization acts—were compiled so long after the immigrant's arrival in this country that some of the information regarding his transit must necessarily be thrown in doubt. As types of inferrential passenger lists, such records are markedly inferior to the more contemporaneous records which derive from documents of source. These consist of ships' logs, account books, captains' lists, cargo lists, debt lists, manifests, baggage lists, and formal agreements of passage—records which have a direct bear ing on the actual voyage, literally placing the immigrant in the milieu of the ship.

Another category of passenger records a step or so removed from the ship, though frequently consulted for evidence of passage, would include newspaper notices of arrival. Still other evidence can be found in the records of the great trading companies such as the Virginia Company and the West India Company. And of a miscel laneous nature, references to embarkation and arrival can be found among land records—in patents and deeds—and among certain court records—wills, suits, and depositions, for example. These references constitute a heterogeneous group, however, and cannot reasonably be considered passenger lists.

Of the fifteen articles included in this consolidation from *NYGBR*, only half may be accounted proper ship passenger lists—some of them, no doubt, admitting of too liberal an interpretation of the phrase. The others, mainly inferrential passenger lists, consist of lists adapted from records of naturalization, waivers of citizenship, printed sources, and miscellaneous colonial records. Even the Board of Trade lists, compiled by John Tribbeko and George Ruperti, certainly the centerpiece of this collection, fall somewhat foul of a literal construction of the phrase ship passenger list.[4] The Board of Trade lists, compiled at the instigation of the Secretary of State, Charles Spencer, third Earl of Sunderland, are enumerations of Palatines lately arrived in London from Holland and taken at encampments around London in the days and weeks following their arrival. Hence a material loss in contemporaneity. By arrangement with the Government, some few of the Palatines dispersed and settled in the British Isles and did not emigrate to North America. None is identified with a ship. On balance, however, it must be admitted that the Board of Trade lists, like some others in this collection, constitute acceptable substitutes for actual ship passenger lists and, in the absence of alternatives, should be judged on their merits.

There is little wonder, in a journal devoted to New York genealogy and biography, that articles on ship passenger lists should focus attention on immigration to colonial New York which, under Dutch jurisdiction, embraced New Jersey and parts of Pennsylvania, including the area designated the South River, now the state of Delaware. While about half of the articles in this collection deal with Dutch and Walloon immigrants, others are concerned with immigrants of German and English provenance, and some few touch upon Huguenots and Jews. Those articles dealing with immigrants to New Netherland are necessarily fixed on the period of the 17th century, and indeed only four articles in the collection enlarge upon 18th-century arrivals, though these four encompass lists of considerable magnitude. In point of time, the earliest recorded immigration—Dutch, of course—occurs in the 1620s. The latest date of record, concerning immigrants of German, Dutch, French, and Jewish origins, is for the year 1769 and is the terminal date in Richard J. Wolfe's article on naturalizations in colonial New York. (As something of an afterthought, however, we might point out that the second of the two articles in the Appendix, "A Passenger List for the Ship *William*," contains a brief list of Scottish and English immigrants bound for New York in 1817. This article originally appeared in the number for July 1970 and was therefore not cited in the Lancour bibliography, the most recent edition of which was published in 1963.)

Consolidation of the articles, however—themselves often an amalgam of diverse parts—should not suggest contents of a uniform character. As is customary with ship passenger lists the data provided

---

[4] These lists appear in the article "Lists of Germans from the Palatinate Who Came to England in 1709," which was also published as an offset by GPC in 1965.

consists of an uneven mixture of references to ships, ports and dates of embarkation and arrival, wives, children, age, religion, occupation, and places of origin and residence. Documentation is almost equally uneven, spare and copious by turns. The articles also vary in their arrangement of data, some reflecting a chronological approach, others alphabetical, but none suffers thereby, since all 5,000 immigrants are conveniently cited in the Index of Names. Ships, too, are handily located by reference to the Index of Ships.

It would be well at this point to say something, however brief, concerning the bibliography of some of the more characteristic passenger lists in this collection. Few of the lists, at least in published form, are unique, and a glance at other published versions would not be inappropriate and, indeed, may even increase our enthusiasm for the lists as herein constituted. In Charles B. Moore's article, "Shipwrights, Fishermen, Passengers from England," for example, passengers cited also appear, in sundry manifestations, in the published researches of Savage, Drake, Hotten, Somerby, and Banks. Although the author is silent on the matter, his article is presumably based on records originally in the custody of the Master of the Rolls—the very same consulted by the other writers—which appear to derive from Oaths of Allegiance and Supremacy and from church certificates of conformity. Moore's article, however, is in the main restricted to passengers who can be traced to Long Island, to Southold, in particular, and in so narrowing its range is able to concentrate attention on details altogether out of the reach of the other published accounts.

Almost the whole of the passenger list in A.J.F. Van Laer's "Settlers of the Colony of Rensselaerswyck, 1637" is discovered in Edward B. O'Callaghan's *History of New Netherland*[5] in the section headed "Names of Settlers in Rensselaerswyck from 1630 to 1646" (reprinted in entirety in the *Year Book of the Holland Society of New York*) (1896); and all of the passengers are noted in Van Laer's own *Van Rensselaer Bowier Manuscripts* (Albany, 1908) in the chapter entitled "Settlers of Rensselaerswyck, 1630-1658," which was published as an offprint in 1965 by GPC. The present Van Laer article is based on a memorandum which was discovered two years after the publication of the *Van Rensselaer Bowier Manuscripts,* and while the passengers named are the same as those appearing in the list of passengers of the ship *Rensselaerswyck* in that book, the memorandum, in Van Laer's words, "affords . . . a means of testing the accuracy of the printed list."

[5] New York, 1846, I, 433-441. Reprinted Spartanburg, S.C.: The Reprint Company, 1966.

Yet more curious is the list of passengers contained in Van Brunt Bergen's "A List of Early Immigrants to New Netherland," which purports to be a consolidation from the manuscripts of Teunis G. Bergen of the passengers identified in three previously published lists —all by O'Callaghan—specifically, "Names of Settlers in Rensselaerswyck from 1630 to 1646," cited above, and "The Roll off Those Who Haue Taken the Oath off Allegiance in the Kings County in the Province off New Yorke . . . 1687" and "Early Immigrants to New Netherland; 1657-1664," both printed in *The Documentary History of the State of New-York.*[6] The Bergen list is coded with the O'Callaghan lists to designate vessels of conveyance, but it does not always correspond with them in matters of transcription, and one of the O'Callaghan lists, "The Roll," is only partially represented in the Bergen list. Speculation about the origin of the data in the Bergen list is perhaps idle—whether it derives from O'Callaghan's printed lists or from the manuscript source material from which he worked, or a combination of the two—but one is nevertheless curious about the method of selection. It is probable, however, that either Teunis Bergen or Van Brunt Bergen consulted the original source material, since the list incorporates entries for 1654-1657 which were omitted by O'Callaghan in his "Early Immigrants to New Netherland; 1657-1664," but which do, in fact, exist in the original account book from which the O'Callaghan list derives.[7]

In any event, the three O'Callaghan lists were reprinted in the *Year Book of the Holland Society of New York* (1896) and the list entitled "Early Immigrants to New Netherland; 1657-1664" was subsequently published in a revised translation by A. J. F. Van Laer in the 1902 *Year Book of the Holland Society of New York.* The article contributed by Rosalie Fellows Bailey, "Emigrants to New Netherland," based on the notes of the historian James Riker, is yet a further refinement and clarification of this same list, adding, according to

---

[6] Albany, 1849, I, 659-661 and Albany, 1850, III, 52-63 respectively.

[7] Dr. Kenn Stryker-Rodda, who kindly provided the editor with an index to Dutch proper names which appear in four of the articles incorporated in this collection, writes: "I am concerned about the Bergen list (pp. 31ff). Van Brunt Bergen was not a Dutch scholar. Consequently, many of the "Van" names he listed never occur as such, the "Van" indicating place of origin. (On p. 48, Van Aerts Daalen became Vanarsdale, and Van Amach remained as Van Amack, but the Van Amersfoorts, Van Amsterdams, Van Edams and more than two-thirds of the others would never have been listed under the Vs by Teunis Bergen. Their names appear in other lists under their patronymics.)"

And on a related matter, Dr. Stryker-Rodda observes: "Most of the omissions from "The Roll" in the Bergen list are accounted for by the men's being natives, or the name's being disguised."

Miss Bailey, "new names, new marriages and relationships, new occupations or employers, new residences and deaths."

A much less bewildering picture emerges from an account of Gordon Ireland's "Servants to Foreign Plantations from Bristol, England, 1654-1686." This article consists of a nearly complete abstract of those portions of the Bristol record books known as "Servants to Foreign Plantations" concerning emigrants to Maryland, Virginia, New York, and Pennsylvania. Names of the emigrants in "Servants to Foreign Plantations," transcribed by R. Hargreaves-Mawdsley, were first published in 1929 in a volume entitled *Bristol and America: A Record of the First Settlers in the Colonies of North America, 1654-1685*,[8] which work failed to provide a number of substantive particulars embodied in the original records, omitting, commonly, the date of entry, place of origin, bondmaster's name, and names of ships and ship masters. With regard only to the 155 passengers bound for the above-named colonies, our article redresses these shortcomings. It might be observed that the contributor elsewhere gives much the same consideration to the servants bound for New England, his article appearing in *The New England Historical and Genealogical Register* (XCIII) and reprinted in *Passengers to America*.[9]

We have already made some preliminary observations about the Board of Trade lists appearing in the article "Lists of Germans from the Palatinate Who Came to England in 1709," but something of their subsequent publishing history is worth adumbrating, if only to demonstrate the superiority of the lists in this present collection. Apart from the GPC reprint, which itself suffers from want of an index, these lists appear in an alphabetical and curiously abridged form in Lou D. McWethy's *The Book of Names; Especially Relating to the Early Palatines and the First Settlers in the Mohawk Valley*.[10] Although copied by Mr. Boyd Ehle from the original records in the library of the British Museum, as were the lists in our article (though by whom we are not informed), there are serious discrepancies in transcription—omissions not the least of them. Perhaps the most expedient means of resolving these discrepancies, short of visiting the British Museum, is to consult Walter Allen Knittle's *Early Eighteenth Century Palatine Emigration*,[11] wherein the first of the lists appears as Appendix B in an alphabetical though much abbreviated form, lacking references to age, occupation, and religion. Knittle was a close

[8] Reprinted Baltimore: Genealogical Publishing Co., Inc., 1969.
[9] Baltimore, 1977.
[10] St. Johnsville, N.Y., 1933. Reprinted Baltimore: Genealogical Publishing Co., Inc., 1969.
[11] Philadelphia, 1937. Reprinted Baltimore: Genealogical Publishing Co., Inc., 1976.

student of Palatine emigration, however, and in spite of the conciseness of his list, it is well regarded. Knittle chose to include only the first of the Board of Trade lists in his book because the persons enumerated are not named in "The Embarkation Lists from Holland," constituting Appendix C. It might be inferred, therefore, that persons named in the other three Board of Trade lists turn up in the Embarkation Lists, though this is mistaken, for only about half of them appear there. (The remaining Palatines, presumably, made their way to London out of the reach of official enumerators.) These Embarkation Lists were prepared in Rotterdam by the Dutch commissioners Hendrik van Toren and Jan van Gent and reflect the influence of Dutch orthography on German names. Interestingly enough, the Board of Trade lists, compiled in London by the German ministers Tribbeko and Ruperti, bear evidence of anglicization.

Still another article in this collection, the last, save only the two brief articles in the Appendix, is an improvement, in part, on a previously published work. Richard J. Wolfe's "The Colonial Naturalization Act of 1740; With a List of Persons Naturalized in New York Colony, 1740-1769" is a more complete and comprehensive record of New York naturalizations than that found in Montague S. Giuseppi's *Naturalization of Foreign Protestants in the American and West Indian Colonies (Pursuant to Statute 13 George II, c. 7),*[12] where an imperfect copy of the present list was used as a source. The Wolfe article is based on the original record book of naturalizations maintained by the Secretary of the Colony of New York between 1740 and 1769 (now in the possession of the New York Public Library[13]); the Giuseppi work on a copy of the returns transmitted to the Commissioners of Trade and Plantations in London—at least two stages removed from the original records. And, so Wolfe observes, "Because the information recorded in the original is so much more complete and obviously more correct than the transcriptions printed in the Giuseppi volume, it is published here." In common with other articles in this collection, then, the Wolfe article is a refinement and extention of existing literature, of which, it is hoped, the genealogist may make modest use, and for which purpose this consolidation has been undertaken.

[12] Volume XXIV of *Publications of the Huguenot Society of London* (London, 1921). Reprinted Baltimore: Genealogical Publishing Co., Inc., 1969.

[13] Coincidentally, this same manuscript volume was one of the chief sources employed in a recently compiled work by Kenneth Scott and Kenn Stryker-Rodda—*Denizations, Naturalizations, and Oaths of Allegiance in Colonial New York* (Baltimore: Genealogical Publishing Co., Inc., 1975).

ACKNOWLEDGEMENTS

The editor is indebted to the Board of Trustees of The New York Genealogical and Biographical Society for permission to reproduce articles from the *Record*; to the indefatigable Elizabeth Petty Bentley for her work on the index of names; and to Dr. Kenn Stryker-Rodda for his invaluable assistance in indexing Dutch names.

NEW YORK "KNICKERBOCKER" FAMILIES; ORIGIN AND SETTLEMENT.

By JOEL N. ENO, A.M.

Though Verrezzani in 1524 probably entered the lower bay, Henry Hudson, captain in the employ of the Dutch East India Company, in Sept., 1609, guided the first ship, the *Half Moon*, past Manhattan, and up the Hudson river nearly to Albany. The company began a trading post, called Mannahatta (Manhattan) in 1614; and in 1615 another at Fort Orange (now Albany). In 1624, the Dutch West India Company made a permanent settlement on Manhattan; it sent Peter Minuits as governor, who arrived 1625 with a company who settled Breukelen (Brooklyn). In 1629, the West India Company inaugurated a system of settlement by what are now called manors, somewhat like the plantation system of Virginia, with Wouter Van Twiller as agent, to buy tracts from the Indians, and then to grant to the leaders of colonies, who were called patroons, each a manor with 16 miles front on the rivers, and extending back as far as needed. Minuits was recalled in 1633, and led a Swedish colony to Delaware in 1638; Van Twiller governed till 1638, Wm. Kieft from 1638 till 1647, and Peter Stuyvesant from 1647 till 1664, when the Dutch surrendered their claims to the Duke of York. Col. Nichols governed till 1667; Lovelace, from 1667 till 1674, succeeded in Oct., 1674, by Sir Edmund Andros; he by Col. Thomas Dongan, 1683; he in 1688 by Francis Nicholson, who in 1689 was imprisoned by Jacob Leisler till March, 1691, when Col. Sloughter, the new royal governor, arrived; Fletcher succeeded in 1692; the Earl of Bellamont in 1698, and so on, a succession of royal governors till the Revolution. The Dutch settlements were mostly confined to the Hudson valley below Troy, and western Long Island, with a few in northeastern New Jersey, for the early immigration was not nearly as large nor as widely distributed as that to Massachusetts, though drawn from the whole south coast of the North Sea. The settlers belonged mainly to the Dutch Reformed church, Presbyterian in organization, but there was general toleration of religious beliefs.

Barheit, Jeronimus Hanse, m. at Albany, 1684. Barkeloo (Borckelloo, Borkelo), Wyllem Jansen van; his family originally from Bor(c)keloe, a community near Zutphen in Gelderland; he came to New Amsterdam before 1662; settled at Flatlands, L. I., 1683. Beeckman, Martin Hendricksen, from Hamelwaard in the Duchy of Bremen, 1638, to serve the patroon Van Rensselaer at Rensselaerwyck near Albany; 3 sons and 3 daus. Beekman, Wilhelmus, from Hasselt in Overyssel, Holland, settled at New Amsterdam, 1647. Benson, Dirck, from Groningen to New Amsterdam, 1648; to Beverwyck (Albany), 1654. Bergen, Hans Hansen van (alias H. H. van Bergen in Noorwegen, and H. H. Noorman=H. H. v. B. of Norway, or H. H. the Norseman), via Holland to New Amsterdam, 1633. Bergen, Martin Gerretsen

1

van, from Holland to Beverwyck, 1630; descendants on the Hudson, above the Highlands. Bleecker, Jan Janse, 1658 from Meppel in Overyssel to Beverwyck. Bogardus, Everardus, 1633 in New Amsterdam. Bogart, Cornelis van der, from Schoenderwoert, near Leerdam, Holland, before 1640 to Rensselaerwyck; children in Albany. His brother, Gysbert, was in New Amsterdam, 1640; in Catskill before 1661; four sons. Boerum, Remsen (van) (son of Remmert Jansen Vanderbeek), in Brooklyn,1647. Bontecou, (Du. Bontekoe, brindled cow), Pierre, via France and England to New York, 1689. Brevoort, Hendrick J., 1630 at New Amersfoort, L. I. Brokaw=Broucard, Bourger (Huguenot), from Mannheim in the Rhine Palatinate to Bushwick, L. I., 1684. Brower=Brouwer Kerckhoven, Adam, 1647 in Brooklyn. Buskirk, see Van Buskirk.

Conover=Couwenhoven, Wolfert Gerretsen van, from Amersfoort in Utrecht province to Rensselaerwyck, 1630; orig. from Couwenhoven or Kauwenhoven, a village 9 miles southwest of Amersfoort.' Cortelyou=Corteljau, Jacques (Hug.), to New Utrecht, N. Y., 1652; at Flatbush, L. I, 1684. Cuyler, Hendrick, 1664, Albany.

De Forest, Henry and Isaac (sons of Jan), from Amsterdam, to Harlem, N. Y., 1636. Delamater (de la Maitre), Claude, from Artois, France, via Amsterdam, to Flatbush, L. I. Delancey=Étienne de Lanci, Caen, Normandy, 1686, to N. Y. De Peyster, Johannes, from Haarlem, Holland, to New Amsterdam about 1645. Devoe=De Veaux, Frederick, in N. Y., 1675. Dewees, Cornelius, Lewis and Willem, three sons of Gerrett Hendrickse De Wees (the orphan), born at Leeuwarden, Friesland; they were in Germantown, Pa., in 1690. Douw, Volckert Janszen, from Leeuwarden to Beverwyck, 1638. Duyckinck=Duyckingh, Evert, Holland, to New Netherland.

Flagler=Fleigler, ——, from Westheim in Franconia, 1711, to Holland; 1735 to Dutchess Co., N. Y. Flypsen, Frederick, 1647 Bolswaert, Friesland, to New Amsterdam, ancestor of Philipse family. Frelinghuysen, Rev. Theodorus Jacobus, from Friesland to the vicinity of Somerville, N. J., 1720.

Gansevoort, ——, from Groningen, Holland, to Albany. Girard, Stephen, born near Bordeaux, France; to N. Y., 1774; Philadelphia, 1776. Goelette, Francois, from France to New York City, 1676. Groesbeck, Claes, Rotterdam to Beverwyck, 1624; N. Y. City, 1696. Gouverneur, Nic. Pierre, 1663, New Amsterdam. Gulick, Hendrik, Netherlands to New Netherland, 1653.

Hardenbergh, Gerrit Janse, 1667 at Albany; of Hardenberg, town, Overyssel. Hasbrouck, Isaac, from France (orig. Hazebrouck, in dept. Nord=Flemish Haesebroek), to Ulster Co., N. Y., 1673. Haughwout (Hoogwood or Hauwert, village near Hoorn in N. Holland), Pietersen van, to N. Y. Hegeman, Adriaan, from Amsterdam to Flatbush, L. I., 1650 or 1651. Hoagland= Hoogland, Cornelis Dircksen, Holland to New Amsterdam before 1645; Hooglant, Dirck Janse, m. in N. Y., 1662 (orig. from Hoogland, a village near Amersfoort). Hoffman, Martin H., born in Esthonia; 1657 New Netherland. Houghtaling=Du. Hoogteling, Mathys, 1676 Albany=high begetting. Hun, Harmen T., 1661, Beverwyck, from Amersfoort, Hol.

Kip=Kype, Henry de, Amsterdam to New Amsterdam, 1635.
Knickerbocker=Knickerbacker, Herman Jansen, from Friesland
to New Amsterdam, before 1700. Koeymans, Barent Pieterse,
1636 from Utrecht to Coeymans.

Lansing, Gerret, from Hasselt in Overyssel, to New Amsterdam before 1640, with 3 sons and 3 daus., thence to Rensselaerwyck, 1650. Lawrence, Wm., from Mass. to Flushing, L. I., 1644.
Le Conte, Guillaume (Hug.), from France to New Rochelle, N. Y.,
1698. Lefferts, from a son of Leffert Pietersen van Haughwout;
see also Haughwout. Livingston, Robert, born at Ancrum in
Roxburghshire, Scotland; in Charlestown, Mass., 1673; thence to
Albany, N. Y. Lockermans, Govert, 1633, Jacob and 1642, Pieter,
in New Netherlands, brothers, from Turnhout, Holland. Lott,
Pieter, from Reynerwout village in Drenthe province, Holland,
to Flatbush, L. I., 1652-3.

Metselaer, Teunis Teunisse, Holland to Beverwyck, 1641.
Polhemius, Theodorus, Holland to New Amsterdam before
1680. Provoost, Willem, Amsterdam to New Netherland, 1624.

Quackenbos(ch), Pieter van, from Oostgeest, Holland to New
Amsterdam about 1670; thence to Albany before 1688.

Rapalje, Joris Jansen (Hug.), Ft. Orange, 1623; New Amsterdam, 1626. Remsen, from a son of Rem(mert) Jansen Vander
beeck, from Holland to Beverwyck, 1642. Roosevelt=Rozenvelt,
Klaas Martensen van, from Holland to New Amsterdam, 1649.
Rutgers, Capt. Harmen, Holland to New Netherland, 1642-45.
Ryerson=Reyerse(n), Ryerse, from Amsterdam; m. at New Amsterdam, 1663.

Schenck, Roelof Martense, from Amersfoort, Holland, to New
Amsterdam, 1650. Schermerhorn, Jacob Janse, from Waterland,
Holland, to Beverwyck, 1636. Schoonmaker, Henry, Germany to
Ulster Co., N. Y., before 1653. Schuyler, Philip Pieterse, from
Holland; his first m. in Beverwyck, Dec. 12, 1650; wife Marz. van
Schlechtenhorst. Stoothoff, Elbert Elbertse, from Nieukerken in
N. Brabant to New Amsterdam about 1632. Stuyvesant, Pieter,
from Friesland to New Amsterdam, 1647. Stryker, Jan, from
Ruinen in Drenthe province to Flatbush, L. I., 1652. Suydam, Hen-
drick Reycke, from Suytdam or Zuytdam, Holland, to N. Y., 1663.
Swartwout, Roelof, and Thomas, Holland to New Netherland, 1651.

Tappan=Tappen, Jurian Teunisse, Holland to Beverwyck,
1662; another Tappan=Eng. Toppan or Tapping, in Milford,
Conn., 1639; settled at Southampton, L. I.

N. B.—The regular mode of forming family names in the
Low Countries or Netherlands (Holland and Belgium), as in
Denmark, Norway, Sweden and Iceland was patronymic; that is,
the Christian-name of the father was the basis of the last name
of the son; so Remsen, the son of Rem(mert) Jansen; the ending—
sen, the same as son, in English John-son, is varied to -zen, and
often shortened to -se; as in Jan-se=son of Jan (Eng. John);
Dirck-se, son of Didrik or Dedrick; Teunis-se, son of Teunis
(Antony); but this mode resulting in many duplicate names,
there grew into use, as a temporary expedient for distinguishing
between duplicate names, the affixing of the native place of each;

with the preposition of location, usually van=of; occasionally te, ten, ter=at the; as in the following:

Ten Broeck, Johannes (=J. at the Marsh), of Holland; had a son born at Albany, 1686. Ten Eyck, Coenradt (=C. at the Oak), Amsterdam to New Amsterdam, 1653. Terhune, Albert Albertse (=A. A. at Huinen, a village in Gelderland), at Gravesend, L. I., 1631; another baptized at New Amsterdam, 1651. Terwilliger, —— (=at Willige, a parish in Utrecht province); in Schenectady, 1700. Tunison=Teunisen, son of Teunis Nyssen or Duyse, from Binnick or Benneken, village near Arnhem in Gelderland, to New Amsterdam, 1638. Updike=Du. op dyk or dijk, (dwelling) upon the dike. Van Allen=of Allen, parish in Westphalia; Lourens, thence to Beverwyck, 1630? Van Alstyne, see Van Olstine or Hulsteyn. Van Amburgh=of Hamburgh; to New Amsterdam. Van Arsdale=Du. van Arsdalen, Symon Jansen, from Holland, 1653 to Flatslands, L. I. Van Benschoten=Du. van Bunschoten, a village in Utrecht province; to New Netherland. Van Brunt, Rutger Joosten, Holland to New Utrecht, L. I., 1653. Van Buren (Beuren), Hendrick Cornelis, orig. of Buren, a town in Gelderland; to L. I., 1683. Van Buskirk=Du. van Beskerck; Holland to New Netherland. Van Camp=Du. van Campen=of Kampen, a town in Overyssel province, Holland; to New Netherland. Van Cleef, Van Cleeve, Du.=of Cleves, a town in Rhenish Prussia; to New Netherland, 1630. Van Corlear (Carrelaar)=Van Curler, Arendt, Holland to Rensselaerwyck, 1630; Jacobus at Harlem on Manhattan, 1653. Van Cortlandt, Oloff Stevense, Holland to New Netherland, 1638. Van Cott, Claes Cornelise, Holland to New Netherland, 1652. Vandeleur=Du. van de Leur=of Leur, village in N. Brabant. Van der Beek or Vanderbeeck, Rem(mert) Jansen, from Holland to Beverwyck, 1642; orig. from Beek (=brook), a parish in Belgium. Vanderbilt=van der Bylt, Jan Aertsen, from Holland to Flatbush, L. I., about 1640; in New Amsterdam, 1653; orig. probably from het Bildt, a bailiwick in Friesland, which certainly gives name to a famed Du. family; but there is a parish, de Bilt, near Utrecht. Van den Bergh (alias van Wesep), Gysbert Cornelisen, Holland to Rensselaerwyck, 1645. Van der Burgh, Du.=of the city. Van der Donck, Adriaen, from Belgium to Beverwyck, 1641; orig. from Donck, a parish in Lunburg, Belgium. Vanderlyn=Du van der Lijn=of the rope or flax. Van der Poel, Wynant Gerretse, Holland to Beverwyck, 1647. Van der Veer (Vandever), Cornelis Jansen, from Alckmaar, N. Holland, to Flatbush, L. I., 1659: (Ver=ferry). Vandervoort,—from Vandermonde in Vlaenderen, Netherlands; m. at New Amsterdam, 1640. Van Deursen (Deusen, Duursen), Abraham, from Holland to New Amsterdam, thence to Fort Orange or Beverwyck, where was Pieter Abrahamsen, in 1657; m. at N. Y., 1666: (Deursen is a hamlet in N. Brabant). Van Devanter=van Deventer, a town in Overyssel. Vandewater, Jacobus=Du. van de Water=of the water; to New Amsterdam, 1653. Van Dorn= Du. van Doorn, a parish near Utrecht. Van Driessen, Revs. Johannes and Petrus (sons of Petrus of Belgium); P. to Albany,

1712; J. later. Van Dyke=van Dyck, Jan Thomasse, at New Utrecht, L. I., 1652; brothers Claes and Hendrick Thomasse (sons of Thomas Janszen van Dyck), in New Amsterdam before 1662. Van Dyne (Dine, Tine)=Van Duyn, Gerret Cornelise, of Neukerck, Zeeland, Netherlands, with his brother-in-law, Jacques Corteljau, to New Amsterdam, 1649; orig. from Duin or Dun, a hamlet in N. Brabant. Van Haughwout, Leffert Pietersen, from Netherlands to Flatbush, L. I., 1660; hence Haughwout and Lefferts families. Van Horn,—e=van Hoorn, a town in N. Holland. Van Hulsteyn (Olstine, Alstyne), to New Amsterdam=of Holstein. Van Kirk=van Kerck, Du.=of the church. Van Lennep=of Lennep, a town, river and district in Rhenish Prussia. Van Meter=Du. van Meteren. Van Name=Du. van Namen, a parish in Westphalia. Van Ness, Hendrick Gerritzen, from Emberland, Holland, m. at New Amsterdam, 1654=of Nes, a village in Friesland. Van Nest (Ness), Pieter, Pieterse, Utrecht, Netherlands to New Amsterdam, 1647; Brooklyn, 1687. Van Norden=Du. van Noórden=of the north. Van Nostrand=van Noordstrand (=north strand or shore), Jan Hansen, Holland to Flatbush, L. I., 1639. Van Rensselaer, Kiliaen; was granted a tract, Rensselaerwyck, in Albany Co.; his son Jeremias arrived there 1658. Van Rozenvelt, probably=Rosenfeld in Holstein; see Roosevelt. Van Sandt or Sant, see Van Zandt. Van Schaick, Gozen Gerritse, in Beverwyck about 1652. Van Schuyler, see Schuyler. Van Sicklen, Antonie, 1635, New Amsterdam, from Ghent. Van Slyck or Slyke=of Slijk—Ewijk in Gelderland. Van Vechten (Vecht, Veghte), Claes Arentse, from Drenthe province to New Amsterdam, 1660; settled in Brooklyn. Van Vechten, Teunis Dirckse, settled at Greenbush, opposite Beverwyck, 1638;=of Vechte, river in Oldenburg. Van Valkenburg,—h =of Valkenberg, mountain in S. Holland, and another in Limburg. Van Vleck=of the vlek, or market town. Van Vliet (Fleet)=of the channel. Van Voorhies, see Voorhies. Van Wickle=van Wickelen, Evert, from Holland to New Netherland, 1665; settled at Flatlands. Van Winkle,—to New Netherland=van de Winkel, a parish in N. Holland. Van Woert, shortened from Schoenderwoert. Van Wyck, Cornelis B., at Flatbush, 1659. Van Zandt=of 't Zandt (sand), a parish in Groningen, Holland. Vedder, Harmen Albertse, Holland to Beverwyck, 1657. Vermilye,—at Kingsbridge, N. Y., 1662. Ver Planck, Abraham Isaacse, in New Amsterdam about 1633. Vinhagen, Jan Dirckse, from Geeman, Holland, to Albany, 1669. Vischer, Harmen Bastiaanse, from Hoorn, Holland, to Rensselaerwyck, before 1644; at Albany, 1678. Voorhies, Stephen Coerte van (son of Coerte Albertse van V., who resided in front of Hies (voor Hies), hamlet near Ruinen in Drenthe province), to Flatlands, L. I., 1660; (Voorhees, Voorhis, Voorhes). Vreeland, Jan Jacobsen, in New Amsterdam, 1633; another in N. J.; from Michael Jansen V. of Brockhuysen, Holland, 1636. Vroom, Cornelis Pietersen; oldest son baptized at New Amsterdam, 1645.

Wyckoff, Pieter Claesen, Netherlands to Flatlands, L. I., 1636. Wendell, Evert Jansen, of Emden, Hannover, to New Amsterdam about 1642. Wynkoop, Pieter, from Holland to New Netherland, 1639.

REPRESENTATIVE PIONEER SETTLERS OF
NEW NETHERLAND AND THEIR ORIGINAL HOME PLACES.

CONTRIBUTED BY RICHARD SCHERMERHORN, JR.

The original thought leading to the writing of this article came about quite naturally. A tourist concern in England (Muirhead Guide Books, Ltd.) inquired of the historian, James Truslow Adams, if he would recommend sources in America from which they could secure information as to the original Holland homes of the early New Netherland settlers. This Company proposed to call attention to these home places in Holland, in their Guidebook, to attract the particular interest of American tourists (their new book contains this information). Mr. Adams, with whom the author has been acquainted for many years, communicated with the latter and asked if he would furnish this information. The author consented, little realizing the amount of work that was necessary.

It would be natural to assume that the passenger lists, which most genealogists know have been published, contain the most substantial information as to the home places of the Dutch emigrants. This is so to some extent, but on the other hand the names of the Dutch emigrants on these passenger lists do not conform with the names of their families a generation or two later, except in a comparatively few cases. The patronymic for a surname was used in most cases, the actual family name being adopted not earlier as a rule than the second or third generation in this country. Then they would usually adopt the name of the original home place or estate of the family rather than the place in which they lived immediately preceding their departure to America.

Another point which must be considered is that not all by any means of these original settlers who may be considered Dutch were actually Dutch. As we know, many (the Walloons) came from France, having settled temporarily in Holland before they came to America. The latter are not included on the lists appearing in this article as France was not to be considered in this particular work. It is further found that a great many of those who are assumed to be Dutch, actually came from what are now sections of Germany. The latter were principally the independent duchies or principalities of Oldenburg, Hanover, Rhine Province, Westphalia and Schleswig-Holstein. All of these were independent governments at the time of the Dutch emigration to America. This does not mean the emigrants from these places were not originally Dutch, as in the 16th Century many of the Dutch fled to these provinces during the Spanish persecutions. It is also true that in the second half of the 17th Century people from the Palatinate and the Rhine Province fled into the Netherlands to escape the French religious persecutions. Therefore in many cases the actual place of residence at any particular time could not positively determine the actual nationality of a family.

To go into a detailed study of all these different phases of families' migrations is a task in itself, but for all practical purposes it is still reasonable to judge that the original settlers of New Netherlands were mainly Dutch or of Dutch blood, and for general purposes it was practical to include in this research the provinces now part of Germany where many New Netherland Settlers resided at the time of their emigration. It might be added, however, that even the Walloons, having lived in Holland and having imbibed Dutch customs and traditions and in this country having intermarried consistently with the Dutch,

6

became to all intents and purposes as Dutch as anything could make them. This applies also to such families as Livingston, Yates and others that grew up in the Dutch settlements.

The sources of information looked into for the compilation of this material were original records as far as time would permit (the material was desired at an early moment). The Dutch Church marriage records of New Amsterdam, Kingston and Bergen were first examined, these giving definite information regarding the continental homes of many early settlers. The standard works of Pearson, Bergen and Riker were also studied, these having covered many of the early public records, and the published public records of New York State relating to the early Dutch (these are voluminous) were also looked into as far as practical, to complement the former. The individually published family genealogies were also referred to, although with a measure of caution, as some of these cannot be classed as infallible. It is surprising how comparatively few Dutch genealogies there are. Other authorities are noted in the list appended and it is believed that they are mainly trustworthy, although it is quite possible that once in a great while an error in deduction might have crept in. Even such an authority as Pearson made a slip occasionally and unfortunately errors are to be found in nearly all genealogical works. Mr. A. J. F. van Laer, N. Y. State Archivist, has been particularly kind and helpful to the author in this work, and his knowledge of this subject is known to be unsurpassed.

The list is, of course, not complete. It was necessary to leave out many important families, because the location of their original homes could not be determined. Other families have been omitted because their names died out early and have no present day significance. A few families, however, whose names do not exist in America today, were included on account of their being well known in the early history of New Netherland. Some other families were perhaps neglected because while not having actually died out, their names are encountered so seldom as to be of little interest. A few perhaps also have been included which have no real significance, but the author could hardly be expected to be an authoritative judge of the noteworthy characteristics of each and every one of the pioneer families. He has simply done the best he could, and has endeavored to furnish a list of those families which have been representative of the best known of the pioneer stock.

ORIGINAL PLACES OF RESIDENCE IN HOLLAND, BELGIUM AND GERMANY
OF
THE PIONEER NEW NETHERLAND SETTLERS (1620-1664)

Abeel, Christoffel Janse, born in Amsterdam (25) (39).

Ackerman, David, from Berlicum, district of Bois-Le-Duc, in N. Brabant (also Abraham and Lodewyck Ackerman) (46) (47).

Adriance (Adriaen Reyerse emigrated from Amsterdam, prob. son of Reyer Elberts from Utrecht) (54) (11).

Amermann, Dirck Janse from Amsterdam (11).

Bancker, Gerrit, prob. from Amsterdam (48).

Banta, Epke Jacobs, from vicinity of Harlingen, in Friesland (3).

Beeckman, Willem, from Hasselt, Overyssel (N. Y. Ref. D. Ch. says from Zutphen) (39) (46).

Beeckman, Marten Hendrickse, from Hamelwaerde (prob. Hammelwarden in Oldenburg) (38).

Benson, Dirck, originally from Groningen, later Amsterdam. The name Bensing, or Bensinck, occurs several times in Court records, 1518-1604, of the Prov. of Drenthe (11) (39) (54).

8   *Representative Pioneer Settlers of New Netherland.*

Bergen, Hans Hans from Bergen, Norway (59).
Blauvelt, Gerret Hendrickse from Deventer, Overyssel (54).
Bleecker, Jan Jansen, from Meppel, Drenthe (45).
Bloodgood, Frans Jans, prob. from Gouda, S. Holland (39).
Boerum, Hendrick Willemse, from Amsterdam (11).
Bogardus, Rev. Everardus, born at Woerden, Utrecht (55).
Bogart, Jan Laurensz, from Schoonderwoert, S. Holland (39) (54).
Bogart, Pieter Jansen, from Leerdam, S. Holland (56).
Bogart, Tunis Gysbertse, from Heikop, Utrecht (or Heikop, near Leerdam,
S. Hol.) (11) (18).
Bradt (Bratt), Albert Andriese, from Frederickstadt, Norway, at mouth of
Glommen River (38).
Brevoort (van), Hendrick Janszen, born at Breevort, near Amersfoort,
Utrecht (54).
Brinckerhoof, Joris Diercksen, from Drenthe (Abraham Joris b. at Flush-
ing, Zeeland) (4) (11).
Brinckerhoff, Jan Dircksen, b. in Drenthe, living some time in Flushing,
Zeeland (11) (39).
Brink, Lambert Huvbertse, from Wageningen, Gelderland (28) (37).
Byvanck, Jan, from Oldenzeel (Oldenzaal, Overyssel) (46).
Brouwer, Adam, from Cologne, Rhine Province (11).
Brouwer, Thomas Harmensen, from Zevenbergen (17).
Coeymans, Pieter: his sons came from Utrecht (16).
Cortelyou, Jacques, from Utrecht (11).
Couwenhoven (van), Wolfert Gysbertsen, from Amersfort, Utrecht.
(Couwenhoven a farm or estate near Amersfort.) (Name also found as Con-
over, N. J. branch) (38).
Covert (Coevert), Teunis Janse, from Heemstede, N. Holland (11) (18).
Coykendall (van Kuykendaal), Jacob Luursen: prob. from Wageningen,
Gelderland (see Kiik-in-t-dal, near Wageningen) (8) (42).
Cuyler, Hendrick, b. in Hasselt, Overyssel. His brother, Reinier Cuyler,
lived in Amsterdam (26) (41).
De Decker, Johan, prob. from Amsterdam (16).
De Groot, Willem Pietersen, from Haerlem, N. Holland (46) (11).
De Witt, Tierck Claase, from Grootholdt, Zunderlandt (possibly Sonderen,
Westphalia, E. Friesland, though also possible Embderland, Friesland) (46)
(41).
Denise (De Nyse), Teunis Nyssen, from Utrecht (62).
Dingman, Adam, b. in Haerlem, N. Holland (41).
Ditmars, Jan Jansen, from Ditmarsen, Schleswig-Holstein (11).
Doremus, Cornelis Cornelise, b. at Middleburg, Zeeland (56).
Douw, Volkert Janse, from Stapelholm, near Frederickstadt (Friedrich-
stadt), in Schleswig-Holstein (40) (46).
Durie (Duryea), Joost, from Mannheim, in Baden, on the Rhine. (There is
also a small place, Mannheim, in the Palatinate, but not on the Rhine) (11).
Duyckinck, Evert, from Borken. Borken is a village in Westphalia. The
place in N. Brabant is called Borkel. (See Borchen, N. Brabant) (46) (11) (6).
Dyckman, Johannes, from Benthem (Bentheim.? Hanover) (45) (54).
Elmendorf, Jacobus (Conradt), b. in Rynborch, S. Holland, near Leyden
(19).
Elting, Jan, from Sweghteler (now Zwiggelt), Drenthe (18) (11).
Freelinghuysen, Domine Theodorus Jacobus, b. Wolfenbuettel, E. Friesland
(5) (22).
Freeman, Domine Bernardus, b. at Gilhuis (Gildehaus, near Bentheim,
Hanover) (48).

Gansevoort, Harmen Harmense, supposed to have come from Groningen (16).

Gardinier, Jacob Janse, from Campen (Kampen in Overyssel) (38).

Goewey, Salomen Abelse, b. in Amsterdam (45).

Groesbeck, Claes Jacobse, from Rotterdam, S. Holland (see also Groesbeek, Gelderland, near Nijmegen) (39) (40).

Hallenbeck, Caspar Jacobse, from Hollenbek, Schleswig-Holstein (40).

Hardenbergh, Gerrit Janse, from Maerssen (Maarssen), near Utrecht (24) (40).

Hardenbroeck, Johannes, from Elbervelt (Elberfeld, Rhine Province) (17).

Haring, Pieter, from N. Holland (60) (one record says from Amsterdam) (56).

Hegeman, Adriaen, from Amsterdam (11).

Heermans, Jan Focken, from Ruinen, Drenthe (18).

Hoes, Jan Tyse, son of Matthys Janse (see Goes, Zeeland) (58).

Hoffman, Martinus, from Revel, Gulf of Finland, then Finland, later Russia (46).

Hoogland, Dirck Janse, from Maarssenveen, Utrecht (11).

Hoogland, Cornelius Andriesen, from The Hague, S. Holland (46).

Hoogland, Stoffel, from Haerlem, N. Holland (46).

Hun, Harmen Thomassen, from Amersfoort, Utrecht (41).

Huyck (Huyghen), Jan, from Wesel, Rhine Province (58).

Kettelhuyn, Joachim, from Cremyn (Kremmin, near Stettin, Pomerania) (41).

Kiersted, Dr. Hans, from Magdeburg, Prussian Saxony (46).

Kip, Hendrick Hendrickse, from Amsterdam (53).

Knickerbacker, Harmen Janse, from Bommel (Zalt-Bommel, Gelderland) (7); family perhaps originally from Wie (now Wyhe), near Zwolle, Overyssel (18).

Lansing, Gerrit Frederickse, from Hasselt, Overyssel. He died in Holland and never came to New Netherland. His widow and 5 children came over in 1655. N. Y. Col. Doc. 14: 334 (45).

Lefferts (Leffert Pieterse), from Drenthe. (Bergen says from Haughwout (Hoogwoud), N. Holland) (18) (11).

Lowe, Jan Bastiansen, from Leerdam, S. Holland (63).

Leisler, Jacob, from Frankfort (46) (17).

Low (Louw), Pieter Cornelissen, from Schleswig-Holstein (62).

Loockermans, Govert, Pieter and Jacob brothers, from Turnhout, Antwerp (46).

Marcelis Jansen, from Bommel, Gelderland (17) (45).

Marselis, Pieter, from Beest, Gelderland (17).

Megapolensis, Domine Joannes, b. Koedyk, N. Holland (11).

Middagh, Aert Antonisse, from Heikop, Utrecht (62).

Minuit, Peter, from Wesel, Westphalia (49).

Moll, Huybert Lambertsen, from Arnhem, Gelderland (also Abraham Lambertse Moll) (46).

Moll, Jan Jansen, from Amsterdam (46).

Mynderse (see van Every).

Nevius, Johannes, from Zoelen, Gelderland (11 says in error Solin, Westphalia), b. at Zoelen (62).

Opdyck, Gysbert, from Wesel, Rhine Province (11) (46).

Osterhout, Jan Jansen, from Oosterhout, N. Brabant (47).

Ostrander, Pieter Pietersen, from Amsterdam (28).

Oudewater, Frans Jacobsen, prob. from Oudewater, S. Holland, on Ysel River, between Utrecht and Leyden (18).

Pels, Evert, from Stettin, Pomerania (38).

Philipse, Frederick, from Bolsward, Friesland (46).

Polhemus (Polheim), Rev. Johannes Theodorus. He had been a minister in the Palatinate, at Meppel, Drenthe, and in Brazil, before he came to N. Netherland, prob. born in Germany (16) (55).

Post, Adriaaen, from The Hague, S. Holland (56).

Post, Lodewyck Corneliszen, from Amsterdam (64).

Pruyn, Frans Jansen, said to have come from Maastricht, Limburg, but family originally from Antwerp (16).

Quackenbos, Pieter (Pieter Bont alias Quackenbos), from Oestgeest, near Leyden, S. Holland (46) (12).

Remsen (Rem Jansen Vander Beeck), from Jeveren (Jever), Oldenburg (46) (11).

Roosevelt, Claes Martensen, prob. from Zeeland (16).

Roosa, Albert Heymans, from Herwijnen, Gelderland (17) (Hol. Soc. Yrbk. 1907).

Rutgers (see Van Woert) (39).

Schaets, Rev. Gideon, b. at Leerdam, S. Holland.

Schenck, Jan and Roeloff Martensen, brothers; Roeloff, b. in Amersfoort, Utrecht. (Johannes Schenck from Middleburg, Zeeland) (58) (21) (36).

Schermerhorn, Jacob Janse, from Amsterdam (originally from Village of Schermerhorn, N. Holland).

Schoonmaker, Hendrick Jochemsen, b. in Hamburg (28) (37).

Schuyler, Philip Pietersen, from Amsterdam (also David Pietersen Schuyler) (20) (38) (46).

Sebring (Seberinge), Jan Roelofse, prob. from Drenthe (61).

Slingerland, Teunis Cornelis from Amsterdam (58).

Springsteen, Johannes and Joost Casparse, brothers, from Groningen (11).

Staats, Major Abraham (Staes), from Amsterdam (38).

Steenwyck, Cornelis, from Haarlem, N. Holland (46).

Stoutenburgh, Pieter, from Stoutenburch, near Amersfoort, Utrecht (16).

Stoutenburgh, Jacob Jansz, from Stoutenburch, near Amersfoort, Utrecht (38).

Strycker, Jan and Jacob Gerritse, prob. brothers; Jan, from Ruinen, Drenthe (11) (18) (22).

Stuyvesant, Pieter, probably originally came from Dockum (Dokkum), Friesland (51).

Sutphen (van), Derick Jansen, from Zutphen, Gelderland (11) (13) (22).

Suydam, Hendrick Rycke, from Suyt-dam or Zuyt-dam (11).

Swart, Gerrit, prob. from Amsterdam (16).

Ten Broeck, Dirck Wesselse, Hendrick Wesselse and Wessel Wesselse, brothers; the last came from Wessum, Munster, Westphalia (18) (37).

Ten Eyck, Coenraet, family prob. from Amsterdam (16) (37).

Terhune, Albert Albertse, prob. from Huinen (Gelderland) (63).

Traphagen, Willem Janszen, from Lemgo (Lemgow, Hanover) (46).

Van Alen, Pieter and Lourens, brothers, from Utrecht, prob. originally from Aelen or Haelen, Waterloo, Brabant, Belgium (1) (17).

Van Alstyne, Jan Martensen, from Meppel, Drenthe (44).

Van Antwerp, Daniel Jansen, from Antwerp, b. at Amsterdam (16) (58).

Van Benthuysen, Paulus Martense, from Benthuizen, near Leyden, S. Holland (40).

Van Bergen, Marten Gerritsen, from Bergen, in Norway (16).

Van Boskerck (Buskirk), Lourens Andriessen, from Schleswig-Holstein (22).

Van Brugh (Verbrugge), Johannes Pieterse, from Haarlem, N. Holland (45).

Van Brunt, Rutger Joosten (from Bruntinge, Drenthe?) (16).

Van Bunschoten, Theunis Eliasen, supposedly from Benschoten, Utrecht (39).

Van Buren, Cornelius Hendricksen, from Buurmalsen, Gelderland (38).

Van Cleve (van Cleef), Jan, from Amsterdam (52).

Van Cortlandt, Oloff Stevense, from Wyck by Duurstede, Utrecht (46).

Van Curler, Arent, from Nykerck, Gelderland (38).

Van Dam, Claes Ripsen (see Damme, W. Flanders).

Van Deusen, Abraham Pietersen (Van Deursen), b. in Haarlem, N. Holland (18) (39).

Van Deventer, Jan Pietersen, from the "Steght." Stegeren is a small place near Deventer, in Overyssel (11).

Van Dolsen, Jan Gerritsen, from Dalfsen or Dalsen (Overyssel) (54).

Van Doorn, Pieter, from 's-Gravezande, S. Holland (see also Doorn, Utrecht) (33).

Van Duyn, Abraham Gerritse, from Zwolle, Overyssel (11).

Van Duyn, Gerrit Cornelissen, from Niewerkerk, Zeeland (see Duin or Duen in Brabant) (18).

Van Dyne (van Dien), Dirck Gerritz, from Tricht (Tricht is a small place in Gelderland) (17).

Van Dyck, Hendrick, from Utrecht (45).

Van Dyck, Jan Jansen, from Amsterdam (also Dirck Jansen Van Dyck and Jacobus Fransen Van Dyck) (46).

Van Etten, Jacob Jansen, from Etten, N. Brabant, near Breda (47).

Van Every (van Iveren, Jeverden), Myndert Frederickse, from Jeveren, Oldenburg (see also Mynderse family) (46).

Van Gaasbeeck, Rev. Domine Laurentius, from Leyden, S. Holland (28) (37).

Van Geisen, Reynier Bastiansen, prob. from Giessen, N. Brabant, but perhaps from Giessen, S. Holland (11).

Van Giesen, Johannis, from Utrecht (56).

Van Guysling, Elias, from Zeeland (17).

Van Hoesen, Jan Fransen, prob. from Husum, in Schleswig-Holstein (40).

Van Horn, Jan Cornelissen, "a citizen of Amsterdam," prob. from Hoorn, N. Holland (22) (31).

Van Houten, three brothers, one, Helmigh Roelofs, from Gelderland. Houten is a village in the Prov. of Utrecht (18).

Van Keulen (Keuren), Mattys Jansen, from Amsterdam (28).

Van Leeuwens (van Lieuw), Frederick Hendricksen, from Utrecht, and Leeuwen, Gelderland (10).

Van Loon, Jan, from Luik, or Liege, Belgium (46).

Van Meteren, Jan Joosten, from Thielerwaardt, Gelderland (44).

Van Meteren, Jan Gysbertsen, from Bommel, Gelderland. Bommel lies on the River Waal, which forms the dividing line between the Tielerwaard and the Bommelerwaard (44) (21) (11) (5).

Van Namen, Jochem Engelbert, from Heusden, N. Brabant (54).

Van Ness, Cornelius Hendrickse, from Vianen, S. Holland (41).

Van Noort, Goosen Jansen, from Beest, Gelderland (17).

Van Norden, Pieter Glaesen, supposedly from Norden, Germany, near Ems, or from Norden near Putten, Gelderland? (36) (16).

Van Nostrand, Jacob Janse, from Nordstrand, island off coast of Schleswig-Holstein (35) (39) (40).

Van Pelt, Teunis and Matthys Jansen Lanen, brothers, from Luik (Liege), Belgium (15). (Lane family descended from Matthys Jansen.)

Van Petten, Claes Frederickse (see Petten, N. Holland, North Sea).

Van Rensselaer, Kiliaen, from Nykerck, Gelderland. Kiliaen van Rensselaer did not come to N. N. His family originally came from the vicinity of Nykerck but he resided at Amsterdam (38).

Van Ripen, Juriaen Tomassen (Ripen is or was in N. Jutland, Denmark) (23).

Van Schelluyne, Dirck, b. in Gorckum, S. Holland; came from The Hague, S. Holland (18) (49).

Van Santvoord, Rev. Cornelius, b. at Leyden, S. Holland; family of Belgium origin, Ypres (18) (48).

Van Schaick, Goosen Gerritsen, from Westerbroeck (Westbroek, Utrecht?). The name van Schaick was prominent in Amersfoort, Utrecht, in the 17th Century (38) (16).

Van Schoonhoven, Geurt Hendrickse, from Schoonhoven, S. Holland (16).

Van Slichtenhorst, Brant Aertz, from Nykerck, Gelderland (38).

Van Slyck, Cornelis Antonissen, from Breuckelen, Utrecht (38) (17).

Van Slyck, Willem Pieterse, from The Hague (Munsell Alb. Colls. v. 4-1849).

Van Steenbergh, Jan Jansen, from Amersfoort, Utrecht (37).

Van Tassell (van Tessel), Jan Cornelise, b. in Schoonderwoert, near Leerdam, S. Holland, prob. originally from Island of Tessel (The Texel), S. W. of Frisian Islands.

Van Twiller, Aert Goosense, from Nykerck, Gelderland (16) (17).

Van Twiller, Wouter, from Nykerck, Gelderland (49).

Van Valkenburg, Lambert Jochemse, b. at Valkenburgh, Limburg (36).

Van Vechten, Teunis Cornelissen, prob. from Vechten, near Utrecht (2) (38).

Van Vechten (Vecht, Vechte), Klaes Arentse, from Norg, Drenthe (11).

Van Vleck, Tielman, from Limburg (16).

Van Vliet, Adriaen Gerritsen, from Utrecht (22).

Van Voorhies, Steven Koerts, from Hees, near Ruinen, Drenthe. Ruinen is the name of a place, as well of former manor of very large extent, in the S. W. part of the Prov. of Drenthe (16) (39).

Van Voorhout, Cornelis Segerse (van Egmont), from Voorhout, S. Holland, but probably originally from Egmont, N. Holland (38).

Van Voorst, Cornelis, from Utrecht (16).

Van Voorst, Willem, from Arnhem, Gelderland (17).

Van Vredenburgh, Willem Isaacsen, from The Hague, S. Holland (46).

Van Wagenen, Aert Jacobsen, from Wageningen, Gelderland (34).

Van Winkle (van Winkel), Jacob Walingen and Symon, brothers, sailed from Hoorn, N. Holland; also said to have come from Middleburg, Zeeland. Winkel is a place in N. Holland (23).

Van Woert, Rutger and Teunis Jacobse, brothers (see also Rutgers family). Woert is a short form of Schoonderwoert, or Schoonrewoerd, in S. Holland (38).

Van Wyck, Cornelis Barentse, prob. from Wijck, N. Brabant (see also Wyk, Utrecht, and Wyck, Limburg) (11) (9) (18).

Van Zandt (Sant), Adam Wenzel, b. in Arnhem, Gelderland (18).

Vanderbilt, Jan Aertsen; family prob. from "Het Bilt," Friesland, or possibly deBilt, suburb of Utrecht (32).

Vanderheyden, Jacob Tyse. (Jan Cornelissen vander Heyden came from Zevenbergen, in N. Brabant (45).

Vanderlinde, Roelof, from Wageningen, Gelderland (56).

Vanderpoel, Wynant Gerritse, from Gorcum, S. Holland (50).

Vanderveer, Cornelis Jansen, from Alkmaar, N. Holland (30) (11).

Vanderveer, Pieter Corneliszen, b. at Amsterdam (14).

Vander Linden, Pieter, from Belle, Flanders (Bael, Baelen, Antwerp) (11).

Vander Donck, Adriaen, from Breda, N. Brabant (38).

Vander Volgen, Claas Lourentsen (van Purmerend) (Purmerend, N. Holland) (40) (48).

Vander Voort, Michael Pauluszen, from Dermond, Flanders (11).

Van de Water, Hendrick, from Amsterdam (also Pieter Van de Water) (46).

Varick, Jan, from Rhenen, Utrecht (18).

Vermeule, Adriaan, b. at Vlissingen (Flushing), Zeeland (56).

Viele, Cornelis Cornelise, from Kniphuysen (Kniphausen), Oldenburg (16).

Visscher, Harmen Bastiaense; his father lived in Hoorn, N. Holland (45).

Vreeland, Michiel Janszoon, from " 's Heer Abtskerke" (Schrabbekerke), Island of S. Beveland, Zeeland (also said to be from Broeckhuysen, N. Brabant) (23) (49).

Wendell, Evert Jansen, from Embden, E. Friesland (now Hanover, Germany) (46).

Westervelt, Willem Lubbertsen, from Meppel, Drenthe; also Roeloff Lubbertse Westervelt (56) (57).

Westfall, Juriaen (Bestval), from Leiderdorp, near Leyden, S. Holland (38).

Winne, Pieter, from Ghent, East Flanders (38).

Witbeck, Jan Thomase, b. at Witbek (Wittbek), Schleswig-Holstein (45).

LOCALITIES IN HOLLAND, BELGIUM, GERMANY, ETC., NAMES OF WHICH HAVE BEEN CONCERNED WITH THE NEW NETHERLAND SETTLERS.

NOTE: The numerals before the places designate the number of emigrant families from these places.

North Holland

23	Amsterdam
	Alkmaar
	Blarikum
	Bloemendaal
	Broek
	Egmond aan Zee
	Hoogwoud
2	Hoorn
6	Haarlem
	Heemskerk
1	Heemstede
1	Koedyk
	Ilpendam
	Naarden
	Ouderkerk
1	Petten
1	Purmerend
1	Schermerhorn

Velzen
Weesp
Winkel

Friesland

1	Bolsward
1	Dockum
1	Harlingen
1	Het Bilt
	Huizum
	Leeuwarden

Groningen

3	Groningen

Drenthe 4

1	Bruntinge
	Coevorden
	De Wyk
1	Hees
	Linde
4	Meppel

1 Norg
2 Ruinen
1 Zwiggelt
Overyssel
  1 Dalsen
  1 Deventer
    Hardenburgh
  4 Hasselt
  1 Kampen
    Raalte
  1 Stegeren
    Steenwyk
  1 Zwolle
  1 Oldenzaal
Gelderland
    Aalst
  3 Arnhem
  2 Beest
  3 Bommel
    Brakel
  1 Buurmalsen
    Doesburg
    Est
    Groesbeek
  1 Huinen
    Huizen
    Ingen
    Leeuwen
  5 Nykerck
  1 Thielerwaardt
  1 Tricht
    Voorst (small)
  4 Wageningen
    Wessel
  1 Zoelen
  2 Zutphen
Utrecht
  6 Amersfoort
  1 Breukelen
  1 Bunschoten
  1 De Bilt
    Doorn
  2 Heikop
  2 Maarsen
    Hooghland
  1 Houten
  1 Rhenen
    Tienhoven
  8 Utrecht
  1 Vechten
    Vreeland
    Waal
  1 Westbroek
  1 Woerden
    Wky by Duurstede

    Zuilen
1 Brevoort
South Holland
  1 Benthuisen
    Giessen
  2 Gorinchem (Gorcum)
  1 's-Gravesande
  3 's-Gravenhage (The Hague)
  1 Gouda
    Ketel
  3 Leerdam
  3 Leyden
  1 Leyderdorp
    Noorden
  1 Oegstgeest
  1 Oudewater
    Ouderkerk
  1 Rotterdam
  1 Rynsborch
    Scheveningen
  3 Schoonerwoerd
  1 Schoonhoven
    Tienhoven
    Valkenburg
  1 Vianen
  1 Voorhout
Zeeland
  1 Goes
  1 Middelburg
  1 Nieuenkerk
    Ouwerkerk (small)
  1 S. Beveland Island
    Veere
  1 Vlissingen (Flushing)
North Brabant
    Aalst (small)
  1 Berlicum
  1 Breda
  1 Broeckhuysen
    den Bosch (Bois-le-Duc)
    Donk
  1 Etten
    Esch (small)
  1 Giessen
    Haring (small)
    Heusden
    Hoeven
    Ledeakker (small)
    Loon-op-Zand
  1 Oosterhout
    Schaik
    Steenbergen
  1 Wijck
    Zevenbergen

Limburg 1
   Bergen
   Halen (small)
   Hees
   Horst
   Maas
  1 Maastricht
   Poel
  1 Valkenburg
   Weert
   Wessem
   Wyck
      BELGIUM

West Flanders
  (On French border)
  1 Damme
   Oudenbourg

East Flanders
   Deynze
  1 Gand (Ghent)
   Lokeren
   Wynkel

Antwerp
  1 Bael (Baelen)
   Antwerp (Anvers)
   Hoogstraten
   Moll
  1 Turnhout

Brabant
  1 Waterloo

Flanders
  1 Dermond

Liege 2
      GERMANY

Oldenburg
   Ammerland
  1 Hammelwarden (small)
  2 Jever in Jeverland
  1 Kniphausen (Kniphausen-
     sieb)
   Neuenburg
   Oldenburg
   Vechta River

Schleswig-Holstein 2
  1 Ditmarschen
   Flensburg (large)

  1 Hamburg (large)
   Heide
  1 Hollenbek
  1 Husum
  1 Nodstrand
  1 Stapelholm
  1 Witbek
   Wyk

Westphalia
  1 Borken
   Buren
   Freadenburg (small)
   Heiden
   Munster
  1 Sondern
  2 Wessum

Rhine Province
   Beeck
   Bruggen (small)
  1 Cologne
  1 Elberfeld
   Essen
   Geldern
   Kleve
   Niewkerk
   Vorst (small)
  2 Wesel

Hanover
  1 Bentheim
  1 Emden
  1 Gildehaus
   Meppen
  1 Lemgow

Germany, General
  1 Frankfort
  1 Magdeburg, Saxony
  1 Mannheim, Baden
  1 Stettin, Pomerania
  1 Kremmin, Pomerania
  1 Norden, near Ems

Other Countries
  2 Bergen, Norway
  1 Frederickstadt, Norway
  1 Ripen, N. Jutland, Denmark
  1 Revel, Gulf of Finland
   (originally Finland)

REFERENCES

1. Early American Families. W. A. Williams.
2. Geneal. Records of Van Vechtens. P. Van Vechten, Jr.
3. Banta Genealogy. T. M. Banta.
4. Brinckerhoff Genealogy. R. Brinckerhoff.
5. Duke, Shepherd, Van Metre Genealogy. S. G. Smith.
6. Duyckinck Geneal. W. C. Duyckinck.
7. Families of Knickerbacker-Viele. K. K. Viele.
8. Cuykendall Family. G. B. Kuykendall.
9. Descendents of Cornelis Bar. Van Wyck. A. Van Wyck.

10. Van Liew Genealogy. T. L. V. Liew.
11. Early Settlers of Kings Co. Bergen.
12. Quackenbush Geneal. A. S. Quackenbush.
13. Van Buren Geneal. H. C. Peckham.
14. Vander Veer Family in the Netherlands. L. P. De Boer.
15. Van Pelt Geneal. E. M. Smith.
16. A. J. F. van Laer data.
17. Holland Society Yearbook, 1902 (passenger lists).
18. N. Y. Geneal. & Biographical Record.
19. Heroes of American Revolution. H. Whittemore.
20. Colonial New York. G. W. Schuyler.
21. Early Dutch Settlers Monmouth Co., N. J., G. C. Beekman.
22. Early Germans of New Jersey. T. F. Chambers.
23. History of Hudson Co., N. J. C. H. Winfield.
24. History of New Paltz. Le Fevre.
25. Abeel Geneal. H. Whittemore.
26. Earliest Cuylers. M. C. Nicoll.
27. Ackerman Geneal. K. K. Viele.
28. Old Ulster Magazine.
29. Van Horn Family—History. F. H. Marvin.
30. Vander Veer Family. J. J. Vanderveer.
32. N. Y. Evening Post, May 4, 1901.
33. Van Doorn Family. A. V. D. Honeyman.
34. Van Wagenen Geneal. G. H. Van Wagenen.
35. Americana Magazine.
36. Washington Ancestry. E. L. McClain.
37. History of Kingston. M. Schoonmaker.
38. Van Rensselaer—Bowier Mss.
39. St. Nicholas Society Geneal. Record—1916.
40. Early Records Albany—V. 2—1916.
41. Early Records Albany—V. 3—1918.
42. Court Minutes Ft. Orange & Beverwyck V. 2—1923.
43. Court Minutes Albany, Rensselaerwyck & Schenectady—V. 2—1928.
44. New Netherland Register Magazine.
45. Pearson's First Settlers of Albany.
46. New York Ref. Dutch Church Marriage Records.
47. Kingston Ref. Dutch Church Marriage Records.
48. Pearson's First Settlers of Schenectady.
49. Valentine's History of New York.
50. Vanderpoel Genealogy.
51. New York Historical Soc. Bulletin, April 1926.
52. Early Settlers of Trenton, N. J.
53. Kip Genealogy.
54. History of Harlem. Riker.
55. Manual Reformed Church in America. Corwin.
56. Bergen Marriage Records—Holland Soc. Yearbook, 1914.
57. Westervelt Genealogy. W. T. Westervelt.
58. Holland Society Yearbooks (Biographical Memoirs).
59. Bergen Family. T. G. Bergen.
60. Hist. Bergen & Passaic Counties, N. J. Clayton.
61. Somerset Co., N. J. Historical Quarterly—Vol. 3.
62. Somerset Co., N. J. Historical Quarterly—Vol. 5.
63. Somerset Co., N. J. Historical Quarterly—Vol. 6.
64. Somerset Co., N. J. Historical Quarterly—Vol. 7.

SHIPWRIGHTS, FISHERMEN, PASSENGERS FROM ENGLAND.

By Charles B. Moore.

Many interesting particulars are known of the first settlers of New England and of New York. Their perilous enterprises were recorded, reported, and studied, especially to guide others.

But after the arrivals and settlements became numerous, it was more difficult and perhaps less necessary to preserve historic or characteristic descriptions, either of persons or families, enterprises or voyages. And now, it is not easy to find where many of the people came from to Long Island, or New York, or had lived in England, Ireland, Scotland, or the Netherlands, before they came here.

Brief sketches of some early settlers are contained in Young's Chronicles, and in the histories of Southampton, and of Long Island, and the introduction to the *Corwin Genealogy*. The *New England Historical and Genealogical Register* contains other sketches. The New York Genealogical and Biographical Record has, to some extent, pursued the idea. There are many others, and almost every family pedigree contributes to aid a general view. (See 1 *Essex Institute*, 97, the *Wells Genealogy*, &c.)

But each writer takes particular notice of his own class. The clerical writers, and a few connected with the government, wrote and preserved the earliest accounts. Their own class, of course, was described in greatest detail. Other classes also deserve notice. Some seem to have been very poorly described.

In 1618, Capt. John Smith reported to Lord Bacon his voyages and views. He claimed that, from four years' voyages to New England, in three things they had been successful. First, a great plenty of *fish*, easily caught, by two months of fishing. Second. The French and English, by trading off cheap articles to the Indians (such as hooks and lines, beads and glass) had obtained near thirty-six thousand *beaver* skins; which were very valuable. And third, all sorts of *timber for shipping* were most plentiful. He gave the Hollanders as an example to be imitated: "whose endeavours by fishing," he said, "cannot be suppressed by all the king of Spain's golden powers." Perhaps to please Bacon and King James, he said, "Truth is more than wealth, and industrious subjects are more available to a king than gold." (*Historical Magazine*, Vol. 5, p. 195.) On the

17

coasts of Scotland, the success of the Dutch in getting fish and beaver was noticed, and attempts were made to compete with them.

Sir Wm. Alexander, a native of Scotland, afterwards Earl of Stirling, was a member of King James' Privy Council. He, representing his Scotch constituents, aided to form an incorporated company *for fishing,* and sought land in the colonies for settlement. The sea-coast was the attractive part—doubtless by reason of the fish—and the most convenient harbor for ships, and islands were liked by him quite as well as the main-land. (*Life,* by Slafter.)

The Virginia Company, at the outset, intended to send over *shipwrights.* So early as January, 1622, the governor and council in this country, entreated the company at London to go on with their purpose of sending the shipwrights, giving their reasons in these words : " for this country is yet seated on the river's side. They (the shipwrights) will be here, men of singular use for the building of ships, pinnacies, and small vessels, without which we cannot well prosecute our discovery, trade with our neighbours, or transport ourselves or our goods from one place to another." (Neill's *Virginia Company,* 285.)

In June, 1622, the Virginia Company in London, sent over to Virginia " Capt. Tho. Barwick, with 25 persons under his government, for the building of boats, ships, and pinnaces ; " saying, " not anything hath put us to so much trouble and charge as this project hath done." (*Ib.,* p. 308.) And in Virginia, it seems, shipwrights were not very successful.

Capt. Barwick & Co. arrived, and were accommodated at James City. They worked first " in houseing themselves." Many were lost by sickness. (*Ib.,* p. 373.)

There and in other places, the early shipwrights had first to build their own houses. They used large and hard timber for frames, it being plenty ; they sawed their own boards out of hard wood, and hewed the hard timber, before they had saw-mills ;* they used their own tools and plans, which were different from the house-carpenter's, and, as a result, their frames of buildings were stronger, and their houses lasted longer than the others ; some of them have been examined by persons now living ; some of the timber yet exists, though perhaps in granaries and out-houses, or only in forlorn looking old buildings. In other cases the old pattern has been imitated, when descendants familiar with it have removed into new places. A curious one could be seen in the old house of a first settler of Orange County. (Eager's *History of Orange County,* 368.)

The shipwrights thus erected early monuments of themselves ; of their trade and their skill. To comprehend the changed circumstances, we must bear in mind that the small vessels called ships, were then built much stronger than now. We have a description of the frame-work of a ship wrecked on Cape Cod, and buried in the sand for some two hundred years. (In *N. E. Hist. and Gene. Reg.*) Ballasted, so that they could not be capsized, or remain wrong side up ; they were to be framed so strongly that no tossing or gamboling over the waves could break them. And for such long and hazardous voyages, we can imagine how necessary it was to show the inexperienced voyager the strong timbers and braced-frames upon which so much depended. We need not stop to think of the sea sick passenger.

---

* The first saw-mill, it has been written, was in 1643. Pierson Genealogy, p. 54.

At the south, the expected provisions and support of the intended settlers, *by fishing*, failed. Fish were not abundant. Provisions were indispensibly necessary. The prospect of obtaining food, by fishing, was better at the north. This was proclaimed. King James made a grant of Nova Scotia (New Scotland), to Sir William Alexander in 1621. In this grant the king was made to say : "no gain is easier or more safe than the planting of new colonies in uncultivated regions, *where the means of living and food abound.*" Sir William published his " Encouragement to Colonies," in 1624. He took pains to show in this, his northern colony, abundant resources for food ;— " salmon and smelt in the great river ; trout in every little brook ; herrings, in a lake, easily taken, and, all the year over, *shell-fish ;* such as lobsters, crabs, cockles, and mussels."

The Plymouth colony was recommended to the north, especially, for the *present profit of fishing.* (Neill's *Virginia Company*, 131.)

This was the turning point which resulted in success. At first, after arrival, " the famine was very severe," and " the first supply of provisions was obtained from the fishing vessels ; of which 35 came in the spring from England to the coast." (Belknap's *Life of Bradford.*) A few small shallops were retained. " Had we not been in a place where divers sorts of shell-fish are that may be taken by the hand, we must have perished." So wrote their early historian. In 1624 a pinnace was stranded and lost. A ship carpenter having been sent to them, he built " two very good and strong shallops, with a great and strong lighter."

In 1625 one of these was first used on a voyage to the Kennebeck, in Maine ; disposing of surplus corn, and bringing back 700 lbs. of beaver, besides other furs. They engaged also in fishing, and erected buildings for fishing at Nantasket and Cape Ann.

In 1626 the ship carpenter was dead. The shallops were too small and open. The house carpenter undertook to lengthen one of them and put on a deck ; but they dare not venture in her around the end of Cape Cod.

In 1627, they built another pinnace. There was no other history of ship-building.

Two years later, in 1629, 35 families of their relatives and friends arrived from Leyden. They had to be supported for 18 months.

The Massachusetts Company, better provided, arrived. The new company entered early and largely into plans for *fishing* and for *ship-building.* (Young's *Chronicles of Massachusetts*, 185.) The largest arrivals were probably in 1630. We have many accounts of individuals who then came over, but, unfortunately, no general list of passengers at this period. The crowd planned to clear the fields and to form villages and towns. The first difficulties were for food and lodging. The new settlers, generally farmers, were yet without crops, and many without houses. They held or seized the power of ruling on the land, and used this power to help themselves to houses and to food, for which all were straining. They limited by law the price of labor to 1*s.* 6*d.* per day even for skilled carpenters, and when fish were scarce and difficult to secure, they limited also the price for fish. By working hard and failing to secure fish in plenty, or by bringing in more than were wanted, fishermen might lose. But they and the shipwrights were prevented by legal compulsion from obtaining a profit by their skill, or by an extra price on occasions when carpenters or fish were scarce, and difficult, almost impossible, to be obtained. The law-makers were interested judges, and nearly all on one side. Their course did not invite others to bring supplies, but presently drove fishermen and shipwrights away.   And to defend their selfish action they made various harsh charges, which a little cautious examination shows were substantially unfounded.   No man is fit to be a judge against others in his own case.

Shipwrights have been valuable and successful pioneers in many of the new settlements.   They have accompanied fishermen, and all other navigators, and sometimes have preceded them.   They have generally aided to introduce and develop commerce.   Their class certainly deserves attention as well as others.

In this country we can detect and trace the ports and harbors which they have frequented or used.   Can we not trace some of them in England?

It is worth an effort to trace all we can.   Those who have studied in this line assure us it is a rich mine for exploration; and we are ready to believe that knowledge of the past may be useful in the future.   Let us try it.

We have some very doubtful stories that we need not stop to dwell upon; but we have also some very reliable data.

We have the old statutes and ordinances, which, to a careful reader, tell a great many facts.   And we have many old records.   These are the framework, such as an old ship-builder might use for a work that may defy the winds and waves of criticism, and be safe to rely on for our voyage.

An English statute exacted an oath of allegiance from soldiers; an oath was also required from English passengers going abroad from English ports. The object or policy of this we may not fully comprehend.   Perhaps it was merely to prevent Englishmen from becoming foreigners; perhaps to secure all discoveries for the English king.   As it seems, it had little connection with any effort to give Englishmen legal protection when abroad.   Perhaps the wise men in power thought that they could manage the disaffected better at home than abroad.   They did not succeed very well in either place.   An oath was one of their forms of inducing men to do what they otherwise would not.   It proved a very frail reliance.   But it had some effect.   It would bind the honest and religious, but not the most mischievous and dangerous.

MSS. books were kept in London to preserve an account of these oaths. One was entitled "A Booke of Entrie for Passengers by yᵉ Commission, and Souldiers according to the Statutie passing beyond the Seas, begun at Christmas 1631, and ending at Christmas 1632."

The front part of the book contained entries of the names of soldiers. The other end was used for lists of emigrants, traders, travellers, etc. This part happens to be preserved entire.   A few of the persons named can be identified.

This book does not contain the names of passengers by the ship William and Francis, Capt. Thomas, which sailed from England in March, and arrived at Boston on 5th June, 1632, and which brought over Rev. Stephen Batchelor, Rev. Thos. James, sen., Rev. Mr. Welde, Edward Winslow, and others—perhaps 60 passengers.   A part of these are named; and some of them probably removed, afterward, from Lynn, where Mr. Batchelor first settled, to Southampton, L. I.

On 22d June, 1632, among 33 men named in the book, who were "transported to New England to the Plantacon pʳ. cert. from Capten Mason" who (it is stated) had "taken the oath of allegiance according to the Statute," were the names of " Jo. Browne, Jo. Benjamin, Richard Benjamin, and John White." Probably they all settled in this country : perhaps first at Boston or Watertown, Mass. (See Drake's City of Boston, and Bond's History of Watertown.) The last name on this list was "Charles Glouer" (meaning Glover). He was *a shipwright.* In 1639 he was in Salem, Mass., and he ranks as the earliest emigrant to America of those who afterward permanently settled at Southold, L. I. (See Appendix.) A son of one of these Benjamins was probably another early settler of Southold.

The next earliest emigrant to this country perhaps was Matthias Corwin, who was at Ipswich, Mass., in 1634, and afterward a permanent settler at Southold, where he died in 1658. (See CORWIN Genealogy.)

On 15th August, 1633, William Wood, a very intelligent man, after a residence of four years in this country, returned to England. He soon published at London his description of the new country and of the success of the settlements. He encouraged emigration. He estimated 4,000 souls in New England, 1,500 head of cattle, 4,000 goats, and swine innumerable. These first 4,000 we have the smallest means of tracing, in detail, abroad ; but many of them have left strong marks in the woods here ; many trees were cut or blazed, many huts built, much game destroyed ; many farms and villages were planned and marked out, but these took a long period to fill out and settle.

There were kept at London books for oaths of soldiers and passengers, each year, beginning and ending at Christmas. Only a few of these books have been preserved and found, so that they can be referred to.

For the years 1633 and 1634 there were a few scattered lists kept at other ports, which have been found, and many of the passengers named in them have been traced in this country, chiefly at Watertown, Mass.

In February, 1633–4, ten ships bound for New England, and lying in the Thames, at or near London, were stopped until further order, by warrant issued by the Privy Council. The masters of the vessels were called before the Council and charged as to their duties. Each was required to give a bond in £100 conditioned (1st) that they would prevent swearing among the passengers ; (2d) that they would cause prayers from the common prayer-book to be read morning and evening ; (3d) that they would receive no person as a passenger without a certificate of his having taken the oaths of allegiance and supremacy ; and (4th) that upon their return they would report the names of all the passengers. They were then permitted to sail. The bond exhibits rather curiously the predominance of the impractical clerical party in the Privy Council. We have some, but not many names of passengers reported by these ships for that year. The great and wealthy men were keenly alive to the idea of securing large tracts of land, and of becoming lords of manors. The government got little credit for attempting to prevent distress and ruin among the laboring passengers, of which much occurred in Virginia, in Maine, and at Plymouth and elsewhere.

Capt. Thomas Young, and his nephew, Robert Evelyn, were sent from England to Virginia, and afterward to New England, to offer supplies, and to open trade between the two, and guard against famine and distress. Their adventures require a separate description. It is believed they had a material influence upon Southold.

In 1635 we have fuller lists of passengers. The next volume discovered at London commences its entries with the date 29th December, 1634, and

has for its latest date 24th December, 1635. About one-third of it is taken
up with the names of persons going to some port of the low countries
(the Netherlands), some to reside there and some to return. At the other
end of the book are entered the names of passengers for New England,
Virginia, the American (or West India) Islands, and some soldiers. The
vellum wrapper has this inscription : " The Register of the names | of all
yᵉ Passenger wᶜʰ | Passed from yᵉ Port of | London for an whole | yeare
ending at | Xmas 1635."

This book contains many passenger lists, some with numerous names, and
of these a large array can be identified. The king's government required
the additional oath called " the oath of supremacie," to the effect that the
king was the supreme head on earth of the church as well as of the State.
Some of the passengers, besides taking oaths at the shipping port, produced
certificates from the magistrates and clergymen of their parishes, showing
their conformity to the orders and discipline of the English Church. These
were required or favored by the authorities ; and they aid us now in tracing
some of the emigrants to the homes of their nativity, where all of them
were accustomed to the English Church. Two ships brought passengers
from Kent County, as appears by their certificates, dated at Tenterden,
Maidstone, Ashford, Sandwich, Canterbury, and other places in that county.

In one of the early entries in this book, dated 16th March, 1634 (which
we would call 1635), are the names of persons to be transported to New
England, embarked in the Christian, of London, John White, master,
" bound thithei "—"the men having taken yᵉ oath (of) allegiance & supremacie." Of these " Tho. Coop," æt. 18, and " Edward Preston," æt. 13,
probably visited Southold. Others can be traced in New England.

The date 1st April, 1635, introduces passengers in *the Hopewell*, of
London, William Bundocke, master, bound for New England. Among
these were William Purryer, æt. 36, Alice his wife, æt. 37, Mary, æt. 7, Sarah,
æt. 5, and Katheren, æt. 18 mo., his children. This man was one of the
original settlers of Southold, L. I., with his family. He left no son to preserve his name ; but his daughters left many descendants under the names
of Reeve, Mapes, and Osman or Osborn (and perhaps Roe and Wells), and
they are now largely represented in other names. In his will he names his
grandson James Reeve. With him, in the Hopewell, embarked Edmond
Farrington, æt. 47, wife Eliza, æt. 49, and four children ; and John Cooper,
æt. 41, his wife Wibroe, æt. 42, and five children. These three men, Purryer,
Farrington, and Cooper, were described " of Oney, in Buckinghamsher,"
doubtless meaning the Parish of Olney, on the river Ouse, in the north
part of the county of Buckingham, not far from Northampton Co., nor
from Bedford Co., 57 miles from London. At this place Cowper, the poet,
once resided. It was in a central part of England, and had little intercourse
with the coast, with shipwrights, or with fishing.

Philip Kyrtland, æt. 21, and Nathaniel Kyrtland, æt. 19, embarked in
their company, described " of Sherington, in Buckinghamsher," a small
parish about 5 miles S. of Olney, near Newport, Pagnell. They were not
fishermen, nor shipwrights, and they attempted to settle on the western part
of Long Island, where there was wider room for farmers or shepherds, and
were driven off by the Dutch. One was afterward at Southampton, L. I.
The other returned to New England and lived at Salem or Lynn.

In the same vessel came George Griggs, æt. 42, Alice his wife, æt. 32,
and five children. He was described of " Landon," probably meaning

Lavendon, about 3 miles north-east of Olney. He was at Boston in 1636, probably settled at Roxbury, and died in 1660. John Griggs, probably of this family, settled in Gravesend, near the south-west corner of Long Island. This party, it is believed, were of the agricultural class. One of them, Edmond Farrington, was an enterprising man, of whom we should take notice. He settled in Massachusetts. In 1638, at Lynn, he had 200 acres laid off for him. On 29th June, 1639, he obtained an agreement and grant of land on Long Island, from James Farrett, the agent for Sir William Alexander, before named, the first Earl of Sterling, the courtier and poet, who had a grant of all Long Island. Farrett's power of attorney contemplated the approval of his grants by Gov. Winthrop, of Massachusetts. The Governor did not approve of removals from Massachusetts, but heartily opposed them. The grant to Farrington, not approved by Winthrop, by deed dated 26th August, 1639, was approved and confirmed by the Earl of Sterling abroad, and doubtless became the basis of the first regular settlement of Southold.

Emigrants explored the country, but waited to secure a good title before "settling." Farrington did not himself become a settler of Long Island; he sent several sons, and sent or introduced others. He signed the engagement for a plantation at Southampton, with two of his sons, the two Kirtlands, Thomas Terry, and others.

A large number of passengers, from different parts of England, embarked in the same vessel, the Hopewell. Among them were Robert Titus, with wife and children, who became largely represented in the western parts of Long Island. (See Riker's Newtown, p. 327.)

Provisions at Salem became very dear. Some potatoes from Bermuda sold for 2d. sterling a pound.

It was a great object to get stock for farms—cows, horses, hogs, sheep, &c.; and it should be noticed that two Dutch vessels left the Texel in Holland, on 27th April, 1635, and came to anchor at Salem, Mass., on the 3d of June following, bringing live stock, 27 Flanders mares, valued at £34 each, and 3 horses, and provisions, with probably some passengers.

Dutch ships were bringing passengers to New York.* Some Englishmen had lived in Holland, mostly Protestants, persecuted in Queen Mary's reign ; others had traded there. Coming back to England they were Protestants, more advanced perhaps than English residents, in the reformation of the Church. There were "Reformed Dutch Churches" in England and in the province of Canterbury. The Archbishop Laud, sustained by the English king, required all the reforming churches within the province of Canterbury to adopt the English liturgy.† Many did not like that liturgy so well as their own reformed plans, and they sought more liberty in the woods and along the coasts here.

The Dutch, having secured a footing at New York, wanted Englishmen to join them.

Early in 1635, a Dutch ship of 400 tons, bound to New York, was lying at Cowes, an outport of London, ready to sail. Her officers, as reported to the English Privy Council, were drawing as many of His Majesty's subjects as they could to go with them, by offering them large or favorable conditions (embracing land and liberty of worship). The Council at once despatched an order to restrain British subjects from going in that or any

---

* 5 N. Y. Hist. Mag., 354.　　　† Brodhead's Hist., 258.

other *Dutch* vessel "*to the Hollanders plantation on Hudson's River.*"
(3 N. Y. Col. MSS., 19.) But this did not in terms prevent the Dutch
ship from taking passengers to New England and landing them, and then
going to New York.

It seems probable that some were so taken. Some English vessels took
Dutch passengers to New York. (1 Brod. Hist. of N. Y., p. 263.)

The Abigail, Robert Hackwell, master, commenced receiving passengers at London on 15th June, 1635, and continued to receive them on
different days until 10th July; when John Winthrop, Junior, with one brother
and sister, children of Gov. Winthrop of Massachusetts, came on board
(perhaps at Bristol). He had visited Ireland and Scotland, formed many
acquaintances, received an authority from some assignees of the patent for
Connecticut, and he invited emigrants. He was afterward Governor of
Connecticut. Among the passengers by the Abigail was "Jo : Harbert,"
called "shoemaker, æt. 23," and some companions with certificates from
the mayor of Northampton, probably afterward of Salem and of Southold ;
"Christopher Foster, æt. 32," afterward of Southampton, L. I., with wife
Frances, æt. 25, and ch. Rebecca, æt. 5, Nathaniel, æt. 2, afterward of
Huntington, L. I., and John, æt. 1 year. Also "Jo. Terry, æt. 32." This
vessel arrived at Boston by the 5th of October, and it is reported that the
Rev. Hugh Peters came over in her, not named on the passenger list.

We must restrict our sketch, in giving names, to such persons as may be
traced to Southold, or to some part of Long Island, as our main object, but
may include some who settled at Salem, Mass., or who came from ancient
Southwold, England, or from Great Yarmouth in its neighborhood, ports
on the farthest N. E. points of England, by way of gathering the surround-
ings and explaining the movements of those who came early into what
became the State of New York. This would be necessary if we had only
the history of Southold in view.

It appears that men in the northeastern parts of England, who were of
the sea-coast, and the nearest neighbors of the Dutch in Holland, were
more ready than others to settle in this region, along the coast, and near
the Dutch, who then had possession of Brooklyn and Manhattan Island,
and generally of the Hudson river and its neighborhood. Yorkshire, in
several respects, was connected with the same idea; but had some dif-
ferences.

In 1635 we find the passenger lists of fifteen vessels, which sailed from
England for some of the West India Islands. A few of these passengers
can be traced to New England, but not often the same year. In one of
the lists of persons bound from London to St. Christopher's appear the
names of William Salmon, æt. 24, and Thomas Terrill, æt. 18 ; perhaps,
afterward of Southold. In another, of the Dorset, bound to the Bormodes,
(Bermudas), are the names of "Tho. More," æt. 18 ; "John Tustin,"
æt. 16, and "Wm. Casse," æt. 19 ; names that sound very much like Southold. The first Thomas More, who came with Martha Young, his wife, and
several children from Salem, Mass., to Southold, by report was a *shipwright.*
The True Love, of London, Robert Dennis, master, on the 10th of June,
1635, reported the names of 125 passengers to be transported to the
Bermudas, or Somer Islands, the passengers having been examined by the
minister of Gravesend (the shipping port near London) as to their conformity to the orders and discipline of the Church of England, and all taking
the oath of allegiance—only ten of these were reported over thirty years

of age—nearly all were young men ; and among these were William Wells, reported only seventeen years old, who probably came to Southold, and some others, who can be traced in other places.

The Defence, Thomas Bostock, master, commenced taking passengers at London, bound for New England, about the 2d of July, 1635, and continued on the 4th, 6th, 10th, 11th, and 18th. The passengers produced certificates of ministers and magistrates from various different parts of the country, of which the master preserved a note ; several of them are worthy of attention. There were Adam Mott, a taylor, æt. 39, with certificates from Cambridge ; Sarah his wife, æt. 31, and their children (Jo., æt. 14, Adam, æt. 12, Jonathan, æt. 9, Elizabeth, æt. 6, and Mary, æt. 4); John Sheppard, marked husbandman, æt. 36, Margaret his wife, æt. 31, and Thomas, his child, æt. three months; Roger Harlakenden, æt. 25, Eliza his wife, æt. 18, Mable his sister, æt. 21, (afterward the wife of Gov. Haines, of Connecticut); and as their servants, Anne Wood, æt. 23, Samuel Shepherd, æt. 22, Joseph Cooke, æt. 27, and George Cooke, æt. 25'; also, Joh. Jackson, called "a wholesale man in Burchen Lane"; Sara Jones, æt. 34, and six children ; Tho. Donn, æt. 25 ; William Hubbard, æt. 40, and large family; William Read, æt. 30, Mabell Read, probably his wife, æt. 30, and three children ; and many others. This vessel arrived safely at Boston on 3d of October, and we can trace many of the passengers. John Sheppard, called a husbandman, was the Rev[d] John, thus concealed, who has written a graphic account of himself, his hazards and escapes, and of his voyage, and who has described several of his companions above named, the courses pursued in England, the settlement of Cambridge, Mass., and the forming of Harvard College. The Rev[d] Mr. Jones (see 6 N. Y. GEN., AND B. REC., 57) and Rev[d] Mr. Wilson came by the same vessel, but their names do not appear on the list. (Young's Chron. of Mass.) The wife of Rev[d] Mr. Jones is named above. Mr. Wilson had before been driven by foul weather upon the coast of Ireland ; visiting Galway first, and then starting again, he had been forced back by tempest to Kinsale, in Ireland, where he "gave much satisfaction to the Christians there about New England." (1 Winth. Journal, 172.)

There were two vessels called "The James." One started in company with the Gabriel; it was of London, of 220 or 300 tons, William Cooper, master, and sailed on 4th of June, having about 100 passengers, called "honest people of Yorkshire." It arrived at Boston on 16th August. The Rev[d] Richard Mather was one of the passengers, and wrote an account of the voyage. (Young's Chronicles of Mass., 447), describing his adventures and naming some of his companions. Many of the vessels, crowded with passengers, were old and leaky and poorly supplied. There was a great deal of suffering. One, John Bayle, came in the True Love ; another, John Bailey, and John Bailey Jr., came in the Gabriel, which was wrecked at Pemaquid (H. 2). Escaping from the wreck, they tried several places, but settled at Newbury, Mass. (23 N. E. Hist. and Gene. Reg., 150, 152, &c.) One, John Bayley, afterwards came to Southold.

The other vessel, called the James, John May, master, received passengers at London, on 22d July, 1635, bound for New England. Among them were Thomas Terry, æt. 28 ; Robert Terry, æt. 25, and Richard Terry, æt. 17 ; names which can be easily recognized at Southold. This vessel arrived in October, and in her came, among others, the Revd William Leverich, a graduate of Cambridge College, England, who, after

stopping at various places, came to Long Island and settled, first at Huntington, and afterward at Newtown, L. I.

About the same time, the Blessing, John Lester, master, received
passengers to be transported to New England; among whom were
" Jo. Jackson, *fisherman*, æt. 40 ; Margaret Jackson, æt. 36, and John,
their son, æt. 2. (See App'x.)   Richard Hollingworth, *shipwright*, æt. 40 ;
Susan, æt. 30, and ch., William, æt. 7, Richard, æt. 4, Susan 2 and Eliza
3 ; Richard Moore, æt. 20 ; Robert Turner, æt. 24 ; John Hart, *shoemaker*, æt. 40, and Mary, probably his wife, æt. 31 ; all of whom apparently
settled first at Salem, Mass., but soon had some connection with Southold.
There were many came over named Jackson.   The first man who had a
deed for land in Southold was *Richard Jackson;* he probably remained in
Massachusetts, married the widow of Richard Brown, and lived until 1672,
when he was ninety years of age.   The land conveyed was near Green-
port, afterward owned by Thomas More.   In the same vessel came some
of the Vassall family, who were disappointed or were badly treated, and
who returned by the way of Barbadoes, to England.   Revd Joshua Hobart,
afterward of Southold, married into this family.

The next vessel which received passengers at London, between 13th
and 23d July, 1635, to be transported to New England, was one particularly interesting to us.   It was " The Love," Joseph Young, master.
Only eight passengers, besides the master, were named on the book.   Two
names, " Willm. Cherrall, baker, æt. 26, and Ursula Cherrall, æt. 40, were
probably copied erroneously, for William Charles and his wife, mother or
sister, who arrived at Salem and were at Marblehead in 1648.   (See App'x.)
Four others, Francis Harman, æt. 43 ; Jo. Harman, æt. 12, and Sara, æt.
10, and Walter Parker, æt. 18, are not traced.   The remaining two passengers named were " Willm. Browne," called " fisherman," æt. 26, and
" Mary Browne," æt. 26, doubtless his wife.   (See App'x.)

Recent investigations demonstrate that this Capt. Joseph Young, master
of the Love, was of Southwold, in England, and married there Margaret,
daughter of the Rev. Christopher Young, who from 1611 to 1626 was
Vicar of Reydon, the parish in which the seaport of Southwold, on the east
coast of England, was situate.

They, Capt. Joseph Young and Margaret his wife, had a son Joseph
baptized at old Southwold on 23d January 1633-4, and a son John baptized there on the 23d March, 1635 ; and these four, Capt. Joseph, his
wife Margaret, and sons Joseph and John, all came from England to Salem,
Mass., and afterward to Southold, L. I., and settled and died in Southold.
William Browne, the passenger in the Love, by report, was a son of Francis Browne, of Weybrid Hall, Suffolk Co., England.   He was not a fisherman, but had served an apprenticeship to be a merchant at Southwold,
Eng., and had married there Mary Young, a sister of Capt. Joseph, or of
his wife, not exactly traced.   This William Browne, called a shopkeeper
at Salem, is supposed to be the one who settled and flourished there, leaving a
family which acquired distinction (see App'x.), and not the one at Southampton, L. I., in 1648 ; who died there in 1650, and whose daughter Mary
married Robert Marvin; but this is not quite certain.   He had a brother
Richard Brown, in London, who had descendants.   It should be noted
that in 1626, Revd Christopher Young was succeeded as Vicar of Reydon
by Revd John Goldsmith.   The first clergyman of Southold, L. I., the
Revd John Youngs, was married there, and had his son Thomas baptized
there.   The exact relationship, if any, to the old Vicar Christopher, does

not appear, but he named one of his sons Christopher, and so did Capt. Joseph. The maiden name of his first wife is given as Lewington, perhaps Livingston; she was a young widow when he married her. Her daughter by her first husband was named Ann Palgrave, and came over with him and married Nicholas Woodbury, of Massachusetts.

Another interesting vessel was the " Batchelor," of London, Thomas Webb, master, which on 11th August, 1635, received "Lyon Gardiner," æt. 36, " Mary his wife," æt. 34, " Eliza Colet, their maid servant," æt. 23, and "Wm. Jope," æt. 40, who were to pass to New England, having brought certificate of their conformity. The vessel, called a " Norsey bark," brought over 12 men. The lasting memorial of this passage is our Gardiner's Island and its inhabitants.

Many vessels, of course, sailed from other English ports. Weymouth was then one of the seaports nearest to this country. Some ports in Wales and Ireland were nearer. In a list of passengers bound for New England, kept at Weymouth, dated 20th March, 1635, appeared the names of Joseph Hull, of Somerset, minister, with wife, seven children and three servants; and of William King, Dorothy his wife, and four children. Mr. King stopped at Salem. His son Samuel and several daughters settled in Southold. He has been largely represented both in Southold and in Salem by descendants. " Mr. Joseph Hull" was in Salem in 1637, and asked to be received as an inhabitant. An entry was once made that he was so received, but it was afterward erased. He was a preacher at Weymouth. He, at a later date, had descendants at Southold.

The vessels and passengers of 1635 were very numerous. The arrivals exceeded the expectations of the previous settlers, and exceeded all preparations made for them or by them, either for food or house-room. Many circumstances combined to occasion this crowd, and, as a result, much suffering. There was not only no glass for windows, but no houses at all of any kind for the strangers, nor food for their hungry stomachs. The cold, much greater than in England farther north, was not anticipated; nor the hunger sufficiently estimated to be provided for or guarded against. Some of the vessels which brought passengers had not supplies sufficient to last their crews for the voyage back, and had the greatest difficulty to obtain them. The lives of many depended upon fish and fishermen. The grand difficulty was the want of sufficient food and covering to sustain life until many other things could be secured.

A second edition of the work of William Wood was published and circulated in England in 1635, and it doubtless aided the result by which more emigrants left for New England than in any other year. He dedicated the book "to the right worshipful, my much honored friend, Sir William Armyne, knight and baronet." The latter was created a baronet 28th Nov., 1619, and called " Airmine of Osgoodby," a joint parish with Kirkby, near Market Rasen. He was M. P. for Grantham, Lincolnshire, in the Long Parliament, and became a member of the Council of State.

The defect of Wm. Wood's book and of other communications made to England was that they did not report the extreme difficulties and wants about food, houses, and clothing. They found plenty of land—(which had become scarce and dear in England). They were sanguine and enthusiastic, and the early sufferers who had mastered the difficulties—resorting to hunting and fishing—probably thought they had been overcome and were ended. But, if overcome for the first set, they were not so for such an unexpected crowd.

SETTLERS OF THE COLONY OF RENSSELAERSWYCK,
1637.

CONTRIBUTED BY A. J. F. VAN LAER.

Among the Rensselaerswyck manuscripts which were salvaged from the fire in the state capitol of March 29, 1911, is a memorandum in the handwriting of Arent van Curler which adds some interesting details to our knowledge of the final stages of the voyage of the ship *Rensselaerswyck*. The heading of the memorandum reads as follows: "The following persons are indebted to the owners of the ship *Renselaerswyck* for board, beginning on the first of October anno 1636 and ending anno 1637 on the date when each person landed in New Netherland." The memorandum contains the names of 33 men, women and children and gives the exact date when each person left the ship. From the log of the ship, which is printed on pages 355–89 of the *Van Rensselaer Bowier Manuscripts*, it is known that the ship left Amsterdam Sept. 25, 1636, and the first of October anchored at the island of Texel to await a favorable wind and make final arrangements before proceeding on its voyage to New Netherland. The ship arrived at Manhattan on March 4, 1637. It sailed up the Hudson river on March 26, and on April 3 came to anchor half a mile below Beren Island. It remained there on account of calms and contrary wind until April 6, and then continued its voyage to Fort Orange, where it arrived on April 7, 1637. The log states that on March 24, Pieter Cornelissen went up the river in a yacht. The memorandum shows that he did not sail alone, but took with him seven men, one boy, one woman and two children. Most of these men were carpenters. The natural inference is that as soon as a sloop could be procured they were sent ahead to put up some temporary shelter for the farmers, in accordance with the patroon's instructions, as contained in a letter to Jacob Albertsen Planck, dated Oct. 3, 1636. The next group of men left the ship when it came to anchor below Beren Island. They were farmers who settled on or near Papscanee Island, on the east side of the river, not far from Fort Orange. They may have gone up in the ship's boat or reached their destination over land. Quite likely, they did not start until April 6, and took with them Tys Barentsen, the shoemaker, who left the ship on that date. The two other men who are mentioned under date of April 6, did not reach the colony. Cornelis Thomassen, the smith, was killed by his helper, Hans Sevenhuysen, at Ilfracombe, in England, on Dec. 8, 1636, and Sevenhuysen was arrested. The final group of passengers includes those who left the ship after its arrival at Fort Orange.

The memorandum belongs to a collection of letters and miscellaneous papers which were turned over to the New York State Library in Dec., 1910, more than two years after the publication of the *Van Rensselaer Bowier Manuscripts.* Its existence was not known when the list of passengers of the ship *Rensselaerswyck* which is printed on pages 809–16 of that volume was prepared. It affords therefore a means of testing the accuracy of the printed list. It will be found that every name in the memorandum is accounted for in the book, with the exception of that of Thomas Jansz, which occurs at the end but seems to be entered by mistake, being apparently a repetition of the name of Thomas Jansz van Bunnick. It should be noted however that in the printed volume the names of Cornelis Maersen and his wife are entered under the year 1631, when Cornelis Maersen first came to New Netherland, and that the "Cuyper," or cooper, who was with him is not definitely identified and may be any one of a number of persons who are listed in the book but not given in the present document. The fact that the names of these settlers do not appear in the memorandum is no proof that they did not come over in the ship *Rensselaerswyck.* We know from the patroon's letter to Jacob Planck that he had engaged 38 persons for his colony. The memorandum includes only such persons as were indebted for their board.

The document brings out the fact that Jean Labatie, or "Johan Latyn," as his name is written in the manuscript, came from Verdun, in France. He was a carpenter by trade and in a letter to Planck, of May 10, 1638, is referred to as in the service of Albert Andriessen, who with Pieter Cornelissen and Claes Jansen van Naerden had a special contract with the patroon. The words "In compagnie," after Jean Labatie's name, seem to

indicate that he was associated with the men whose names pre-
cede his, in other words, that Claes Jansen van Nykerck had
taken the place of Claes Jansen van Naerden, who sailed a year
later, and that Jean Labatie had been admitted to the partnership.

The following is a complete copy of the memorandum, which
on the back, in the handwriting of Mr. Berthold Fernow, is
marked as number 1002 of the Rensselaerswyck manuscripts.

> D'naervolgende p[er]soenen syn schuldich aende reders
> vant Jacht vant Jacht [sic] renselaerswyck voor
> cost pen[ningen] beginnende 1 Octob[er] a° 1636
> en[de] eyndigende a° 1637 op yders datum wanneer
> in Nieu-Nederlant, syn aen Lant gegaen

	A° 1637 tot 24 marty	a 6 stu: daechs yder*
Pieter Cornelissen van munnekedam	. .	f 52 — 4
Albert Andriessen	. . . . . .	f 52 — 4
Annitgen syn huysvrou	. . . . .	f 52 — 4
2 van dito Aelberts kinderen	. . .	f 52 — 4
Claes Jansz van nyckerck	. . .	f 52 — 4
Johan Latyn van verduyn In compagnie	.	f 52 — 4
Arent Andriesen van vrederickstadt	. .	f 52 — 4
Jacob Jansz van Amsterdam	. . .	f 52 — 4
Gysbert Claesz van Amsterdam Jongen	. .	f 52 — 4
Dirck Jansz van Edam	. . . .	f 52 — 4
Reynier Timansz van Edam	. . .	f 52 — 4
		574 : 4
	Tot 3 April a[°] 1637	
Simon Walingen	. . . . .	f 54 — 12
Cornelis Maersen e[nde] Catelyn syn huysvrou		f108 — 12
Mauris Jansz van Broeckhuysen	. . .	f 54 — 12
Den Cuyper by Cornelis Marsen	. . .	f 54 — 12
	Tot 6 April	
Tys Barentsz Schoenmaecker van Edam	.	f 55 — 10
Cornelis Tomasz Smit voor 38 dagen†	. .	f 20 — 2
Hans Sevenhuysen syn knecht	. . .	f 20 — 2
	Totten 8 April	
Solder [Arent Pietersen]	. . . . .	f 56 — 2
Rutger Jacobsz	. . . . . .	f 56 — 2
Adriaen Hubertsz	. . . . . .	f 56 — 2
Cornelis Tuenisz van Westbroeck	. . .	f 56 — 2
Tomas Jansz van Bunnick	. • . .	f 61 — 4
Jacob Pietersz van Utrecht	. . .	61 — 4
Arent Steveniersz syn huysvrou en[de] twe kinderen	. . .	183 — 12
Cristen Cristensz van vleckeren mit syn huysvrou	. . . . .	122 — 8
Tomas Jansz	. . . . . .	61 — 4

---

* At 6 stivers a day each. One florin, or guilder, equals 20 stivers.
Fl. 52—4 corresponds therefore to 174 days.
  † This should be 68 days.

A LIST OF EARLY IMMIGRANTS TO NEW NETHERLAND.

Alphabetically Arranged, with Additions and Corrections, from Manuscripts of the late Teunis G. Bergen.

Communicated by Van Brunt Bergen, of Bay Ridge, N. Y.

EXPLANATIONS.

List of Ships.—*See* Documentary History of the State of New York, Quarto, Vol. III., pp. 33–42.

31

Immigrants in the ship Broken Heart, Jan. 20, 1664, marked.................... 42
"   "   Beaver, Jan. 20, 1664, marked...................... 43
"   "   Concord, April 17, 1664, marked....................... 44

Names of settlers in Rensselaerwyck, from 1630 to 1646.—*See* O'Callaghan's History of New Netherland, Vol. I., pp. 433–441. *a.*

Names taken from "The Roll of Oaths of Allegiance in Kings Co., N. Y."—*See* Documentary History of the State of New York, Quarto, Vol. I., pp. 429–432 *b.*

A

b Aaten, Adriaen Hend., 1651.
34 Abels, Hendrick, from New Netherland, Mar., 1663.
1 Aboaf, Jacob, Jew, July 8, 1654.
19 Abrahams, Annetje, maiden, Mar., 1660.
24 Abrahams, Cornelis, from Gelderland, farmer, April 27, 1660.
11 Abrahamsen, Francois, from Flissingen, June, 1658.
16 Abrahamsen, Marten, from Bloemendael, wife, and 2 children, Dec., 1659.
32 Ackerman, Davit, from the Maiery of Bosh, wife, and 6 children, ag. 20, 18, 16, 12, 8, 6, Sept. 2, 1662.
36 Adriaensen, Joris, from Leerdam, April 16, 1663.
30 Aertsen, Adriaen, from Tielderweert in Guilderland, May 24, 1662.
16 Aertsen, Jan, from Amersfoort, Dec., 1659.
b Aertsen, Reynier, 1653
16 Aertsen, William, from Wagening, Dec., 1659.
15 Aertz, Louis, from Bruges, planter, April, 1659.
40 Alberts, Peter, from Flissingen, wife, and 2 children, Oct., 1663.
b Albertse, Ruth, 1662.
a Albertsen, Hendrick, 1642.
32 Albertsen, Hendrick, laborer, Sept. 2, 1662.
32 Albertsen, Jan, from Steenwyck, wife, and child, ag. 2¼, Sept. 2, 1662.
31 Aldertsen, Hendrick, from the Thillerwaerd, farmer, and 2 children, May 24, 1662.
a Allertsen, Francis, 1658.
12 Amelhofsen, Jan Barents, from Amsterdam, Feb., 1659.
b Ammerman, Dirck Janssen, 1650.
27 Andriesen, Andries, May 9, 1661.
27 Andriesen, Govert, May 9, 1661.
27 Andriesen, Teunis, May 9, 1661.
44 Andriessen, Claes, from Holsteyn, April 17, 1664.
14 Andriessen, Matthew, from Peters-houck, April, 1659.
32 Anthonis, Annetje, wife of Gerrit Mannaet, and child, ag. 5, Sept. 2, 1662.
41 Arens, Lysbet, from Amsterdam, and child, Jan. 20, 1664.
15 Arents, Lysbeth, wife of Cornelis Barents, and daughter, April, 1659.
20 Arentsen, Claes, from Drenthe, wife, 3 children, and boy, April 15, 1660.
30 Arentsen, Hendrick, from Tielderweert in Guilderland, May 24, 1662.
36 Arien, Jean, from Monpellier, wife, and child (removed to the Islands), April 16, 1663.
a Arissen, Claes, 1630.
39 Aukes, Douwe, Sept., 1663.

B

a Bakker, Willem Juriaensen, 1637.
b Bale, Vincent, 1683.
36 Barents, Elje, wife of Adam Bremen, and servant-girl, April 16, 1663.
31 Barents, Harmtje, from Meppel, maiden, May 24, 1662.
25 Barents, Jannetje, widow of Jan Quisthout, Jan. 11, 1661.
16 Barentsen, Andries, from Twent, wife, and child, Dec., 1659.
32 Barentsen, Claes, from Dordrecht, Sept. 2, 1662.
a Barentsen, Gilles, 1639.
6 Barentsen, Jan, house carpenter and workman, May, 1658.
31 Barentsen, Jan, from Meppel, farmer, wife, and 5 children, ag. 12, 8, 5, 3, May 24, 1662.
27 Barentsen, Tys, from Leerdam, wife, and 3 children, May 9, 1661.
1 Barsimson, Jacob, Jew, July 8, 1654.
20 Bartels, Cornelis, from Drenthe, April 15, 1660.
19 Bartelson, Jonas, wife, and 2 children, Mar., 1660.
44 Bartholemeus, Hendrick, and 5 children, April 17, 1664.
36 Bastiaensen, Giel, from Leerdam, wife, and 4 children, ag. 9, 8, 5, 1, April 16, 1663.
26 Bastiaensen, Jacob, from Heycop, May 9, 1661.
39 Bastiaensen, Jacob, from Newerveen, Spet., 1663.
36 Bastiaensen, Jan, from Leerdam, wife, and 4 children, ag. 19, 15, 12, 5, April 16, 1663.
15 Belet, Dirch, from Breda, cooper, April, 1659.
39 Berghman, Anthonie, from Gorckum, Sept., 1663.
a Berghoorn, Adriaen, 1638.
12 Bevvis, Carel, from Leyden, wife, and 3 children, ag. 8, 6, 3, Feb., 1659.
21 Beyard, Pieter, from Nieupoort, soldier, Mar. 9, 1660.
27 Bielliou, Peter, from Pays de Vaud, wife, and 4 children, May 9, 1661.
24 Blanchan, Matthews, from Artois, farmer, wife, and 3 children, April 27, 1660.
5 Bleyers, Christina, from Stoltenau, May, 1658.
36 Bocke, Jerome, from Walslant, wife, and 5 children, ag. 18, 15, 9, 6, 3, April 16, 1663.
39 Boelhont, Gysbert Krynne, Sept., 1663.
29 Boer, Teunis Dircksen, wife, and 3 children, Jan. 28, 1662.
36 Boerhaus, Barent, April 16, 1663.
36 Boerhaus, Jan, April 16, 1663.
b Bogaert, Theunis Gysbertse, 1652.
b Borcklo, Willem Willemse, 1653.
a Borrelingen, Joris, 1641.
a Bos, Cornelis Teunissen, 1631.
16 Bos, Hendrick, from Leyden, wife, and 2 children, Dec., 1659.
32 Bossch, Jan, from Westphalen, Sept. 2, 1662.
6 Bouche, Simon, May, 1658.
a Bradt, Albert Andriessen, 1630.
4 Breemen, Adam, from Aecken, Dec., 1657.
a Brigham, Richard, 1645.
a Bronck, Pieter, 1646.
b Broulaet, Bourgon, 1675.

22 Brouval, Michiel, from Berg Cassel, soldier, April 15, 1660.
b Brouwer, Adain, 1642.
39 Brouwer, Jan, and brother, Sept., 1663.
b Brouwer, Jan, 1657.
10 Brouwers, Lyntie, Dec., 1656.
30 Brouwers, Thomas Harmensen, from Sevenbergen, farmer, May 24, 1662.
b Bruynenburg, Jan Hanssen, 1639.
b Bruynsen, Ruth, 1653.
31 Buer, Albert, from Gulicke, May 24, 1662.
39 Burger, Johannes, from Geemen, Sept., 1663.
5 Buyers, Geertrie, May, 1658.
22 Buys, Christian Bartels, from Amsterdam, soldier, April 15, 1660.
b Buys, Jan, 1648.
2 Buyskes, Dirk, April, 1657.
6 Buytenhuys, Jan Gerretsen, baker, wife, and sucking child, May, 1658.
a Bylvelt, Juriaen, 1635.

C

10 Carsten, Jansen, Dec., 1656.
39 Carstensen, Peter, from Holsteyn, and son, ag. 16, Sept., 1663.
a Carstenssen, Andries, 1630.
20 Cartens, Coert, from Drenthe, farmer's servant, April 15, 1660.
b Casperse, Johannis, 1652.
b Casperse, Joost, 1652.
24 Cassier, Philip, from Calais, farmer, wife, and 4 children, April 27, 1660.
14 Christians, Grietje, from Tonningen, April, 1659.
11 Claes, Maria, maiden, June, 1658.
32 Claesen, Ammerens, maiden, Sept. 2, 1662.
a Claessen, Claes, 1630.
34 Claesen, Cornelis, from Amsterdam, Mar., 1663.
34 Claesen, Fredrick, from Meppelen, Mar., 1663.
34 Claesen, Fredrick, from Norway, Mar., 1663.
15 Claesen, Geerty, April, 1659.
b Claesen, Hendrick, 1654.
23 Claesen, Jan, from Outbeventer, soldier, April 27, 1660.
32 Claesen, Jan, laborer, Sept. 2, 1662.
6 Claessen, Peter, from Holstein, farmer, wife, and 2 children, May, 1658.
39 Claesen, Reinier, from Francken, Sept., 1663.
12 Clement, Bastiaen, from Doornick, Feb., 1659.
b Clement, Jan, 1665.
a Clock, Abraham, 1645.
b Cockevaer, Alezander, 1657.
16 Coenraet, Hans, baker ; the wife of, and 2 children, Dec., 1659.
12 Coerten, Harmen, from Voorhuysen, wife, and 5 children, Feb., 1659.
27 Coerten, Meyndert, from Aernhem, May 9, 1661.
33 Colff, Jacob, from Leyden, wife, and 2 children, ag. 5, 3, Oct., 1662.
36 Cool, Theunis Bastiaensen, and child, April 16, 1663.
36 Corneliss, Hendrick, from New Netherland, April 16, 1663.
44 Corneliss, Bastiaen, from Maersen, April 17, 1664.
12 Corneliss, Peter, from Holstein, laborer, Feb., 1659.

23 Cornelis, Reinier, from Utrecht (to be discharged whenever he requests it, to follow his trade).
a Cornelissen, Cryn, 1639.
12 Cornellissen, Evert, from the vicinity of Amersfoort, Feb., 1659.
a Cornelissen, Hendrick, 1634.
a Cornelissen, Jan, 1635.
b Cornelissen, Matthys, 1663.
30 Cornie, Symon, from Gene, France, farmer, and wife, May 24, 1662.
a Corstiaenssen, Johan, 1642.
b Cortejou, Jacques, 1652.
33 Cossaris, Jacques, wife, and 2 children, ag. 5, 1½, Oct., 1662.
6 Cousseau, Jaques, May, 1658.
b Couverts, Luijcas, 1663.
b Couverts, Theunis Janse, 1651.
12 Craneburen, Catalyntje, maiden, Feb., 1659.
a Creynen, Jan, 1640.
22 Croos, Conraet, from Switserland, April 15, 1660.
a Crynnesen, Cornelis, 1642.
29 Cuyck, Peter Jansen, from Heusden, farmer, Jan. 28, 1662.

D

a Dam or Damen, Jan Jansen, 1634.
b Damen, Jan, 1650.
b Daniel, Pieter, 1677.
b Davies, Willem, 1653.
a Davits, Christoffel, 1638.
32 Davitsen, Davit, from Maestricht, Sept. 2, 1662.
a De Backer, Herry, 1642.
b Debaene, Joost, 1683.
b De Beauvois, Jacobus, 1659.
39 De Bruyn, Albert Adriaense, from the Betawe, Sept., 1663.
11 De Bruyn, Huybert, June, 1658.
b De Camp, Laurens Janse, 1664.
2 De Chousoy, Marcus, wife, 2 workmen, and 2 boys, April, 1657.
26 De Clein, Hugh Barentsen, wife, and 7 children, May 9, 1661.
33 De Conchilier (now Conselyea), Oct., 1662.
9 De Conick, Harman, Mar. 12, 1656.
b De Consilie, Jean, 1662.
12 De Goeyer, Tryntje, maiden, Feb., 1659.
11 De Gordosa, Francisco, from Davingen, June, 1658.
36 De Groot, Staes, from Tricht, April 16, 1663.
31 De Groot, Willem Pietersen, wife, and 5 children, ag. 9, 7, 5, 3, 1½, May 24, 1662.
b De Hart, Simon Aertsen, 1664.
a De Hooges, Antonie, 1642.
32 De la Main, Robbert, from Dieppe, Sept. 2, 1662.
32 De la Warde, Jan, from Antwerp, Sept. 2, 1662.
45 De Lorie, Christiaen, from St. Malo, Dec. 23, 1661.
36 De Maire, David, from Picardy, wife, and 4 children, ag. 18, 11, 6, 1 April 16, 1663.

32 De Mare, Piere, from Roan, shoemaker, and wife, Sept. 2, 1662.
 a De Metselaer, Teunis, 1641.
 6 De Mil, Anthony, from Haerlem, wife, and 3 children, May, 1658.
33 De Mulder, Ferdinandus, Oct., 1662.
 a De Neger, Jan, 1646.
 a De Reus, Gerrit Teunissen, 1631.
41 De Roode, Lysbet, from Dantzick, wife of John Saline, and child,
       Jan. 20, 1664.
37 De Rues, Jean Paul, June 27, 1663.
 a De Vos, Andries, 1640.
31 De Vos, Balthasaer, from Utrecht, and wife, May 24, 1662.
32 De Witt, Leendert, from Kumunt, Sept. 2, 1662.
 b De Witt, Pieter Janse, 1652.
14 Diesvelt, Peter Arentsen, tailor, April, 1659.
11 Dingeman, Jansen, from Dordrecht, and his bride, Catharine Douwers,
       June, 1658.
35 Dirap, Annetje, from Vianen, widow, and child, ag. 4, Mar. 30, 1663.
20 Dircks, Burtje, from Drenthe, maiden, April 15, 1660.
20 Dircks, Egbertje, from Drenthe, maiden, April 15, 1660.
12 Dircks, Feytje, Feb., 1659.
 5 Dircks, Ursel, from Holstein, and 2 children, May, 1658.
 b Dirckse, Paulus, 1651.
32 Dircksen, Anthony, from Brabant, Sept. 2, 1662.
35 Dirksen, Evert, from Vianen, and 2 children, ag. 13, 6, Mar. 30, 1663.
23 Dircksen, Gysbert, from Schaustevoorn, soldier, April 27, 1660.
11 Dircksen, Harmen, from Norway, wife, and child, June, 1658.
12 Dircksen, Jan, from Alckmaer, wife, and 3 children, Feb., 1659.
31 Dircken, Peckle, from Friesland, May 24, 1662.
13 Dircksen, Roelof, from Sweden, Feb., 1659.
13 Dirxsz, Sweris, from Sweden, Feb., 1659.
 a Dries, Hendrick, 1642.
 b Dorland, Jan Gerrise, 1652.
36 Dorlant, Lammert Jansen, April 16, 1663.
 4 Douwe, Claessen, from Medemblick, mason, Dec., 1657.
 b Dreths, Josias, 1661.
 a Dries, Gertrude, 1642.
12 Drune, Symon, from Henegouw, wife, and 2 children, Feb., 1659.
 b Du Chaine, Anthony, 1663.
33 Du Pui, Nicolas, from Artois, wife, and 3 children, ag. 6, 5, 2, Oct.,
       1662.
 b Durie, Joost, 1675.
33 Du Tois, Arnou, from Ryssel (Lisle), wife, and child, ag. 19, Oct.,
       1662.
22 Dyck, Hendrick, from Nahuys, soldier, April 15, 1660.

E

36 Egberts, Barent, from Bentein, wife, and 2 children, ag. 3, 1, April 16,
       1663.
20 Egberts, Gerrit, from Meppelt, farmer's servant, April 15, 1660.
31 Engelbergh, Jochem, from Heussen, May 24, 1662.

22 Engsinck, Harman Jansen, from Oldenseel, soldier, April 15, 1660.
44 Enjoert, Carel, from Flanders, wife, and 3 children, April 17, 1664.
34 Everts, Dirck, from Amersfoort, wife, and 3 children, ag. 7, 3, 1, Mar., 1663.
12 Eyckers, Jannetje, from East Friesland, Feb., 1659.

F

a Ferlyn, Jasper, 1631.
a Flodder, Jacob, 1638.
a Flodder, Jan Jansen, 1642.
6 Fonteyn, Charel, a Frenchman, and wife, May, 1658.
14 Fontie, Amader, Frenchman, farmer, April, 1659.
20 Foppe, Beletje, April 15, 1660.
21 Forbiet, Adrianus, from Brussel, soldier, Mar. 9, 1660.
12 Fournoi, Adriaen, from Valenciennes, Feb., 1659.
12 Franckese, Arent, from Ioeren, baker, Feb., 1659.
b Franssen, Joost, 1654.
b Fredricks, Jan, 1652.
25 Furmont, Jacob, wife, and child, Jan. 11, 1661.

G

11 Garet, Charles, June, 1658.
26 Genejoy, Estienne, from Rochelle, wife, and 3 children, May 9, 1661.
25 Gerlossen, Cornelis, from East Friesland, tailor, Jan. 11, 1661.
36 Gerrits, Grietje, wife of Dirck Jansen Van Vliet, April 16, 1663.
31 Gerrits, Luytien, from Friesland, farmer, May 24, 1662.
12 Gerrits, Vroutje, wife of Cosyn Gerritsen, wheelwright, Feb., 1659.
44 Gerritse, Claes, wife, and child, ag. 4, April 17, 1664.
30 Gerritse, Jan, from Emderland, Mar. 24, 1662.
34 Gerritse, Roeloff, from Meppelen, Mar., 1663.
30 Gerritsen, Adriaen, from Utrecht, farmer, wife, and 5 children, ag. 13, 12, 11, 8, 7, May 24, 1662.
a Gerritsen, Adriaen, 1634.
16 Gerritsen, Albert, from Wagening, Dec., 1659.
42 Gerritsen, Claes, son of Gerrit Lubbertsen, from Wesel, Jan. 20, 1664.
a Gerritsen, Claes, 1640.
27 Gerritsen, Gerrit, from Beucurn, May 9, 1661.
16 Gerritsen, Gerrit, from Wagening, wife, and child, Dec., 1659.
44 Gerritsen, Gerrit, from Swol, April 17, 1664.
39 Gerritsen, Hendrick, from Aernhem, Sept., 1663.
12 Gerretsen, Stoffel, from Laer, Feb., 1659.
34 Gerritsen, Theunis, from Buren, painter, Mar., 1663.
a Gerritsen, Wolfert, 1630.
a Glen, Sander Leendertsen, 1639.
24 Glissen, Bastiaen, from Calemburg, farmer, wife, and 5 children, April 27, 1660.
21 God-frind, Jan, from Brussels, soldier, Mar. 9, 1660.
36 Goffou, Guilliam, from Sweden, April 16, 1663.

6 Gouwenberch, Jan, fiom Hoorn, May, 1658.
27 Goverts, Laurens (died on the passage), May 9, 1661.
27 Goverts, Roeloft, May 9, 1661.
a Govertsen, Jacob, 1630.
39 Govertsen, Jacob, and son, ag. 18, Sept., 1663.
32 Grand, Joost, from Walslant, Sept. 2, 1662.
14 Grisant, Pierre, Frenchman, farmer, April, 1659.
16 Groenevelt, Leendert Arentsen, and wife, Dec., 1659.
34 Groesvelt, Bay, wife, and sucking child, Mar., 1663.
b Gulick, Jochem, 1653.
a Gysbertsen, Claes, 1641.
a Gysbertsen, Lubert, 1634.
20 Gyseling, Elias, from Zealand, April 15, 1660.
21 Gysen, Peter, from Doornick, cadet, and wife, May 9, 1660.

H

b Haecks, Simon, 1671.
2 Haen, Jacob Hendricksen, April, 1657.
b Hafften, Jacob Henk, 1664.
16 Hagel, Jan Gerritsen, Dec., 1659.
22 Hamelton, John, of Hamelton, soldier, April 15, 1660.
34 Hansen, Hendrick, from Germany, Mar., 1663.
31 Hardenbroeck, Abel, wife, and child, ag. 4, May 24, 1662.
45 Hardenbroeck, Adolph, wife, and son, Dec. 23, 1661.
41 Hardenbroeck, Johannes, from Elbervelt, wife, and 4 children, ag. 8, 6,
    5, 3, Jan. 20, 1664.
31 Hargerinck, Gerrit, from Newenhuys, and 2 sons, ag. 15, 9, May 24,
    1662.
39 Hargeringh, Grietje, from Newenhuys, Sept., 1663.
39 Hargeringh, Jan, from Newenhuys, Sept., 1663.
16 Harmans, Jan, wife, and sucking child, Dec., 1659.
20 Harmens, Annetje, maiden, April 15, 1660.
34 Harmens, Grietje, from Alckmaer, Mar., 1663.
12 Harmens, Jan, from Amersfoort, tailor, wife, and 4 children, Feb.,
    1659.
17 Harmens, Laurens, from Holstein, and wife, Mar., 1660.
30 Harmens, Lysbeth, from the Tiaert, Mar. 24, 1662.
11 Harmensen, Douwe, from Friesland, wife, and 4 children, June, 1658.
12 Harmensen, Hendrick, from Amsterdam, Feb., 1659.
11 Harmensen, Jan, June, 1658.
45 Harmensen, Lubbert, from Overyssel, Dec. 23, 1661.
a Harmensen, Raynert, 1630.
22 Hayen, Claes, from Bremen, cadet, April 15, 1660.
b Hegeman, Hendricus, 1651.
b Hegeman, Jacobus, 1651.
b Hegeman, Joseph, 1650.
14 Hellerick, Hendrick Theunisz, and wife, April, 1659.
23 Hellingh, Harmen, from Reeda, soldier, April 27, 1660.
44 Hendricks, Adriaentje, and child, April 17, 1664.

39 Hendricks, Annetje, wife of Fredrick Hendricks Cooper, Sept., 1663.
b Hendricks, Ephraim, 1654.
34 Hendricks, Grietje, wife of Jan Arentsen Smith, in Esopus, and daughter, ag. 4, Mar., 1663.
21 Hendricks, Harmen, from Deventer, soldier, Mar. 9, 1660.
12 Hendricks, Jacob, from the Highland, and maid-servant, Feb., 1659.
34 Hendricks, Jacob, nephew of Adrian Lammertsen, Mar., 1663.
16 Hendricks, Roeloff, from Drenthe, Dec., 1659.
12 Hendricks, Saertje, from Delft, Feb., 1659.
30 Hendrickse, Adriaen, from Berckeloo, farmer, May 24, 1662.
b Hendrickse, Albert, 1662.
32 Hendricksen, Albert, from Maersen, house carpenter, Sept. 2, 1662.
16 Hendricksen, Femmetje, maiden, Dec., 1659.
27 Hendricksen, Gerrit, from Swoll, May 9, 1661.
a Hendricksen, Gerrit, 1638.
34 Hendricksen, Hendrick, from Westphalia, Mar., 1663.
32 Hendricksen, Lysbet, Sept. 2, 1662.
a Hendricksen, Robert, 1634.
31 Hendricx, Annetie, wife of Jan Evertse, shoemaker, and 5 children, ag. 14, 12, 9, 7, 6, April, 1662.
32 Hermansen, Roelof, from Germany, and wife, Sept. 2, 1662.
11 Hermens, Jannetje, maiden, and her brother, Jan Harmensen, June, 1658.
a Herrick, Jacob, 1646.
20 Heymans, Albert, from Gelderland, farmer, wife, and 8 children, April 15, 1660.
a Higgéns, Tomas, 1646.
a Holmes, Johan, 1642.
34 Holst, Barent, from Hamburgh, Mar., 1663.
30 Homes, Precilla, her brother, ag. 9, and one suckling, May 24, 1662.
36 Honink, Adriaen Jansen, from Well, wife, and 4 children, ag. 8, 6, 4, ½, April 16, 1663.
30 Hooft, Barent Wilten, from Munster, tailor, May 24, 1662.
6 Hoogland, Cornelis Andriessen, tailor, May, 1658.
31 Hooglant, Cornelis Dircksen, farmer, wife, son, and daughter, ag. 24 and 21, May 24, 1662.
b Hooglant, Dirck Jan, 1657.
36 Houpleine, Joost, from Flanders, wife, and son, ag. 18, April 16, 1663.
36 Houpleine, Joost, Jun, wife, and sucking child, April 16, 1663.
a Houten, Joris, 1634.
a Hubertsen, Adriaen, 1636.
a Hubertsen, Andries, 1640.
b Huijcken, Willem, 1663.
20 Huyberts, Ariaen, from Jena (in the service of Roeloff Swartwout), April 15, 1660.
38 Huyberts, Geertje, from Marken, wife of Jan Gerritsen, and nephew, June 27, 1663.
24 Huyberts, Joost, from Gelderland, farmer, wife, and 2 children, April 27, 1660.
45 Huybertsen, Lammert, from Wagening, wife, and 2 children, Dec. 23, 1661.

I

27 Imans, Andries, from Leyden, May 9, 1661.
12 Isacksen, Deunys, from Wyck by Daurstede, Feb., 1659.
11 Isbrands, Jan, rope maker, June, 1658.
32 Ive, Gerardus, from Walslant, Sept. 2, 1662.

J

38 Jacobs, Annetje, from Gornichem, June 27, 1663.
24 Jacobs, Canster, the wife of, and daughter, from Hoesem, April 27, 1660.
12 Jacobs, Epke, from Harlingen, farmer, wife, and 5 sons, Feb., 1659.
26 Jacobs, Gideon, May 9, 1661.
32 Jacobs, Jacomyntje, daughter of Jacob Swart, Sept. 2, 1662.
12 Jacobs, Peter, from Holstein, laborer, Feb., 1659.
20 Jacobs, Peter, from East Friesland, April 15, 1660.
16 Jacobsen, Aeltje, maiden, Dec., 1659.
31 Jacobsen, Gerrit, from Meppel, farmer, May 24, 1662.
12 Jacobsen, Jan, from Utrecht, farmer, wife, mother, and 2 children, Feb., 1659.
34 Jacobsen, Jan, from East Friesland, wife, and 2 children, ag. 7, 5, Mar., 1663.
 a Jacobsen, Jan, 1634.
 a Jacobsen, Nys, 1640.
 a Jacobsen, Pieter, 1639.
 4 Jacobsen, Thys, Dec., 1657.
24 Jacobsen, Willem, from Haerlem, farmer, April 27, 1660.
36 Jans, Gerrit, from Arnhem, and wife, April 16, 1663.
33 Jans, Judith, from Leyden, maiden, Oct., 1662.
19 Jans, Maria, orphan, Mar., 1660.
40 Jans, Marritje, from Amsterdam, Oct., 1663.
44 Jans, Sicke, from Amsterdam, April 17, 1664.
14 Jans, Vaintie, from Amsterdam, maiden, April, 1659.
20 Janse, Focke, from Drenthe, farmer, wife, and 7 children, April 15, 1660.
 b Janse, Jan, 1651.
 b Janse, Lambert, 1665.
 b Janse, Pieter Guil., 1642.
 b Janse, Willem Guil., 1640.
11 Jansen, Adriaen, from Zea-land, fisherman, June, 1658.
30 Jansen, Albert, from Steenwyck, tailor, May 24, 1662.
17 Jansen, Bart, from Amsterdam, mason, wife, and 3 children, Mar., 1660.
33 Jansen, Carsten, Oct., 1662.
27 Jansen, Claes, from Uithoorn, wife, and child, May 9, 1661.

A LIST OF EARLY IMMIGRANTS TO NEW NETHERLAND.

Alphabetically Arranged, with Additions and Corrections, from Manuscripts of the late Teunis G. Bergen.

J

39 Jansen, Claes, from Amsterdam, wife and 3 children, ag. 15, 12, 6, Sept., 1663.

14 Jansen, Claes, from Parmerend, wheelwright, wife, servant, and child, April, 1659.

31 Jansen, Dirck, from Bommelderweert, and 2 children, May 24, 1662.

22 Jansen, Dirck, from Bytwelt, soldier, April 15, 1660.

35 Jansen, Elias, from Fiel, Mar. 30, 1663.

39 Jansen, Grietien, from Weldorp, Sept., 1663.

18 Jansen, Hendrick, from Amersfoort, wife and 4 children, Mar. 9, 1660.

16 Jansen, Hendrick, from Wagening, Dec., 1659.

34 Jansen, Hendrick, painter, Mar., 1663.

21 Jansen, Jacob, from Mullem, soldier, Mar. 9, 1660.

31 Jansen, Jacob, of New Netherlands, farmer, May 24, 1662.

16 Jansen, Jacob, from Amersfoort, Dec., 1659.

6 Jansen, Jan, house carpenter, wife and 5 children, Maria, Magdalena, Arien, Sophia, Christina, May, 1658.

42 Jansen, Jan, from Amsterdam, Jan. 20, 1664.

21 Jansen, Jan, from Dunker, soldier, Mar. 9, 1660.

39 Jansen, Jan, from Norway, and wife, Sept., 1663.

39 Jansen, Jan Jun., wife and child, ag. 2½, Sept., 1663.

34 Jansen, Jeremias, from Westerhoot, Mar., 1663.

11 Jansen, Joris, from Hoorn, house carpenter, June, 1658.

32 Jansen, Jouriaen, from Holsteyn, Sept. 2, 1662.

17 Jansen, Maritje, maiden, Mar., 1660.

12 Jansen, Nettert, from Embden, Feb., 1659.

34 Jansen, Peter, from Amersfoort, and 4 children, ag. 19, 16, 7, 3, Mar., 1663.

29 Jansen, Peter, from Amsterdam, farmer, Jan. 28, 1662.

20 Jansen, Peter, from Drenthe, shoemaker, wife and 4 children, April 15, 1660.

34 Jansen, Theunis, from the country of Luyck, wife and 6 children, ag. 18, 16, 14, 9, 7, 2, Mar., 1663.

34 Jansen, Thys, from the country of Luyck, and 4 children, ag. 17, 15, 13, 11 (his wife died on passage), Mar., 1663.

15 Jansen, Thys, from the Gooy, farmer, April, 1659.

16 Jansen, Tys, from Amersfoort, Dec., 1659.

a Jansen, Volckert, 1638.

15 Jansen, Willem, from Rotterdam, fisherman, wife, sucking child, and maid servant, April, 1659.
20 Janss, Albert, from Drenthe, April 15, 1660.
2   Janssen, Arent, house carpenter, wife and daughter, April, 1657.
b Janssen, Hans, 1640.
12 Janssen, Lawrens, from Wormer, Feb., 1659.
b Janssen, Swaen, 1654.
35 Jaspers, Grietje, from Fiel, maiden, Mar. 30, 1663.
44 Jeppes, Jentje, wife and 3 children, April 17, 1664.
26 Jochems, Hendrickje, May 9, 1661.
26 Jochems, Geertje, May 9, 1661.
12 Jochems, Geertruy, from Hamburgh, wife of Claes Claessen, from Amersfoort, and 2 children, Feb., 1659.
39 Johannis, Foppe, servant of Schout Olferts, Sept., 1663.
39 Johannis, Minne, wife and 4 children, ag. 8, 8, 6, 1, together with his wife's sister and his servant, Sept., 1663.
32 Joosten, Jan, from Tielderweert, wife and 5 children, ag. 15, 12, 9, 6, 2½, Sept. 2, 1662.
a Joris, Burger, 1637.
36 Journai, Moillart, from Walslant, April 16, 1663.
b Juriaense, Barent, 1658.
41 Juriaensen, Jannecken, from Grevckeur, Jan. 20, 1664.

K

b Kamminga, Hendrick Janse, 1679.
b Kat, Claes Cornelissen, 1662.
20 Keirs, Jan, from Drenthe, and wife, April 15, 1660.
22 Kemmes, Brant, from Dockum, soldier, April 15, 1660.
a Kenningh, Tomas, 1646.
36 Kerve, Jacob, from Leyden, and wife, April 16, 1663.
b Kiersen, Jan, 1649.
b Klock, Pelgrom, 1656.
10 Kock, Jan Gillessen, from Utrecht, wife and 3 children, Dec., 1656.
23 Kockuyt, Joost, from Bruges, soldier, April 27, 1660.
b Kockuyt, Joost, 1660.
b Koeck, Laurens, 1661.
20 Koorts, Steven, from Drenthe, wife and 7 children, April 15, 1660.
Koerten, see Coerten.
a Korn, Nicolaus, 1642.
a Koyemans, Barent Pieterse, 1636.
2   Kraey, Teunis, from Venlo, wife, 4 children, and 2 servants, April, 1657.
32 Kraffort, David, mason, wife and child, Sept. 2, 1662.
a Krol, Bastiaen Jansen, 1630.
24 Krypel, Anthony, from Artois, farmer, and wife, April 27, 1660.
40 Kume, Ariaen Peters, from Flissingen, Oct., 1663.
b Kume, Adriaen, 1660.

L

a Labbadie, Jan., 1634.
b La Febre, Isaack, 1683.

b La Forge, Adriaen, 1672.
b Lamberse, Thomas, 1651.
34 Lammerts, Hendrick, from Amersfoort, Mar., 1663.
34 Lammertsen, Adrian, from Tielderveen, wife and 6 children, ag. 17, 15, 11, 7, 5, 3, Mar., 1663.
26 Lammertsen, Jan, from Bremen, May 9, 1661.
16 Langelens, Philip, farmer, wife and 2 children, Dec., 1659.
36 Laurens, Jans, from Rypen, April 16, 1663.
35 Laurens, Maria, Mar. 30, 1663.
39 Laurense, Jan, from New Netherland, Sept., 1663.
a Laurenssen, Laurens, 1630.
12 Lawrense, Jan, Noorman, and wife, Feb., 1659.
32 Le Chaire, Jan, from Valenciennes, carpenter, Sept. 2, 1662.
15 Leenders, Aertje, from Amsterdam, widow, April, 1659.
a Leendertsen, Cornelis, 1658.
a Leendertsen, Willem, 1646.
23 Lengelgraaff, Daniel, from Amsterdam, soldier, April 27, 1660.
11 Lequie, Jan, from Paris, June, 1658.
b Lequie, Jean, 1657.
22 Levelin, Johannes, from Milhausen, soldier, April 15, 1660.
23 Leysseler, Jacob, from Francfort, soldier, April 27, 1660.
23 Locker, Conraet, from Nieuenburg, soldier, April 27, 1660.
b Lott, Pieter, 1659.
33 Louhman, Louis, wife and 3 children, ag. 6, 4, 2, Oct., 1662.
36 Lourens, Jan, from Schoonder Woort, wife and 2 children, ag. 7, 4, April 16, 1663.
18 Lourens, Peter, the wife of, Mar. 9, 1660.
32 Lourensen, Adriaen, from Loenen, carpenter, Sept. 2, 1662.
b Loyse, Cornelis, 1651.
b Lubberse, Thys, 1637.
31 Lubbertsen, Lubbert, from Meppel, farmer, wife and 4 children, ag. 17, 13, 9, May 24, 1662.
31 Lubbertsen, Willem, from Meppel, farmer, wife and 6 children, ag. 19, 16, 9, 7, 4, May 24, 1662.
35 Lucas, Dirck, Mar. 30, 1663.
27 Luten, Walraven, from Flanders, wife and suckling, May 9, 1661.
13 Luycas, Jan, from Oldenseel, shoemaker, wife and suckling, Feb., 1659.
40 Luycase, Willem, from Maeslands-sluys, Oct., 1663.
b Luyster, Pieter Cornelis, 1656.

M

15 Mandeville, Gillis, April, 1659.
22 Mannaet, Gerrit (Van Haen), soldier, April 15, 1660.
a Mannix, Geertje, 1642.
10 Marritje, Juriaens, Dec., 1656.
12 Marschal, Evert, from Amsterdam, glasier, wife and daughter, Feb., 1659.
12 Marschal, Nicholas Gillissen, Feb., 1659.
20 Martensen, Arent, from Gelderland (in the service of Roeloff Swartwout), April 15, 1660.

34 Martensen, Peter, from Ditmarsum, and child, ag. 7, Mar., 1663.
32 Martin, Piere, from Walslant, Sept. 2, 1662.
22 Mattens, Peter, from Laeren, soldier, April 15, 1660.
36 Matthysen, Peter, from Limborgh, April 16, 1663.
 a Megapolensis, Dominie Johannes Jr., 1642.
39 Megelio, Hessel, from Friesland, Sept., 1663.
44 Mellis, Claes, from Great Schermer, wife, 2 children, and servant,
        April 17, 1664.
16 Melyn, Cornelis, and 2 sons, Dec., 1659.
33 Merlitt, Gideon, wife and 4 children, ag. 15, 8, 6, 4, Oct., 1662.
 b Messcher, Adam Machielse, 1647.
36 Mesurole, Jean, from Picardy, wife and sucking child, April 16, 1663.
23 Mettermans, Paulus, from Louren, soldier, April 27, 1660.
12 Meynderts, Egbert, from Amsterdam, wife, child, and servant, Feb.,
        1659.
12 Meynderts, Jan, from Joeren, farmer, and wife, Feb., 1659.
 a Meynten, Willem, 1638.
14 Michielsen, Cornelis, from Medemblick, April, 1659.
26 Middagh, Aert Teunissen, May 9, 1661.
 b Middagh, Jan Aertsen, 1659.
 b Miseroll, Jean Jun, 1667.
27 Mol, Dirck, May 9, 1661.
20 Mol, Jan Jansen, April 15, 1660.
14 Monier, Jacques, Frenchman, farmer, April, 1659.
14 Monier, Pierre, Frenchman, farmer, April, 1659.
16 Moors, Maria, from Arnhem, maiden, Dec., 1659.

N

19 Niesen, Cornelis, the wife of, Mar., 1660.
36 Niu, Pierre, from Pays de Vaud, sister, wife, and sucking child, April
        16, 1663.
21 Norman, Andries, from Steenwyck, soldier, Mar. 9, 1660.
 a Nostrandt, Jacob Jansen, 1638.
 a Nyssen, Wolf, 1646.

O

39 Olferts, Schout, from Friesland, wife and child, ag. 2½, Sept., 1663.
 a Oosterum, Gerrit Willems, 1631.
31 Ooencamp, Casper, servant of Abel Hardenbroeck, May 24, 1662.

P

 b Palmentier, Michiel, 1664.
 b Para, Pieter, 1659.
36 Parmentie, Pierre, from Pays de Vaud, wife and son, ag. 9, April 16,
        1663.
27 Paulessen, Gommert, from Antwerp, May 9, 1661.
33 Paulus, Claus, from Ditmarsen, and wife, Oct., 1662.

22 Peters, Peter, from Amsterdam, cadet, with his wife and 3 children, April 15, 1660.
15 Petersen, Albert, mason, April, 1659.
35 Petersen, Andrees, from Fiel, Mar. 30, 1663.
22 Petersen, Claes, from Detmarsen, cadet, April 15, 1660.
26 Petersen, Evert, the son of, Consoler of the sick, May 9, 1661.
15 Petersen, Gerrit, April, 1659.
22 Petersen, Jan, from Detmarsen, soldier, April 15, 1660.
31 Petersen, Jan, from Deventer, tailor, wife and 3 children, ag. 9, 6, 4, May 24, 1662.
21 Petersen, Marcus, from Steenwyck, soldier, Mar. 9, 1660.
15 Petersen, Peter, alias Para, from Picardy, wife and daughter, April, 1659.
29 Petersen, Siewert, from Hoesem, maltster, Jan. 28, 1662.
16 Petersen, Willem, from Amersfoort, Dec., 1659.
 6 Pieters, Tryntje, maiden, May, 1658.
 b Pieterse, Lefferd, 1660.
30 Pietersen, Reynier, from Idemland, farmer, May 24, 1662.
 a Pietersen, Wybrant, 1638.
 a Plauck, Jacob Albertzen, 1634.
11 Ples, Michiel, from Holstein, wife and 3 children, June, 1658.
37 Pont, Vieu, from Normandy, June 27, 1663.
 a Poog, Johan, 1639.
 a Pos, Simon Dircksen, 1630.
 3 Pouuelson, Claes, from Detmarsum, mason, Dec., 1657.
21 Princen, Matthys, from Waltneel, soldier, Mar. 9, 1660.
 b Probasco, Christoffel, 1654.
22 Pronck, Johan, from Bonn above Ceulen, soldier, a smith, and baker, April 15, 1660.
16 Pynacker, Joost Adriaensen, from Delft, Dec., 1559.

R

17 Reinders, Wiggert, from the Grouw, farmer, Mar , 1660.
14 Reneau, Jacques, Frenchman, farmer, April, 1659.
36 Renare, Martin, from Picardy, wife and child, April 16, 1663.
36 Richarvie, Pierre, from Parys, April 16, 1663.
 b Ridder, Barent Joosten, 1652.
23 Riet, Jan, soldier, April 27, 1660.
12 Roelofs, Sophia, Feb., 1659.
40 Roelofs, Boel, from Friesland, Oct., 1663.
12 Roelofs, Matthys, from Denmark, wife and child, Feb., 1659.
12 Roelofsen, Boele, joncker, wife, 3 children, wife's sister, and a boy, Feb., 1659.
27 Roelofsen, Jacob, May 9, 1661.
27 Roelofsen, Jan, May 6, 1661.
39 Roelofsen, Jan, from Norway, Sept., 1663.
 b Romeyn, Stoffel Janse, 1653.
35 Rosens, Clement, Mar. 30, 1663.
 a Rutgersen, Ryckert, 1636.
14 Ruytenbeeck, Annetje, maiden, April, 1659.

a Ruyter, Claes Jansen, 1638.
b Ryerse, Adriaen, 1646.
c Ryersen, Jan, 1637.

S

32 Saboriski, Albert, from Prussia, Sept. 2, 1662.
27 Samsons, Geertje, from Weesp, May 9, 1661.
27 Santvoort, Jacob Abrahamsen, May 9, 1661.
36 Sardingh, Hans Jacob, April 16, 1663.
14 Savariau, Matthieu, Frenchman, farmer, April, 1659.
17 Schaets, Cornelis Davitsen, wheelwright, Mar., 1660.
b Schamp, Pieter, 1672.
b Schenck, Jan Marteuse, 1650.
b Schenck, Roeloff Marteuse, 1650.
a Schermerhorn, Jacob Jansen, 1645.
35 Schiltman, Dirck, from Tiel, Mar. 30, 1663.
32 Scholts, Symon, from Prussia, Sept. 2, 1662.
35 Schot, Willem, Mar. 30, 1663.
a Scuth, Jan Willemsen, 1646.
b Seeu, Cornelis Jansse, 1660.
33 Setshoorn, Abelis, Oct., 1662.
28 Slecht, Barent Cornelissen, Nov., 1661.
b Sleght, Hendrick, 1652.
b Smack, Hendrick Mathysse, 1654.
30 Smet, Stoffel, from Keurle, farmer, May 24, 1662.
2 Smetdes, Johannis, April, 1657.
11 Smith, Dirck, ensign, wife of, and a sucking child, June, 1658.
34 Smith, Edward, from Leyden, Mar., 1663.
a Smith, Lucas, 1642.
4 Snedick, Jan, wife and 2 children, Dec., 1657.
20 Souvanich, Jan, from Byle in Drenthe, April 15, 1660.
31 Spiegelaer, Jan, and wife, May 24, 1662.
b Spiegelaer, Jan, 1662.
a Spierinck, Cornelis, 1639.
a Spierinck, Jacques, 1630.
45 Spiers, Hendrick Jansen, wife and 2 children, Dec. 23, 1661.
a Staes, Abraham, 1642.
15 Steenhuysen, Englebrecht, from Soest, tailor, April, 1659.
21 Steffen, Johan, from Herborn, soldier, Mar. 9, 1660.
16 Stepfer, Harmen, from the Duchy of Cleef, Dec., 1659.
16 Sterrevelt, Adriaen Huybertsen, farmer, Dec., 1659.
a Steveniersen, Arent, 1636.
a Stevensen, Abraham, 1637.
7 Stevenson, Jacob, cooper, and wife, Aug. 3, 1654.
20 Stintham, Peter, from Nimwegen, tailor, April 15, 1660.
2 Stoeff, Hertwich, April, 1657.
b Stoffelse, Dirck, 1657.
b Stoffelse, Gerrit, 1651.
11 Stoffelsen, Machteld, widow, June, 1658.
a Stoffelsen, Ryer, 1639.
a Stol, Jacob Jansen, 1630.

13 Stolten, Marten Warnarts, from Swoll, Feb., 1659.
b Stoothoof, Elbert Elbertse, 1637.
32 Storm, Dirck, from the Maiery of Bosh, wife and 3 children, ag. 6, 2,
   1¼, Sept. 2, 1662.
b Strycker, Jacob, 1651.
b Strycker, Jan, 1652.
b Stryker, Gerrit Janse, 1652.
4 Sudeich, Claes, Dec., 1657.
b Suydan, Hendrick Rijcken, 1663.
20 Swartwout, Roeloff, farmer (on his return to N. Netherland, his former
   residence), April 15, 1660.
22 Swetermik, Hendrich, from Osenburg, soldier, April 15, 1660.
32 Symonsen, Willem, from Amsterdam, Sept. 2, 1662.

T

41 Tack, Evert, from the Barony of Breda, Jan. 20, 1664.
44 Taelman, Jan, April 17, 1664.
32 Ten Houte, Souverain, baker, Sept. 2, 1662.
12 Teunis, Magalantje, from Voorhuysen, Feb., 1659.
41 Teunis, Sara, Jan. 20, 1664.
27 Teunissen, Aerent, from Amsterdam, wife and 2 children, May 9, 1661.
39 Teunissen, Cornelis, from Norway, Sept., 1663.
a Teunissen, Claes, 1645.
a Teunissen, Jan, 1640.
a Teunissen, Jannitje, 1640.
23 Teunisen, Peter, from Fleensburgh, soldier, April 27, 1660.
45 Theunissen, Claes, from Goreum, servant and boy, Dec., 23, 1661.
27 Theunissen, Jan, from Amsterdam, wife and 2 children, May 9, 1661.
26 Thysen, Wouter, from Hilversom, May 9, 1661.
b Tierckse, Thomas, 1652.
a Tiers, Johan, 1631.
31 Tinmer, Jan, from Gorchum, and wife, May 24, 1662.
14 Tollenaer, Peter, from Hasselt, April, 1659.
a Tomassen, Barent, 1630.
a Tomassen, Cornelis, 1636.
36 Tomassen, Juriaen, from Rypen, April 16, 1663.
12 Toonson, Joris Jorissen, from Redfort, mason, Feb., 1659.
b Tull, Pieter Pieterse, 1657.
32 Tymonsen, Hendrick, from Loosdrecht, Sept. 2, 1662.
16 Tysen, Claes, cooper, the wife of, and 2 children, Dec., 1659.
a Tyssen, Claes, 1639.
a Tyssen, Jan, 1630.

U

24 Uslie, David, from Calais, farmer, and wife, April 27, 1660.

48

A LIST OF EARLY IMMIGRANTS TO NEW NETHERLAND.

ALPHABETICALLY ARRANGED, WITH ADDITIONS AND CORRECTIONS, FROM MANUSCRIPTS OF THE LATE TEUNIS G. BERGEN.

V

23 Vaex, Jan, from Nieustadt, soldier, April 27, 1660.
b Van Aerts Daalen, Simon Janse, 1653.
b Van Amach, Theunis Janse, 1673.
a Van Amersfoort, Jan Dircksen, 1638.
a Van Amersfoort, Jan Dircksen, 1642.
b Van Amersfoort, Jan Harmenssen, 1658.
a Van Amsterdam, Albert Jansen, 1642.
a Van Amsterdam, Gysbert Claessen, 1636.
a Van Amsterdam, Jacob Jansen, 1636.
a Van Baasle, Johan Helms, 1642.
a Van Baden, Hans Vos, 1642.
26 Van Beest, Adriaentje Cornelis, widow and daughter, May 9, 1661.
26 Van Beest, Aert Pietersen, Buys, wife and son, May 9, 1661.
31 Van Beest, Annetje Gillis, servant girl, May 24, 16 2.
26 Van Beest, Frans Jacobsen, wife and 2 children, May 9, 1661.
26 Van Beest, Geertje Cornelis, widow and 6 children, May 9, 1661.
26 Van Beest, Geertruy Teunissen, May 9, 1661.
26 Van Beest, Goosen Jansen Van Noort, May 9, 1661.
26 Van Beest, Hendrick Bries, May 9, 1661.
34 Van Beest, Jan Petersen Buys, Mar., 1663.
26 Van Beest, Peter Marcelis, wife, 4 children, and 2 servants, May 9, 1661.
36 Van Beest, Marretje Theunis, April 16, 1663.
26 Van Beest, Neeltje Jans, May 9, 1661.
34 Van Bergen, Andries Pietersen, Mar., 1663.
a Van Bergen, Martin Gerrittsen, 1630.
b Van Boerum, Willem Jacobs, 1649.
41 Van Bommel, Marselis Jansen, farmer, Jan. 20, 1664.
b Van Bosch, Jan Wouterse, 1659.
a Van Breda, Claes Jansen, 1639.
a Van Bremen, Jan Jansen, 1646.
a Van Breukelen, Cornelis Teunissen, 1631.
a Van Broeckhuysen, Mauritz Jansen, 1636.
a Van Broeckhuysen, Michel Jansen, 1636.
b Van Brunt, Ruth Joosten, 1653.
a Van Bersingeren, Adriaen Cornelissen, 1642.

a Van Bunick, Gysbert Adriaensen, 1638.
a Van Bunick, Tomas Jansen, 1636.
a Van Buren, Cornelis, Maessen, 1631.
24 Van Buren, Gerrit Aartsen, farmer, April 27, 1660.
24 Van Buren, Gerrit Cornelissen, farmer, April 27, 1660.
b Van Buren, Jacob Willem, 1649.
a Van Campen, Jacob Jansen, 1640.
b Van Cassant, Isaack, 1652.
b Van Cleef, Jan, 1653.
30 Van Compen, Claes, from Oldenburg, farmer's boy, May 24, 1662.
12 Van Coppenol, Jan. from Ronsen, farmer, wife and 2 children, Feb., 1659.
a Van Cremyn, Joachim Kuttelhuys, 1642.
a Van Curler, Arendt, 1630.
27 Van Denen, Annetje, from Enden, May 9, 1661.
21 Van der Beecke, William, from Oudenaerde, soldier, Mar. 9, 1660.
a Van der Belt, Adriaen Teunissen, 1640.
a Van der Belt, Simon Walings, 1636.
a Van der Bogaert, Harman Mynderts, 1646.
3 Van den Bos, Jan Jansen, mason, and his brother, Dec., 1657.
43 Van der Briel, Anietje Hendricks, Jan. 20, 1664.
a Van der Donk, Adriaen, 1641.
44 Van der Hagen, Seravia, and child, April 17, 1664.
4 Van der Kuyl, Cornelis Barentsen, Dec., 1657.
36 Van der Peich, Matthys Bastiaensen, and daughter, April 16, 1663.
14 Van der Schelling, Jacobus, and his boy, April, 1659.
6 Van der Sluys, Andries, wife of and child, clerk in Fort Orange, May 1658.
14 Van der Spiegel, Laurens, van Flissingen, April, 1659.
13 Van der Veer, Cornelis Jansen, farmer, Feb., 1659.
12 Van der Wielen, Laurens Jacobs, Feb., 1659.
b Van Deventer, Jan, 1662.
b Van de Water, Jacobus, 1658.
14 Van de Wert, Marten, from Utrecht, hatter, April, 1659.
17 Vandieu, Dirck Gerritsen, from Tricht, farmer, Mar., 1660.
a Van Doorn, Cornelis Lambertsen, 1642.
a Van Dublin, Jan Andriessen, 1646.
b Van Duyn, Gerrit Cornelis, 1649.
24 Van Duyvelant, Jan, the wife of, April 27, 1660.
5 Van Duyvelant, Jan Adriaensen, May, 1658.
b Vandyck, Achias Janse, 1651.
b Vandyck, Jan Janse, 1652.
b Vandyck, Karel Janse, 1652.
b Van Dyckhuys, Jan Theunis, 1653.
14 Van Ecke, Peter, from Leyden, planter, April, 1659.
a Van Edam, Dirck Jansen, 1636.
a Van Edam, Jan Michaelsen, 1637.
a Van Edam, Rynier Tymanssen, 1636.
a Van Edam, Tys Barentsen Schoonmaker, 1636.
b Van Ens, Cornelis Hendricksen, May, 1658.
a Van Es, Cornelis Hendricksen, 1642.
a Van Franiker, Jan Terssen, 1635.

a Van Frederickstad, Arent Andriessen, 1636.
12 Van Garder, Gillis Jansen, wife and 4 children, Feb., 1659.
a Van Gertruydenburgh, Paulus Jansen, 1642.
6 Van Gilthuys, Gerrit Gerritsen, tailor, May, 1658.
6 Van Gloockens, Jan Evertsen, May, 1658.
12 Van Gorehem, Weyntje Martens, Feb., 1659.
44 Van Haagen, Maria, and child, ag. 4, April 17, 1664.
22 Van Haen, Gerrit Mannaet, soldier, April 15, 1660.
6 Van Halen, Peter, from Utrecht, wife, 2 children, and a boy, May, 1658.
a Van Hamelwaard, Adam Roelantsen, 1639.
a Van Hamelwaard, Martin Hendricksen, 1638.
33 Van Heyningen, Claes Jansen, Oct., 1662.
8 Van Hooghvelt, Lysbet, Dec. 20, 1656.
a Van Hoosem, Jan, 1646.
a Van Houtten, Cornelis Kryne, 1640.
a Van Houtten, Jan Cornelissen, 1640.
a Van Houtten, Jan Creyne, 1642.
a Van Houtten, Roeloff Cornelissen, 1638.
11 Van Kampen, Jan Brandsen, farmer, June, 1658.
b Van Kerck, Jan Sen., 1663.
12 Van Kootuyck, Wouter Gerritsen, Feb., 1659.
6 Van Laer, Adriaen, from Amsterdam, and servant, May, 1658.
20 Van Leeuwen, Cornelis Jacobs (in the service of Roeloff Swartwout), April 15, 1660.
a Van Leyden, Wm. Fredericksen, 1642.
44 Van Lier, Jan Evertsen, the wife of, and child ag. 8, April 17, 1664.
34 Van Limmigen, Jan Cornelisz, Mar., 1663.
15 Van Loo, Barent, from Elburg, April, 1659.
a Van Luyderdorp, Juriaen Bestval, 1642.
a Van Luyten, Arendt Teunissen, 1642.
a Van Maesterlandt, Roeloff Jansen, 1630.
16 Van Manen, Gerrit, from Wagéning, Dec., 1659.
b Van Meeteren, Kreyn Janse, 1663.
a Van Merkerk, Cornelis Teunissen, 1637.
14 Van Meulen, Geertry, maiden, April, 1659.
a Van Munnichendam, Pieter Cornelissen, 1636.
39 Van Naerden, Beletje Jacobs, Sept., 1663.
39 Van Naerden, Dirck Teunissen, Sept., 1663.
12 Van Naerden, Jan Roelofsen, farmer, Feb., 1659.
b Van Nesten, Pieter, 1647.
a Van Nieukerke, Brandt Peelen, 1630.
15 Van Niewkerk, Gerrit Cornelis, wife, boy, and sucking child, April, 1659.
b Van Noostrant, Simon Hanssen, 1639.
42 Van Norden, Jan Wouterse, Jan. 20, 1664.
a Van Nordinge, Pieter Nicolaussen, 1637.
b Van Nuys, Auke Janse, 1651.
b Van Nuys, Jan Oake, 1651.
42 Van Oy, Govert, wife and 3 children, Jan. 20, 1664.
b Van Pelt, Anthony, 1663.
b Van Pelt, Gysbert Thysen Laenen, 1663.
b Van Pelt, Hendrick Thyssen, 1666.

b Van Pelt, Theunis Janse Laenen, 1663.
b Van Pelt, Wouter, 1663.
a Van Rotterdam, Hans Jansen, 1639.
a Van Rotterdam, Jan Jansen, 1640.
a Van Ruth, Claes Jansen, 1641.
11 Van Sauten, Adam, wife and 2 children, June, 1658.
a Van Schaick, Goosen Gerritsen, 1637.
a Van Schoonderwoerdt, Cornelis Cornelissen, 1641.
a Van Schoonderwoerdt, Cornelis Gerritsen, 1642.
a Van Schoenderwoerdt, Rutger Jacobsen, 1636.
a Van Schoenderwordt, Teunis Jacobsen, 1640.
21 Van Schure, Willem, from Leuren, soldier, Mar. 9, 1660.
b Van Sichgelen, Ferdinandus, 1652.
a Van Sleswyck, Juriaen, 1642.
a Van Slyck, Cornelis Antonissen, 1641.
a Van Soest, Rutger Hendricksen, 1630.
a Van Soest, Seger Hendricksen, 1630.
a Van Steltyn, Evert Pels, 1642.
a Van Stoutenburgh, Jacob Jansen, 1646.
b Van Sutphen, Dirck Janse, 1651.
36 Van Teyl, Jan Otto, wife and child, ag. 2, April 16, 1663.
12 Van Twiller, Goossen, from New-Kerk, Feb., 1659.
a Van Utrecht, Jacob Adriaensen, 1639.
a Van Valckenburg, Lambert, 1645.
a Van Vechten, Teunis Cornelissen, 1637.
a Van Vechten, Teunis Dircksen, 1638.
a Van Vee, Pieter Hertgers, 1645.
24 Van Veen, Gerrit Jansz, from Calemburg, farmer's boy, April 27, 1660.
a Van Veere, Maryn Andriaensen, 1631.
32 Van Venloo, Lendert Dircksen, of Rumunt, Sept. 2, 1662.
a Van Vlecburg, Cristen Cristyssen Noorman, 1636.
b Van Vliet, Dirck Jansen, 1664.
b Van Vliet, Jan Dircks, 1664.
b Van Voorhees, Jan Stevense, 1660.
b Van Voorhees, Luycas Stevense, 1660.
a Van Voorhoudt, Cornelis Segers, 1642.
b Van Voorhuys, Court Stevense, 1661.
6 Van Vrendenburch, Willem, May, 1658.
a Van Waalwyck, Claes Jansen, 1642.
a Van Wesepe, Gysbert Cornelissen, 1645.
a Van Westbroek, Cornelis Teunissen, 1631.
b Van Wickelen, Evert Janssen, 1664.
42 Van Wie, Lysbeth Janssen, near Goch, Jan. 20, 1664.
b Van Wyck, Cornelis Barense, 1660.
12 Van Ysselstein, Jannetje Theunis, Feb., 1659.
b Van Zutphen, Jan Barense, 1657.
b Vechten, Claes Arense, 1660.
b Vechten, Hendrick, 1660.
36 Verbeeck, Gerrit, April 16, 1663.
a Verbeeck, Johannes, 1635.
21 Verele, Johannis, from Antwerp, soldier, Mar. 9, 1660.
12 Verhagen, Josyntje, from Middleburg, and daughter, Feb., 1659.

34 Verkerk, Jan Jansen, from Buren, wife and 5 children, ag. 9, 8, 6, 5, 1, Mar., 1663.

b Verkerk, Roeloff, 1663.

14 Vermeulen, Albert Theunissen, from Rotterdam, wife and 4 children, April, 1659.

33 Verniele, Isaac, wife and 4 children, ag. all over 20, Oct., 1662.

44 Vernoey, Corneliss Cornelisse, wife and sucking child, Jan. 20, 1664.

44 Verplanck, Abigel, and child, April 17, 1664.

39 Verplanck, Susanna, and child, Sept., 1663.

b Verschier, Wouter Gysbert, 1649.

39 Ver Schuren, Lysbet, Sept., 1663.

2 Vincent, Adriaen, April, 1657.

31 Vincian, Adriaen, from Tournay, farmer, wife and 3 children, ag. 18, 12, 5, May 24, 1662.

11 Volckertse, Jannetje, wife of Evert Luykese, baker, and daughter, June, 1658.

39 Voorst, Willem, from Arnhem, Sept., 1663.

23 Vorst, Thomas, from Bremen, soldier, April 27, 1660.

27 Vos, Cornelis Dircksen, wife, mother, and 2 children, May 9, 1661.

39 Vreesen, Jan, from Hamburg, Sept., 1663.

23 Vreesen, Jan, from Hamburg, cadet, wife and 2 children, April 27, 1660.

W

a Wagenaar, Jacob Aertsen, 1642.

b Waldron, Daniel, 1652.

23 Warten, Teunis, from Gorcum, soldier, April 27, 1660.

a Wemp, Jan Barentsen, 1645.

34 Wessels, Hendrick, from Wishem, Mar., 1663.

42 Wessels, S. Vander (wife died on passage), Jan. 20, 1664.

16 Wesselsen,Wessel, from Munster, Dec., 1659.

a Westercamp, Hendrick, 1646.

44 Wienrick, Hendrick, from Wesel, April 17, 1664.

23 Willays, Ferdinandus, from Cortryck, soldier, April 27, 1660.

36 Willems, Arnoldus, brother-in-law of Gerrit Jans, April 16, 1663.

26 Willems, Geertje, from Amsterdam, May 9, 1661.

b Willemse, Hendrick, 1649.

44 Willemse, Arnoldus, April 17, 1664.

b Willemse, Johannis, 1662.

44 Willemse, Maes, from Hooghlant, April 17, 1664.

b Willemse, Willem, 1657.

b Willemsen, Abram, 1662.

a Willemsen, Adriaen, 1642.

27 Willemsen, Jan, from the Loosdrecht, wife and 2 sons, May 9, 1661.

a Willemsen, Matheld, 1642.

b Willkens, Claes, 1662.

22 Wiskhousen, Jan, from Bergen in Norway, soldier, April 15, 1660.

a Witsent, Thomas, 1631.

b Woertman, Dirck Janse, 1647.

11 Wolf, Claes, from the Elve, sailor, June, 1658.

a Wolfertsen, Jacob, 1641.

37 Worster, Peter, June 27, 1663.
34 Wouters, Claes, from Amersfoort, wife and child, ag. 8, Mar., 1663.
30 Wouterse, Jacob, Mar. 24, 1662.
12 Woutersen, Jan, from Ravesteyn, shoemaker, wife and daughter, Feb., 1659.
 b Wyckoff, Peter Claesen, 1636.
 a Wyncoop, Peter, 1642.
 b Wynhart, Cornelis, 1657.

Z

 a Zevenhuyzen, Hans, 1636.

EMIGRANTS TO NEW NETHERLAND

ACCOUNT BOOK 1654 TO 1664

CONTRIBUTED BY ROSALIE FELLOWS BAILEY, F.A.S.G.

This original account book[1] may interest today's social and economic historian for the light it throws on transportation, employment, employee "fringe benefit," and payment customs in New Netherland.

This article comprises important new material found among the notes of James Riker,[2] taken from this document of moneys owing for passage to New Netherland. In its abbreviated form as a list, it is well-known as the only group of passenger listings during the Dutch period. Because two translations have been published[3] and Riker's notes were intended as his own working tools, the present contributor—fearful of perpetuating errors —has made a cursory comparison of Riker's notes with the original Dutch account book,[4] using the microfilm copy recently obtained by The New York Genealogical and Biographical Society.

Riker commented thereon: "I think from the nature of these accounts that they were made up from the records of the [West India] Company, by order of the English rulers after the confiscation of the Company's property in New Netherland, and as assets of or debts due the Company, and to be collected [by the English]. They *are not full lists* of the passengers which came out in said vessels on the respective dates." Also mentioned, is a contemporary comment that New Netherland was "only six weeks' sail from Holland"[5] and that in the account book *the date, as is evident, is the date of embarkation.*"

The material below—even though almost all the emigrants' or voyagers' names have been printed elsewhere—contains new names, new marriages and relationships, new occupations or employers, new residences and deaths. In several accounts, the "newness" is the benefit derived from printing the entries in their original sequence; for, as this is an account book of money due, further entries may have been set down later or, even if entered at the same time, they may not concern the status at the time of crossing the ocean but a later event.[6] Passengers on paid "tickets" naturally are not listed in the account book—unless they owe for others.

In the ship *Wire-Cask*, April 2, 1657:

Marcus de Chousoy,[7] wife, two workmen and two boys, over 12 years old (all six charged at the full rate, 36 florins each). (On the credit* side, 4 lines):

p. Johannes Smedtes who accepted   paid f 36
p. Dirck Buyskes   paid f 36
p. Jan Guion from Leyden[8]
p. Pieter Boutyn.

Teunis Kray,[9] from Venlo, wife and four children (two under 10 years) and two servants (1 male and 1 female).

In the *St. John Baptist*, Dec. 23, 1657:

Adam Breemen, from Aecken. His wife and maid servant came out in the *Spotted Cow* in 1663.

In the *Gilded Bear*, skipper Cornelis Willemsen de Beer, Dec. 30, 1657:

Cornelis Barentsen vande Kuyl. (Added on debit* side): Aug. 9, 1659, To Lysbet Arents by transfer from folio 25. (At folio 25, Lysbet Arents is called "wife of Cornelis Barentsen").

The skipper of the ship *Market Gardener (Moesman)* is Jacob Jansen Staets, May 1, 1658.

In the *Gilded Beaver*, May 17, 1658:

Wife of Jan Jansen,† house carpenter, wife and five children, 11, 12, 13, 17, and 21 years old—Maria, Magdalena, Ariaen Jansen, Sophia, and Christina. (Only two charges, one for the wife and one for the children together). (Added on Dr.): A note written and signed by Jan Jansen, "I agree to pay for all except one daughter of my wife: She shall pay for it."

Pieter van Halen,[10] shoemaker, from Utrecht, wife and two children, 1 and 3 years old, and boy (charge for two children together f 18, for the boy full fare).

Simon Bouche (His fare is the only charge to Jaques Cousseau's[11] account).

Jan Evertsen, from Loockeren. (On Cr.): Jan. 10, 1660, Coenraet Ten Eyck agrees to pay for him.[12]

In the *Brownfish*, June 19, 1658:

Machtelt Stoffelse, widow; is acquainted with farming. (Added on Cr.): April 15, 1661, Gerrit Jansen van Campen,[13] her husband, a soldier; his debt is liquidated.

Wife of Dirck Smith[14] and a nursing child (her full fare is the only charge to account of Dirck Smith, Ensign in the Company's service).

---

*Debit side and credit side hereafter referred to as Dr. and Cr.

†For these "wife of" listings, the account is in the man's name, but the charges itemize whose passage fare is owing.

Maria Claes, maiden. (On Cr.) : Feb. 25, 1664, Claes Hay, her present husband, is charged with it.

In the *Golden Mill*, skipper Barent Jochems, June 7, 1658:
Adam van Santen,[15] wife and two children, 1 and 4 years old.

In the *Faith*, Feb. 12, 1659:
Pieter Jacobsz, farm laborer, out of Holstein.
Stoffel Gerritsen van Laer. (On Cr.) : May 2, 1660,* Adriaen van Laer the brother of Stoffel van Laer engages to settle his account.

In the *Beaver*, April 25, 1659:
Albert Theunissen Vermeulen, from Rotterdam, wife and four children, 4, 9, 16, and 17 years old. (On Cr.) : Received payment in seawant from Cornelis Vermeulen the son of Albert Vermeulen—for which the Treasury of the Receiver Van Ruyven is discharged this day, Sept. 20, 1660.
Laurens van der Spiegel, from Vlissingen. (On Dr.) : Nota. This shall be paid by Christina Hey.[16]

In the *Market Gardener*, April 25, 1659:
Aertie Leenders, widow, from Amsterdam. (On Dr.) : Nota. She lives in Fort Orange.
Willem Jansen, fisherman, from Rotterdam, wife and nursing child, and maid servant. (On Dr.) : Nota. This girl left him and lives in Fort Orange.
Dirck Belet, cooper, from Breda. (On Cr.) : P. Stuyvesant assumes the debt on Sept. 10, 1659.

The following six names stand next in order in the accounts but with no date or allusion to indebtedness for their passage. Each is entered as, "To cash received of the Lords Directors," with very small sums varying between f 3.3 and f 12.10.
Albert Pietersen, mason
Geerty Claesen
Gerrit Pietersen
Gillis Mandeville[17]
Jacob Hendricksen Haen, painter.[18]
Adriaen Vincent.[19]

In the *Faith*, Dec. 22, 1659:
The wife of Jan Harmensz, baker, and her sister.
The wife of Claes Tysen, cooper, and two children, 4 and 7 years old. (The only charges are f 36 for the wife and f 36 for the two children together).

In the *Spotted Cow*, April 15, 1660:
Pieter Simkam,[20] tailor, from Nimwegen. (On Cr.) : On April 15, 1661, placed to credit of Gen. Stuyvesant, to whom Simkam is engaged.

*1669 in Riker's notes, but the account book reads 1660.

Soldiers in the *Spotted Cow*, April 15, 1660:*

Johan Hamelton, from Hamelton. (On Cr.) : Owes David Craffort for transportation.

Johan Spronck,[21] from Bonn above Ceulen; is a smith and baker.

Brant Hemmes, from Dockum. (On Cr.) : Assigns two months' wages per year to his mother.

Harman Jansen Engsinck, from Oldenseel. (On Cr.) : Assigns wages per year to Beertie Jansen, his mother.

In the *Beaver*, May 9, 1661:

Pieter Marselis,[22] from Beest, wife and four children, 13, 6, 4, and 2 years old, and two servants (laborer and servant girl).

In the *St. John Baptist*, May 9, 1661:

Jan Jeuriaensen, out of the Duchy of Cleef. Nota. This person died on the way.

These persons came here at their Masters' cost; workingmen charged to Michiel Muyden.†

In the *Faith*, Dec. 23, 166 (0):

Wife of Hendrick Jansen Spier,[23] and two children, 4 and 5 years old (only two charges, one for her and one for the children together as another full fare).

Jan Aertsen,[24] from Amersfoort. (On Dr.) : Nota. "woont bij" (lives with) Elbert Elbertsen "inde baay" (in Flatlands).

In the *Faith*, March 24, 1662:

Willem Jansz,[25] farmer,‡ from Berckeloo.

Harmen Jansen, farmer, from Berckeloo, wife and two children, 5 and 3 years old.

Symon Cornie, farmer, of those out of France, and his wife. (Added on Cr.) : 1664, was so much deducted because Simon was formerly a corporal at the time of the surrender, and was then permitted to depart or stay, but as he concluded to remain here, so the adjoining sum was not brought into account f 72.

Adriaen Aertsen, farmer, from Tielderweert [country around Tiel], (out of) Gelderland.§

*Original of the soldiers' rolls not compared by this contributor.

† Entire account, names and charges, carefully crossed off (though not mentioned by Riker or van Laer). For the eight workers' names crossed out, see HSYB:1902:19.

‡Farmer is the term by which van Laer translates terms such as: (a) *lantsman* (for patroon Cornelis Melyn and others) ; (b) *lantbouman* (for many, including the above four on the *Faith*; Riker consistently transcribes it as *landbouwer*) ; (c) *bouman*, and (d) *boer*.

§*Uyt*, literally "out of," usually translated like *van*, as "from." In this example, Tielderweert is in Gelderland, so perhaps it is his surname and the entry maybe should read, Adriaen Aertsen van Tilderweert, farmer out of Gelderland.

In the *Hope*, April 8, 1662:

Gerrit Hargerinck,[26] from Nieuwenhuys, and his two sons, 9 and 15 years old. (On Cr.) : "Gerrit de oudst naer (the Older toward) fort Orangue. Christiaen Herregerinck woont bij (lives with) Jacob Backer."

Abel Hardenbroeck,[27] wife and child 4 years old, and servant named Casper Overcamp. (On Cr.) : Dec. 31, 1663 entry concerning Casper Overcamp [see below].

Casper Overcamp (separate account opened for him in 1663 on folio 79, replacing Abel Hardenbroeck for his passage fare,   f 36) .*

Dirck Jansen, farmer, from the Bommelderweert, and his two children.

In the *Fox*, Aug. 31, 1662:

Piere Martin, out of Walsland.†

Piere d'Mare,[28] shoemaker, from Roan (Rouen) , and his wife (charged for two full fares, at this ship's high rate,   f 42) .

In the *Rosetree*, March 15, 1663:

The wife of Pieter Jansen, from Amersfoort, and four children, 19, 16, 7, and 3 years old (charged for 1 adult fare   f 39 and for the 4 children together   f 117) .

Jan Jansen Verberck [Verkerck],[29] from Buren, wife, and five children, 9, 8, 6, 5, and 1 years old—this is a nursing child.

Thys Jansen,[30] from the country of Liège, and wife and four children, 17, 15, 13, and 11 years old. (There is no charge for his wife, and a note opposite her entry says: died in Texel.)

In the *Spotted Cow*, April 16, 1663:

Hans Jacob Sardingh [Hardingh].[31]

In *De Statyn*, Sept. 27, 1663:

Schout Olferts,[32] from Friesland, wife and child, 2 years old, and servant Foppe Johannis. (On Cr.) : Foppe Johannis' charge transferred to him, "as he promised to pay his passage."

Foppe Johannis[33] (separate account opened for him; see preceding account) .

In the *Sacred Heart*, Jan. 20, 1664:

The widow of Govert van Oy, and two children, 9 and 1½ years old. (Added on Dr.) : Nota. Govert van Oy, with wife and three children, was

*Account noticed by this contributor while verifying Riker's notes.

†Riker entered Pays de Vaud as translation of *Walslant*, then doubted it. *Walslant* this contributor has found in records in the Netherlands to refer to its lost southernmost provinces (now southern Belgium and north France) . If it must be translated, it is safer to say "the Walloon country." Of course, any Pays de Vaud refugees in Holland would attend the French-language Walloon churches there.

to come over, but the child aged 5 years died in Amsterdam, and Govert himself in Texel.

The four following are each entered as, "Came out at the cost of the Company."

Jan Jansen, from Amsterdam.

Claes Gerritsen, son of Gerrit Lubbertsen, from Wesel.

Wander Wessels.[34] (Added on Dr.) : Nota. His wife was coming out but died in Texel.

Jan Wouterse, from Nerden.

NOTES

1. New York Historical Manuscripts, Colonial, in the Office of the Secretary of State (now at the State Library) , XIV: 83-123 as arranged, but actually an old liber KK, still carrying its old *paging*, 1-90. In its *Calendar* . . . , Pt. 1, Dutch (1865) : 299.

See also *Ibid*, XIII: 75, 88 & 106, and its *Calendar*, pp. 290, 291 & 292, for three rolls of soldiers sent to New Netherland in March and April, 1660. These have been placed chronologically within the account-book list for printing (see note 3) and in Riker's notes (see note 2) .

Now that microfilm copies are available, intensive study is feasible.

2. James Riker collection, "List of Emigrants to New Netherland 1654 to 1664," MS pamphlet in Box 23, Manuscript Division, New York Public Library; courtesy of Mr. Hill, Chief of that division, and of Mr. Wolfe, of the Editorial Division.

3. E. B. O'Callaghan's *Documentary History of the State of New York*, III (1850) : 52-63, which was reprinted in *Year Book of The Holland Society of New York* (1896) . Revised translation by A. J. F. van Laer, State Archivist, in *Year Book* of *Ibid* (1902) : 1-37. See the last-mentioned publication for the full list of *indebted* passengers.

4. The account book is entirely in Dutch. It has debit and credit entries for each account on facing pages. The debit entry, by official scriveners, opens the account of emigrant or voyager (or whoever was initially responsible for the passage price) , gives the ship, skipper, and date of voyage, lists the persons (usually by relationship rather than by name) who came over, for whom he is responsible and details each charge (normally 36 florins for each adult and older child, often half fare for a young child, and nothing for a nursing infant) , with the total due. An informative, undated note may be at the end of the debit entry, perhaps in a different writing. Many accounts have no credit entry. The credit entry, usually scribbled, concerns payment, including any change in the person responsible for the debt, residence of debtor, etc. Mr. van Laer translated many of these notes and credits, entering the latter in parentheses for his printed list; more are now printed for the first time from the notes of Riker, who was primarily interested in local history and genealogy; many more credit entries remain untranslated.

5. O'Callaghan's *History of New Netherland*, II (1848) : 446.

6. As Mr. van Laer was a Dutchman, an archivist, and studied the account book for publication, his spelling of name and place and his sequence for the passage entry are used for this compilation rather than Riker's, except for the American editor's change to the capital V or D (for van or de) . It will be noted from van Laer's explanation (in HSYB, 1902) that the form of sentence of the passage entry makes it impossible to distinguish if a name refers to a person's former residence or is his surname. Mr. van Laer has very rightly "played safe" by translating them all as origin, and overemphasizing this as he precedes it with any occupation given.

The current contributor departs from Mr. van Laer's (or the editor's?) sequence only if the printed passage entry had been enlarged to include an occupation or residence from another sentence—which, if it happened to refer to a time later than the voyage, could take on a different meaning.

7. De Chousoy settled in Harlem. Ancestor of the Dissosway family of Staten Island.

8. Guion is identified as Jean Guenon who settled in Flushing, ancestor of the Genung family (Riker's *History of Harlem* (1881), 110 & 216).

9. Cray was in New Amsterdam in 1639. This 1657 voyage was his third known trip (J. H. Innes' *New Amsterdam and its People*, 82; CDM, 19 & 162).

10. Van Halen is ancestor of the Van Alen family of Albany and Kinderhook.

11. Cousseau was also on this voyage but had evidently paid his fare. He was an active merchant of La Rochelle and New York City (Riker's *Harlem*, 111 & 425). He signed merely "Cousseau."

12. As Ten Eyck was a shoemaker, perhaps passenger Jan Evertsen was the master shoe-maker of Albany, in 1661.

13. Van Campen settled at Esopus, and three of his sons settled in the Delaware River Valley.

14. Dirck Smith served with credit in the Esopus War, and died in 1660.

15. Van Santen had a permit of the Directors to sail direct to New Amstel on the Dela-ware. This ship carried 100 passengers there (CDNY:2:70 & 72; 12:216 etc.).

16. Van der Spiegel settled in New Amsterdam, dying after fathering ten children (NYGB *Record*, 57:43 & 63:11). The woman who was responsible for his passage fare was his relative, who had come here over ten years before (contributor's own files).

17. Mandeville is in the account book for his 1659 voyage as Van Garder; he settled in Flatbush and Greenwich Village, ancestor of the Mandeville family (Riker's *Harlem*, 111).

18. Haen or Haan became a small burgher of New Amsterdam in 1659.

19. Vincent had built a house in New Amsterdam about 1646 (Innes, *Ibid*, 150) and is in the account book for another voyage in 1662.

20. Van Laer printed the surname as Timkam, and O'Callaghan as Hinkam. However, administration was granted in 1702 on the estate of Peter Sympkam of New York, boulter, and Simkam is the name on the Dutch church records.

21. Van Laer printed the surname as Verpronk. He signed his name "Johannis Sprungh" and settled eventually in Kings County (Bergen's *Early Settlers of Kings County*, 272).

22. Marselis settled at Bergen; the family at Preakness descend from him.

23. Spier settled at Bergen and is ancestor of the family at Passaic.

24. Jan Aertsen and Jacob Jansen (next in the account book) both lived with Elbert Elbertsen. He was *not*, however, Jan Aertsen Vanderbilt, who lived in Flatbush in the 1660's and emigrated before his 1650 marriage. The Jan Aertsen listed here took the oath of allegiance in Brooklyn, as having been in this country 27 years, which agrees with this 1660 voyage.

25. "Willem Jansz van borkello," as he signed his name, had first come here by 1658 when he married. On the 1662 trip he brought his brother (next in the account book) , and from them descend the Van Barkelo family (NYGB *Rec.*: 77:31; 84:70 & 196) .

26. Hargerinck does not seem to be in Pearson's *Settlers of Albany*. But at Esopus, Gerret Herregrens sued for wages in 1662 *(Dutch Records of Kingston,* 37 & 45) .

27. Hardenbroeck was one of the brothers of the wealthy widow Margaret, who in that year 1662 married carpenter Frederick Philipse, later a "multi-millionaire."

28. D'Mare is not the Demarest family of Harlem and Hackensack, who as David de Maire is in this account book on a 1663 voyage. Riker's notes refer to Pearson's *Albany*, but the nearest to that spelling noticed there seems to be a Pieter de Maecker, also called Pieter Janse Lamaker, in the 1650's. On the same ship in 1662 was a Robbert de la Maire who owned land at Harlem in the 1660's as Robert le Maire (Riker's *Harlem*, 232 etc.) . The Dutch word "de" (the) is not an integral part of a Dutch surname, nor is "van."

29. Verberck is clearly written on the account book. However, Riker, Bergen, and this contributor feel it refers to the Verkerck or Van Kirk family who came from that region of Holland to New Utrecht and soon scattered to Pennsylvania, Delaware, and New Jersey.

30. Thys Jansen and his brother Theunis Jansen (who precedes in the account book) are the ancestors of the Van Pelt and Lane families of New York and New Jersey.

31. Though written Sardingh, Riker feels it should be Hardingh. He calls attention to the Harding family of Orange County, descended from the New York City marriage in 1667 of Hans Jacobszen Harty, from Baren (Bern) , Switzerland (Riker's *Harlem*, 407) .

32. Schout or, rather, Sioert Olferts settled in New York City and is the ancestor of the Sioerts or Shourd family (Riker's *Harlem*, 486) .

33. Foppe Johannis, also called Focco Janszen, fathered Fockens and Heermans families *(Amer. Genealogist*, 36:215; contributor's own files) .

34. Wander Wessels, also called Wandel and Warnert Wessels, lived in New York City (NYGB *Record*, 44:322; contributor's own files) .

SERVANTS TO FOREIGN PLANTATIONS FROM BRISTOL, ENGLAND, 1654-1686

CONTRIBUTED BY GORDON IRELAND

On May 9, 1645, the Interregnum Parliament passed an ordinance for the punishment of "all such persons as shall steale, sell, buy, inveigle, purloyne, convey or receive any little Children, And for the strict and diligent search of all Ships and other Vessels on the River or at The Downes." However, it was not until Sept. 29, 1654, that, in the city of Bristol, which had then its own Admiralty jurisdiction and a monopoly of the Virginia trade, the Common Council passed an ordinance for the prevention of kidnapping; it provided that "all Boyes, Maides and other persons which for the future shall be transported beyond the Seas as servants shall before their going a shipboard have their Covenants or Indentures of service and apprenticeship inrolled in the Tolzey Books as other Indentures of apprenticeship are and have used to be."

Enrollment began on the following day, apparently by allotting separate spaces for this class of business in the rough entry books, by appointed clerks during each day's hours of attendance, and then sorting and faircopying the entries into big separate volumes of enrollment kept in the Chamberlain's office. Two volumes of *Servants to Foreign Plantations* with approximately 11,643 entries represent the fair copies under this system of enrollment; one from Sept. 30, 1654 to 1663, with 440 pages of entries (the folios, due to misnumbering, running to 545), and the second from 1663 to August 1679, with 319 pages (318 folios); also, about 500 further scattered entries, among the city apprenticeships, from Mar. 27, 1680 to June 12, 1686. With the waning of this type of emigration, after about thirty years, the entries gradually ceased.

The two transcribed volumes, bound in calf, were found at the back of an ancient wall press when the top floor of the Bristol Council House was rebuilt in 1925, and evidently had not been consulted for more than two centuries. In May 1940, they, with other records, were removed from the Council House to the Bomb Proof Record Rooms, a disused railway tunnel in the rocks of the Avon Gorge, which had been converted into a strong room fully equipped with electric lighting and heating and an air-conditioning plant. They remained there until 1946, when they were brought back to the Bristol Council House, none of them destroyed or damaged in any way. During a heavy raid on Bristol on the night of Dec. 6, 1940, the top floors of the Council House were destroyed by fire; however, the Council Chambers were saved, the archives and strong rooms were not damaged, and the staff remained at the Council House during the war. At the present time the building is temporarily repaired, and will be used until the city can gain permission to continue with the new Civic Buildings which were under construction when the war began.

The two volumes contain 2656 names for Barbados,* approximately 2560

*Printed in the *Journal of the Barbados Museum and Historical Society*, v.XIV, pp.48–69, 143–58, et seq.

for Nevis, 555 for other British West Indian islands, 4876 for Virginia, 163 for New England*, 177 for Maryland, New York and Pennsylvania in the present United States, and 770 without named destination. The servants' names, destinations, vessels where stated, and pages of the record have been published, with expert introductions throwing most interesting lights on the whole story, in *Bristol and America* (R. Sydney Glover, London, 1929.) The system of copying from the original journal entries into the classified volumes may account for some apparent duplications which appear in the lists. Some of the earlier entries give brief particulars of the apprenticeship agreement and later sometimes the servant's prior residence, the name of the ship and of the ship's master; but as business increased the entries become much shorter and often show, besides the servant's name and destination, only the date of the entry and the name of the bondmaster. These emigrants were of all sorts and conditions: a few pardoned criminals, some political prisoners, some children and apprentices who had been kidnapped and sold, but the majority were respectable and industrious men and women; they, chiefly for transportation charges, bound themselves for a fixed term, usually under five years, and they expected to become freeholders, commonly of fifty acres of land, each, at the end of their period of service.

To make the material of the present compilation as useful as possible to historians, genealogists, and others interested, it is given alphabetically in four classifications: (I) by names of the emigrants, showing to some extent possible family groups; (II) by names of the bondmasters, showing servants under the same man; (III) by vessels and captains, showing servants on the same voyage, where known; and (IV) by places from which the emigrants came, showing the comparatively few known cases of same origin.

TABLE I: EMIGRANTS

DESTINATION, MARYLAND

As contributed, this List contained the names of the respective bondmasters, and, in all cases in which the original entries give the information, the names of the vessels and captains and (mostly for 1684 and 1685) the places from which the emigrants came; but to meet the size of our pages these three columns have been omitted from Table I.

			Record	
No.	*Name of Servant*	*Date of Entry*	*Book*	*Page*
I	Ano, Mary	Sept. 23, 1676	II	292
2	Attkinson, Richard	Oct. 3, 1672	II	231
3	Barker, Thomas	Nov. 14, 1678	II	313
4	Barlam, Thomas for Md, or Va.	Aug. 3, 1685	II	180
5	Bayliffe, James	Sept. 29, 1675	II	277
6	Bayly, Dorothy	Oct. 15, 1672	II	232
7	Bayly, Thomas Mariner	Aug. 21, 1660	I	376
8	Bennet, John	Aug. 21, 1660	I	376

*Published in the *New England Historical and Genealogical Register* v.93, pp. 381–88.

No.	Name of Servant	Date of Entry	Record Book	Page
9	Bennett, William for Md. or Va.	Oct. 31, 1685	II	182

William Sanders, No. 114, is the entry next above this. "These two boys came to town with ye soldiers and have been wandering about ye town and offred themselves voluntarily."

No.	Name of Servant	Date of Entry	Record Book	Page
10	Bero, Nathaniell	Aug. 6, 1662	I	507
11	Bevan, Thomas	Sept. 23, 1676	II	292
12	Bevis, Benjamin	Aug. 28, 1675	II	274
13	Bick, John	Oct. 20, 1665	II	63
14	Bird, Alice	July 17, 1677	II	300
15	Boole, Edward	Aug. 26, 1676	II	289
16	Boole, Jane	Aug. 26, 1676	II	289
17	Braye, Susana	Aug. 18, 1676	II	288
18	Brookes, Joseph	Aug. 20, 1680	II	172
19	Camme, Thomas	Oct. 3, 1672	II	231
20	Chechy, Joane	Aug. 5, 1670	II	186
21	Clarvo, Francis	Aug. 14, 1684	II	173
22	Couzens, Mary	Oct. 29, 1678	II	312
23	Crumpe, Joseph	Dec. 4, 1675	II	282
24	Curry, Robert	July 29, 1684	II	173
25	Curtis, Elizabeth	Oct. 15, 1670	II	194
26	Curtis, Robert	Oct. 15, 1670	II	194
27	Daggett, Richard	Oct. 26, 1678	II	312
28	Dammes, John	Oct. 3, 1672	II	231
29	Dangerfield, Edward	Aug. 26, 1665	II	48
30	Davis, Susannah	Aug. 22, 1671	II	211
31	Douding, Ann	Sept. 24, 1680	II	172
32	Evans, Mary for Md. or Va.	Aug. 15, 1685	II	181
33	Foord, Lettice	Dec. 12, 1673	II	243
34	Fowler, Sarah	Oct. 4, 1671	II	215
35	Fowler, Thomas	Nov. 12, 1678	II	313
36	Fowler, Tobias	Aug. 11, 1663	II	12
37	France, Richard	Dec. 2, 1685	II	182
38	Freeman, Oliver for Md. or Va.	Aug. 19, 1685	II	181
39	Fry, James	July 9, 1680	II	171
40	Fry, Joseph	Sept. 28, 1675	II	277
41	Garland, Randolph for Md. or Va.	Sept. 8, 1685	II	181
42	German, Thomas	Aug. 30, 1662	I	516
43	Golden, William for Va. or Md.	Aug. 25, 1684	II	173
44	Griffith, Roger	Nov. 5, 1680	II	172
45	Gwyn, Christopher	Oct. 16, 1684	II	174
46	Hall, William	July 24, 1672	II	225
47	Hardy, James	July 7, 1675	II	270
48	Harris, Jeremy	July 20, 1677	II	300

No.	Name of Servant	Date of Entry	Record Book	Page
49	Harris, Thomas	Sept. 24, 1670	II	193
50	Hartily, John	Oct. 3, 1672	II	231
51	Haskins, John	Aug. 20, 1668	II	135
52	Hayford, Thomas	Aug. 3, 1680	II	171
53	Hennis, Miles	July 25, 1685	II	180
	Glassmaker for Md. or Va.			
54	Hill, John	Mar. 12, 1673	II	246
55	Holland, William	Oct. 3, 1672	II	231
56	Horne, George	July 26, 1672	II	226
57	Hughs, John	Aug. 9, 1677	II	301
58	Hunt, Cornelius	Oct. 2, 1684	II	174
59	James, Alice	Aug. 29, 1676	II	290
	for Pottuxon			
60	James, Thomas	July 17, 1677	II	300
61	Jenkins, David	July 6, 1674	II	251
62	Jenkins, David,	Dec. 2, 1685	II	182
	Carpenter			
63	Jenkins, Mary	Aug. 26, 1676	II	289
64	Jinkin, William	Sept. 22, 1670	II	192
65	Jones, Blanch	June 24, 1675	II	269
66	Jones, Charles	Sept. 23, 1672	II	230
67	Jones, David	Sept. 30, 1675	II	277
	for Md. or Va.			
68	Jones, Evan	Sept. 9, 1674	II	253
69	Jones, Henry	Dec. 2, 1685	II	182
	Husbandman			
70	Jones, Thomas	June 26, 1680	II	171
71	Knowles, Mary,	Aug. 31, 1685	II	181
	Spinster for Md. or Va.			
72	Lewis, Margery	Sept. 4, 1676	II	290
73	Lewis, Watkin	June 30, 1675	II	270
74	Lightwood, Richard	Sept. 19, 1670	II	192
75	Llewellin, Jenkins	Aug. 18, 1685	II	181
	Yeoman for Md. or Va.			
76	Low, William	Oct. 4, 1673	II	240
77	Mills, Humfry	Nov. 2, 1677	II	305
78	Mills, John	Nov. 25, 1673	II	243
79	Mishew, William	July 26, 1672	II	225
80	Morgan, George	July 19, 1680	II	171
81	Morgan, Owen	Sept. 3, 1685	II	181
	for Va. or Md.			
82	Morgan, Philip	Aug. 3, 1680	II	171
83	Morgan, Thomas	Aug. 8, 1670	II	187
84	Napp, Edith	Aug. 21, 1685	II	181
	for Md. or Va.			
85	Napp, Margaret	Aug. 21, 1685	II	181
	for Md. or Va.			
86	Napp, Sarah	Aug. 21, 1685	II	181
	for Md. or Va.			

No.	Name of Servant	Date of Entry	Record Book	Page
87	Nicholls, Elizabeth	Aug. 20, 1685	II	181
	Spinster for Md. or Va.			
88	Nicholls, Joane	Dec. 6, 1678	II	314
89	Peccard, Ann	Aug. 13, 1662	I	510
90	Pegg, Stephen	Oct. 3, 1672	II	231
91	Penbrooke, William	Nov. 6, 1678	II	312
92	Plovey, William	July 24, 1672	II	225
93	Popejoy, William	Aug. 10, 1680	II	172
94	Pottinger, John	Sept. 24, 1684	II	174
95	Powell, Richard	Aug. 26, 1676	II	289
96	Price, Elienor	Aug. 25, 1677	II	301
97	Price, Mary	Dec. 11, 1680	II	172
98	Price, Thomas	Aug. 26, 1676	II	289
99	Pridley, William	Oct. 31, 1673	II	241
100	Pudding, Joane	June 29, 1668	II	131
101	Pullin, Richard	Aug. 21, 1660	I	376
	Yeoman			
102	Pye, Walter	Aug. 13, 1662	I	510
103	Raby, John	Aug. 15, 1685	II	181
	Feltmaker for Md. or Va.			
104	Ragland, Thomas	Dec. 11, 1680	II	172
105	Rawlins, Anthony	Oct. 6, 1666	II	75
106	Rawlins, John	Oct. 6, 1666	II	75
107	Rawlins, Richard	Oct. 6, 1666	II	76
108	Reed, Sarah	Dec. 7, 1685	II	182
109	Rendall, Giles	Oct. 16, 1671	II	216
110	Roe, Thomas	Oct. 3, 1672	II	231
111	Rowneing, Christopher	Oct. 20, 1670	II	195
112	Rudman, William	July 25, 1670	II	186
	Bound for 7 years			
113	Salisbury, Richard	Aug. 5, 1684	II	173
	Mariner			
114	Sanders, William	Oct. 31, 1685	II	182
	for Md. or Va.			
	See note under William Bennett, No. 9, above			
115	Savage, Elizabeth	Aug. 21, 1660	I	376
	Spinster			
116	Seise, William	Aug. 26, 1676	II	289
117	Sely, William	Sept. 4, 1676	II	290
118	Shipboy, Elizabeth	Sept. 24, 1670	II	193
119	Smith, Edward	Oct. 3, 1672	II	231
120	Sparkes, Robert	Sept. 13, 1670	II	191
121	Spiller, John	Sept. 26, 1666	II	75
122	Teverton, Phillip	Aug. 12, 1670	II	187
123	Thomas, John	Sept. 16, 1680	II	172
124	Trottman, Thomas	Aug. 11, 1663	II	11
125	Trow, Alice	Aug. 25, 1677	II	302
126	Turner, Grace	Oct. 3, 1672	II	231
127	Turner, John	Nov. 14, 1678	II	313

			Record	
No.	Name of Servant	Date of Entry	Book	Page
128	Upton, Grace	Sept. 24, 1670	II	193
129	Ward, Thomas	July 24, 1672	II	225
130	Waters, Anne	Dec. 5, 1673	II	243
131	Wathen, John	Sept. 10, 1670	II	191
132	Wattkins, Alicia	Aug. 20, 1680	II	172
133	Webb, William	July 13, 1680	II	171
134	Whiteby, Arthur	Dec. 10, 1675	II	282
135	Whiting, Thomas	Oct. 12, 1671	II	216
136	Wilkins, Mary	July 4, 1663	II	6
137	Williams, Cicely	Sept. 12, 1674	II	253
138	Williams, Edmund	Dec. 7, 1685	II	182
	Labourer, Husband of Mary Williams, No. 144, below			
139	Williams, Elizabeth	Sept. 9, 1685	II	181
	Spinster			
140	Williams, James	Oct. 16, 1684	II	174
141	Williams, John	Oct. 21, 1674	II	257
142	Williams, Joseph	Aug. 11, 1663	II	11
143	Williams, Lewis	Dec. 2, 1676	II	295
144	Williams, Mary	Dec. 7, 1685	II	182
	Wife of Edmund Williams, No. 138, above			
145	Williams, Thomas	Sept. 24, 1680	II	172
146	Williams, Thomas	Oct. 16, 1684	II	174
147	Williams, Welthian	Aug. 4, 1674	II	252
148	Window, William	Nov. 3, 1677	II	305
149	Winson, Richard	Sept. 23, 1676	II	292
150	Winter, William	Aug. 26, 1670	II	189
151	Wood, Robert	Aug. 6, 1662	I	507
152	Woodheard, John	Nov. 1, 1675	II	280
153	Workeman, Samuel	Dec. 11, 1680	II	172
154	Wright, Peter	Jan. 31, 1658	I	181
155	Wyatt, Mary	July 17, 1677	II	300
	See also Joane Curtis, No. 176, below			

DESTINATION, NEW YORK

156	Minor, Samuell	Oct. 9, 1678	II	311
157	Williams, Arthur	Oct. 9, 1678	II	311
158	Williams, Edward	Oct. 9, 1678	II	311

DESTINATION, PENNSYLVANIA

159	Athay, Richard	Aug. 25, 1684	II	173
	Cordwinder			
160	Bosly, Jacob	Aug. 11, 1684	II	173
	Sawyer			
161	Fisher, John	Oct. 15, 1684	II	174
	Labourer			
162	Goldsmith, William	Aug. 25, 1684	II	173
	Labourer			

			Record	
No.	*Name of Servant*	*Date of Entry*	*Book*	*Page*
163	Hoskins, Caesar	Oct. 15, 1684	II	174
	Ribbon Weaver			
164	Jones, Mary	Aug. 21, 1684	II	173
	for Pa. or Va.			
165	Morgan, Benjamin	Sept. 19, 1685	II	181
166	Morgan, Joseph	Sept. 19, 1685	II	181
167	Pearce, Henry	Oct. 2, 1685	II	182

son of Anthony Pearce, late of Calne in Wiltshire, Clothier, by consent of his mother Katharine Pearce, widow of Devizes, bound to Francis Smith, of Devizes, Gentleman

168	Phillpott, Elizabeth	Sept. 19, 1685	II	181
	Spinster			
169	Pinnick, Edward	Aug. 19, 1684	II	173
170	Pinnick, John	Aug. 19, 1684	II	173
171	Roberts, John	Aug. 25, 1685	II	181
	Hosier			
172	Sansom, Francis	June 27, 1684	II	173
	Baker			
173	Thomas, John	June 3, 1684	II	173
174	Thurston, Thomas	Sept. 3, 1685	II	181
	Gardiner			

Son of Thomas Thurston of Twineing, with consent of his said father testified by John Gardiner, Worcester Carrier who brought him to Town to that purpose

175	Veale, Samuel	Oct. 15, 1684	II	174
	Ribbon Weaver			

DESTINATION, VIRGINIA

176	Curtis, Joane	Jan. 3, 1677	II	306
	for Wickacomico in Va. (now in Md.?)			
177	Higgins, John	June 16, 1675	II	269
	for York River			

TABLE II: BONDMASTERS

Name	*Number of Servant*
Andrews, Henry	66, 122
Andrews, Mary	34
Archer, Peter	72, 117
Arnee, John	40
Barrett, Arthur	96, 125
Barton, Edmund	13
Bradford, Ambrose	21
Brian, Lewis	20, 112, 128
Brittain, Richard	6
Broad, Anthony	3, 35, 57, 127
Bryan, Robert	29
Cart, Joshua	165, 166, 168, 171, 174

Name	Number of Servant
Cecill, jun., John	130
Cheter, Humphry	151
Christason, Winlock	49, 118
Cindy, John	132
Clowde, Robert	169, 170
Cowley, George	2, 19, 28, 50, 55, 90, 110, 119, 126
Danby, John	8
Daniell, Thomas	30
Dorrington, Ann	100
Dymen, John	130
Fere, Thomas	7
Fisher, Thomas	47, 134
Gibbs, Richard	64, 74
Harris, John	5, 44, 54
Haynes, Charles	59
Hooke, Abraham	41, 81, 139
Hooker, Thomas	33
Hort, John	103, 159, 160
Jackson, William	97, 104, 153
Jeffries, Jerome	25, 26
Jeffries, John	99
Jenkins, Elinor	14
Jenkins, Jasper	15, 16, 63, 95, 98, 116
Jinkins, Sarah	136
Jones, Thomas	9, 114
King, Mathew	150
Lawrence, Benjamin	1, 11, 149
Lawrence, Thomas	93
Lloyd, Henry	172
Luffman, Daniell	105, 106, 107, 121
Male, Anthony	155
Negar, John	154
Newton, Thomas	46, 56, 79, 92, 129
Otridge, John	143
Parker, George	12
Phelps, David	176
Pickering, John	137
Pope, Jane	75
Pope, Thomas	109
Porter, John	24, 52
Powell, Henry	48, 60
Rawles (Ralles), Francis	69, 94
Read, John	4, 32, 84, 85, 86
Ridout, Nicholas	161, 163, 175
Saunders, Joseph	38, 113
Saunders, William	61
Smith, Francis	167
Smith, Zachariah	71, 78, 87
Sparkes, Peter	120

Name	Number of Servant
Speed, Thomas	177
Steevens, John	162
Stone, Jonathan	43
Stretton, John	22
Taylor, Thomas	65
Telfe, William	76
Thomas, Alexander	73
Thomas, Francis	58
Thomas, Hugh	131, 152
Thomas, Lambrock	37, 62, 108, 138, 144
Thomas, Richard	147
Thurston, Thomas	51
Tompson, Charles	173
Trottman, Elias	36, 124, 142
Tucker, Joseph	83
Twite, Fortune	135
Walls, Joseph	42
Walls, William	77, 148
Walter, John	156, 157, 158
Wathen, John	45, 140, 146
Wellen, John	17
Whitopp, Thomas	53
Wicks, Joseph	9, 89, 102
Wilde (Wylde) Abraham	18, 27, 39, 70, 80, 82, 88, 91, 133
Williams, David	111
Williams, Marmaduke	31, 123, 145
Williams, Robert	68, 141
Willis, Philip	164
Woolaston, Thomas	23
Woolcott, John	101, 115
Wynn, Robert	67

TABLE III: SHIPS AND SHIP MASTERS

Name of Ship	Name of Ship Master	Number of Servant
Agreement	William Stratton	22, 27, 91
Alithea	Edward Watkins	58, 143
Angell Gabriell	John Roach	176
Bristol Merchant	William Smith	159, 160, 169, 170, 172, 173
Comfort	(Master not named)	41, 45, 139, 140, 146
Constant Martha	William Hunman	134
Factor	(Master not named)	171, 174
Francis and Mary	(Master not named)	77, 135, 148
Great Society	(Master not named)	32, 84, 85, 86, 103
Katherine	Robert Dapwell	156, 157, 158
Ketch	William Jones	155
Loues Mireare	John Neads	153
Maryland Merchant	(Master not named)	1, 3, 11, 35, 37, 57, 62, 69, 94, 108, 125, 127, 138, 144, 149

Name of Ship	Name of Ship Master	Number of Servant
Maryland Merchant	(Thomas Smith)	9, 114
Maryland Merchant	George Tyler	44, 96, 161, 163, 175
Patience	Thomas Copner	71, 87
Resolution	(Master not named)	43
Richard and James	(Master not named)	19, 28, 50, 55, 64, 90, 110, 119
Richard and James	William Nicholls (Nicholas)	74, 128
Richard and James	Thomas Opie	31, 123, 132, 145
Samuel	Thomas Warnes	18, 39, 52, 70, 80, 82, 93, 133
Society	(Master not named)	4, 43, 53, 122
Society	—— Burkett	120
Society	Philip Jordan	97, 104, 154
Society	John Read (Reed)	21, 24, 38, 75, 113
Starr	Christopher Barcott	23
Susanna	William Neades	14, 17, 48, 59, 60, 116
Unicorne	—— Cooper	165, 166, 167, 168, 171
Vinchorne	Thomas Coop	25, 26, 111
(Ship not named)	—— Trago	72, 117

TABLE IV: PLACES FROM WHICH EMIGRANTS CAME

Place Name	Number of Servant
Abby Door, Herefordshire	45
Bramsgrove, Worcestershire	38
Brecknockshire	139, 165, 166
Bridgwater	9
Bristol	21, 87, 108, 138, 144, 168
Brockley, Somersetshire	84, 85, 86
Browsley, Shropshire	172
Calne, Wiltshire	167
Canterbury	114
Cardiff, Glamorganshire	32
Cardigan	81
Castle Moreton, Worcestershire	58
Chester	41
Chipping Norton, Oxfordshire	160
Cornwall	162
Creekhowell, Brecknockshire	139
Cromwell, Gloucestershire	37
Devizes	167
Dowchurch	140, 146
Falmouth, Cornwall	162
Flintshire	4
Glamorganshire	32, 70, 75, 164
Gloucester	53, 171
Gloucestershire	37
Handmore, Flintshire	4
Herefordshire	45, 163
Hirsington, Somerset	161

Place Name	*Number of Servant*
Keinsham, Somerset	175
Kent	94
Litten, Somersetshire	159
Llandaff	173
Llandwortid, Brecknockshire	165, 166
Llantrishen, Glamorganshire	70
Llantverne, Herefordshire	163
London	43, 113
Mary Stoke, Somersetshire	24
Monmouthshire	69
Neath, Glamorganshire	75
Oxfordshire	160
Parish of St. Peter, Bristol	138
Parish of St. Phillips	71
Pensford, Somerset	103
Rolstone, Chester	41
St. Brides, Glamorganshire	164
St. Peter's Parish, Bristol	138
St. Phillips' Parish	71
Seane, Wiltshire	169, 170
Shropshire	172
Sittingburne, Kent	94
Somersetshire	24, 84, 85, 86, 103, 159, 161, 175
Swansea	62
Twineing, Worcestershire	174
Whitson, Monmouthshire	69
Wiltshire	167, 169, 170
Worcestershire	38, 58, 174

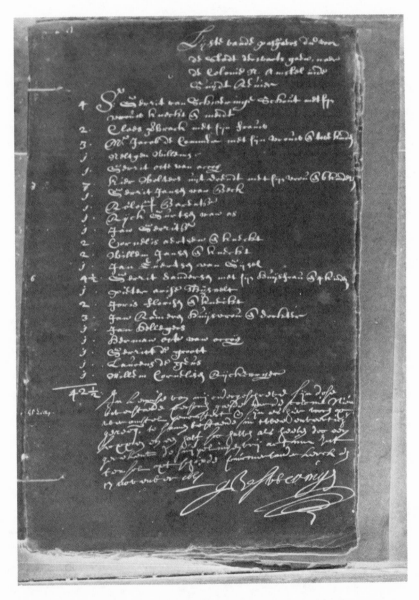

PASSENGER LIST OF "DE PURMERENDER KERCK" ("THE PURMERLAND CHURCH"),
WHICH SAILED FROM TEXEL, NOV. 24, 1661, FOR NEW AMSTEL, DELAWARE.

(For translation see article, "Delaware Papers.")

DELAWARE PAPERS.

Passenger List of Colonists to the South River (Delaware) Colony of New Netherland, 1661.

CONTRIBUTED BY LOUIS P. DE BOER, LL.B., A.M..

It is well known that the settlements on the South River, the Delaware, of New Netherland, often changed hands in the early days of their existence.

After the Dutch had colonies of small proportions and short duration there, the Swedes—chiefly through the guiding hand of Pierre Minuit, at one time Director-General of New Netherland,—in 1638 formed a larger and more lasting settlement there, known in American colonial history by the name of New Sweden.

During Pieter Stuyvesant's administration as Director-General of New Netherland, New Sweden, in 1655, again became a part of New Netherland, the West India Company's colony on the North American continent, under the sovereignty of The High Mighty Lords, the States General of the United Netherlands.

In 1661 the West India Company transferred the ownership of the South River Colony to the City of Amsterdam, and in the records of that city, the colony is often found mentioned as the "Stadt's Colonie" or the "City Colony."

All documents relative to the history of this colony from 1661 till 1664, i.e., till the year of the English occupation of all of New Netherland, are not found among the West India Company papers in the General Archives of the Kingdom of the Netherlands, at the Hague, but in the Old City Archives of Amsterdam.

From the last named collection of documents, which in its entirety deserves to be copied and translated on behalf of early American colonial history, the following data has been taken:

"Lyste van de Coloniers en andere Vryeluyden soo hun reets hebben aengegeven om na deses Stats Colonie in Nieu Nederlant te gaen.

4. Joris Florisse, tot Leyderdorp, met syn jongen en 2 knechts.
3. Cornelis Aertsen, tot Sevenhoven, met syn Jongen en neeff.
1. Jan Leendertsen, in de Bent.
3. Jan Roemers, van Haserwoude, met syn huysvrou en dochter.
2. Gerrit de Grot, van Ryns(a)terwoude, en Jongen.
1. Pieter Adriaensen, tot Sevenhoven.
1. Een Jongman van Sardam.
1. Laurens de Geus, van Amsterdam.
1. Coort de metselaer, tot Amsterdam.
3. personen van Vreelandt.
10. Gerrit Sandersen, van Tuyl, met 10 personen.
4. Joost Noorda, met syn vrou en 2 knechts.
1. Anthony Willemsen, van Vreelandt, synde een metselaer.
1. Arent Arentsen, van Oldenburg, boereknecht.
1. Lourens Cornelissen, van der Wel.
1. Jacob Pietersen, van Brugge, in de Angeliers Streat, boerknecht."
Translation:—
"List of Colonists and other Freemen who have already applied for going to the Colony of this City in New Netherland.
4. Joris Florisse, at Leyderdorp, with his boy and 2 man-servants.
3. Cornelis Aertsen, at Sevenhoven, with his Boy and nephew (or cousin).
1. Jan Leendertsen, in the Bent.
3. Jan Roemers, of Haserwoude, with his wife and daughter.

75

2. Gerrit de Grot, of Ryns(a)terwoude, and boy.
1. Pieter Adriaensen, at Sevenhoven.
1. A young man of Sardam (i.e., Saendam).
1. Laurens de Geus, of Amsterdam.
1. Coort, the mason, at Amsterdam.
3. Persons of Vreelandt.
10. Gerrit Sandersen, of Tuyl, with 10 persons.‡
4. Joost Noorda, with his wife and 2 man-servants.
1. Anthony Willemsen, of Vreelandt, being a mason.
1. Arent Arentsen, of Oldenburg, farmhand.
1. Lourens Cornelissen, of Wel.
1. Jacob Pietersen, of Bruges (living), in the Angeliers Street (at Amsterdam), farmhand."

No date is affixed to this document, which appears to be a preliminary list probably made for the use of some official. That it antedates the following document, is shown from its place in the collection, where it is under No. 65, whereas the following paper falls under No. 88.

(See: S. II L., No. 12 (13), document No. 65, Old City Archives, Amsterdam.)

The following document appears between the numbers 87 and 89, but through some omission is not numbered No. 88 as it should be:

"Lyste van Passagiers die voor de Stadt Amsterdam derwaerts gaen, naer de Colonie N. Amstel in de Suydt Revier.

4. Sr. Gerrit van Schweringe, Schout, met syn vrouw, knecht en meydt.
2. Claes Verbrack, met syn frauw.
3. Mr. Jacob de Commer, met syn vrouw en twee kinderen.
1. Neeltgen Willems.
1. Gerrit Otte, van Accoy.
8. 7. Kier Wolters, uyt Drendt, met syn vrou en 6 kinderen.
1. Gerrit Jansen van Beck.
1. Roelof Barentszen.
1. Ryck Gurtsen van As.
1. Jan Gerritsz.
2. Cornelis Aertsen en knecht.*
2. Willem Jansen en knecht.
1. Jan Evertsen van Gysel.
6. 4½. Gerrit Sandersen, met syn huysfrau en 4 kinderen.*
1. Pieter Arise Thysvelt.
2. Joris Florissen en knecht.*
3. Jan Ramaere, huysvrou en dochter.*
1. Jan Hellegers.
1. Herman Otte, van Accoy.
1. Gerrit de Groott.*
1. Laurens de Geus.*
1. Willem Cornelissen Byckevryer.
45. 42½ Zielen.

In kennisse van my ondergeschreve, syn dese bovenstaende personen gaende nae de colonie Nieuwr Amstel, gemonstert en syn als hier vooren opgereeq, to samen bestaende in twee ent veetich hoppen en een half, soo halven als heelen door een gerekent, de suygelingen vry.†

Actum int Texel, opt Schip "de Purmerender Kerck,"
        den 17 November, 1661.§   G. V. SWERINGEN."

---

‡ "with 10 persons."—This expression in old Dutch is often used to indicate 9 persons beside the one mentioned. This list therefore includes 38 persons, 14 of whom are named.

Translation:—

"List of Passengers who go there for the City of Amsterdam; to the Colony of N. Amstel, on the South River.

    4. Sr. Gerrit van Schweringe, Schout, with his wife, man-servant and maid.
    2. Claes Verbrack, with his wife.
4. 3. Jacob de Commer, with his wife and two children.
    1. Neeltgen Willems.
    1. Gerrit Otte, of Accoy.
8. 7. Kier Wolters, from Drenthe, with his wife and 6 children.
    1. Gerrit Jansen van Beck.
    1. Roelof Barentszen.
    1. Ryck Gurtsen van As.
    1. Jan Gerritsz.
    2. Cornelis Aertsen and man-servant.*
    1. Jan Evertsen van Gysel.
6. 4½ Gerrit Sandersen, with his wife and 4 children.*
    1. Pieter Arise Thysvelt.
    2. Joris Florissen and man-servant.*
    3. Jan Ramaere, wife and daughter.*
    1. Jan Hellegers.
    1. Herman Otte, of Accoy.
    1. Gerrit de Groott.*
    1. Laurens de Geus.*
    1. Willem Cornelisse Byckevryer.
    42½
    45 [in fact, 46] souls.

To the knowledge of me, the undersigned, these above listed persons have been examined, and they are as accounted for above, existing altogether of forty two heads and a half, halves and wholes all counted together; nursing children free.†

Done in the Texel Roadstead, on the Ship
The Purmerland Church,
the 17th of November, 1661.§
(w.s.:) G. V. SWERINGEN."

---

* The names thus marked in the passenger-list also occur in the preliminary list given above. The preliminary list in many instances supplements this passenger-list, by giving the various places of origin of the passengers.
Jan Ramaere is called Jan Roemers in the preliminary list.
There might have been a relationship between Gerrit Otte and Herman Otte, both names occuring in the passenger-list, and both persons from Accoy.

† The number of passengers was taken by "heads," who had to pay full passage, "half-heads," for whom half-fare had to be paid (these were presumably children under the age of five) and infants, who had free passage.
Forty-two and a half heads would make forty-three persons. One infant of Kier Wolters, and one of Gerrit Sandersen were exempt, but they have been accounted for in the margin, this making Kier Wolters' family amount to 8 instead of 7, and Gerrit Sandersen's family to 6 instead of 5 (4½), and making a total of forty-five souls, as given in the margin.
The scribe, however, has omitted in the margin an infant of Mr. Jacob de Commer, the surgeon of the expedition, whose family although consisting of himself, his wife and two children, is counted only for three.
Correcting this error we would reach a total of 46 passengers sailing on 24 November, 1661, on "de Purmerlander Kerck," from Texel Roadsteads for Newer Amstel, Delaware.

§ As a matter of record it must be stated here that the ship remained in Texel Roadsteads for a whole week, not sailing until the 24th of November, 1661, evidently waiting for further cargoes and supplies.
An inventory of the medical outfit and surgical instruments taken by Dr. Jacob de Kommer to the colony, on this ship, would be of interest to students of medical history in America.

WEST JERSEY SETTLERS.

THE following list, compiled from West Jersey records, contains the names of the people who, remaining in England, were sufficiently interested in the territory taken from the Dutch in 1664 to buy land there from the West Jersey Society, John Fenwick or William Penn, or who came over and settled on the land bought by themselves or their families in England or acquired as immigrants under the law of the day.

BERTHOLD FERNOW.

Adams, John, of Reading, Co. of Bucks, clothier, and wife Elizabeth, da. of John Fenwick.

Anderson, Tho., of Parish of St. James, Clerkenwell, Middlesex, bricklayer, and wife Ann.

Antrobus, Benjamin, of London, linen draper.

Ashfield, John, son and heir of Sir Richard Ashfield of Eastwood Park, Co. of Glocester, Knt. and Bart.

Atherton, Thomas, of Dublin, Ireland, shoemaker.

Bacon, Daniel, of Sheffield, grocer.

Burclett, Benjamin, of Westminster, Middlesex Co., gentleman.

Barker, Samuel, of Barlborough, Co. of Derby.

Barkestead, John, of London, merchant.

Barlow, Obadiah, of Sheffield, cutler.

Beal, Henry, of Bradley, Co. of Stafford, maltster.

Beamond, Richd., of London, weaver.

Biddle, Wm., of Bishopsgate Str., London, shoemaker.

Bingham, John, of London, goldsmith, and wife Mary.

Bissell, John, of Loxley, Co. of Warwick, clerk.

Booth, Edward, of Peasinhurst, alias Buntingfield, Parish of Ashover, Co. of Derby, yeoman.

Bourne, Edward, of Worcester, physician.

Bowde, Adlord, of Hertford, draper.

Bowyer, Arthur, of the Parish of Bray, Co. of Berks, baker, and wife Grace.

Bradwav, Edward, of St. Paul Shadwell, Co. of Middlesex, lighterman, and wife Mary.

Breckon, Francis, of Scarborough, Co. of York, mariner.

Brewster, John, of Newcastle-upon-Tyne, Co. of Northumberland, yeoman.

Burgesse, Benjamin, of Bristol, mariner, and wife Jane Buchanan.

Cann, John, of the Parish of St. Martins in the Fields, Middlesex, tailor, and wife Mary.

Centerell, Godfrey, of Rosenalley, Queens Co., Ireland, yeoman.

Carelton, Tho., of Ballincarrick, Co. of Wicklow, Ireland.

Champney, Edward, of Aldmonsbury, Co. of Gloucester, and wife Priscilla, da. John Fenwick.

Chinton, Robert, of Godalming, Co. of Surrey, salesman.

Clarke, Thomas, of London, haberdasher.

Clarkey, Wm., of Dublin, Ireland, merchant.

Cooper, James, of Stratford-upon-Avon, shoemaker.

Cooper, Wm., of Amersum, Buckingham Co., smith.

Cripps, John, of the Parish of St. Martin, Whitechapel, Co. of Middlesex, woolcomber.

Crues, Wm., of Southwark, Co. of Surrey.

Curbie, Recompense, of Dartmouth, Co. of Bristol.

Davenport, Francis, of Whittington, Co. of Derby, milliner.

Dennet, Samuel, of Loxley, Co. of Warwick, yeoman, and wife Susannah.

Dennis, Edw., of London, merchant tailor.

Dennis, John and Samuel, brothers, of Cork, Ireland, joiner and merchant.

Dimsdale, Robert, of Edmonton, Co. of Middlesex, physician.

Dimsdale, Robert, of Bishop Starford, Co. of Hertford.

Duke, Edward, of Aylesbury, Co. of Kent, gentleman.

Duke, Thomas, of London, draper.

Edridge, John, of the Parish of St. Paul Shadwell, Co. of Middlesex, tanner, and wife Elizabeth.

Ellis, George, of Higham, Parish of Shirland, Co. of Derby, maltster.

Elton, Anthony, of Yatsbury Parish, Co. of Wilts, yeoman.

Empson, Cornelius, of Booth, Co. of York, gentleman.

Estell, John, of Langdale, Co. of York, yeoman.

Evans, John, of Great Wigston, Co. of Leicester, husbandman.

Evans, Wm., of South Newenton, Co. of Oxon, carpenter.

Everett, Edward, of St. Saviours, Southwark, skipper.

Ewer, Robert, of Highworth, Co. of Wilts, merchant.

Fairbanks, Robert, of Balnecross, Co. of Wexford, Ireland, tailor.

Farr, Elias, of Spittlefields, Parish of Stepney, cheesemonger.

Fenwick, John, of Binfield, Berkshire, England.

Flemyng, John, of the Parish of St. Dusistan, West London, gentleman.

ffollett, John Casimir, of Shoreditch, Middlesex, chemist.

Ford, Philipp, of London, merchant.

Foster, Mathias, of Dublin, Ireland, merchant.

Fowke, Tho., of Holmegate, Parish of Northwingfield, Co. of Derby, yeoman.

Garbutt, Peter, of Scarborough, Co. of York, draper.

Gerish, Tho., of Bromham, Co. of Wilts, clothier.

Grace, Tho., of Mansfield, Nottingham Co., tailor.

Guy, Richard, of the Parish of Stepney, Middlesex, cheesemonger, and wife Bridgett.

Haddon, John, of Rotherith, Co. of Surrey, blacksmith.

Haige, Wm., of London, merchant.

Hancock, Godfrey, of Woodhouse, Parish of Handsworth, Co. of York, yeoman.

Hancock, Richard, of Bromley near Bow, Co. of Middlesex, upholsterer, and wife Margaret.

Hancock, Wm., of the Parish of St. Leonard Shoreditch, cordwainer, and wife Isabella.

Harding, Edward, of Oakingham, Co. of Berks, weaver.

Harding, John, of Oakingham, Co. of Berks, weaver.

Harding, Tho., of London, boxmaker.

Harris, John, of Goat Acre, Co. of Wilts.

Hedge, Samuel, second son of Samuel Hedge of London, merchant, marries Ann, 2d da. of John Fenwick.

Helmsley, Joseph, of Great Kelk, Co. of York, yeoman.

Heritage, Richard, of Brayles, Co. of Warwick, carpenter.

Hooke, John, of Gray's Inn, Co. of Middlesex, esquire.

Hooton, John, of Skegley, Co. of Nottingham, husbandman.

Hooton, Tho., of Blackfriars, London, chandler.

Hooton, Tho., of Helperingham, Co. of Lincoln, yeoman.

Hopper, Robert, of Scarborough, Yorkshire, master mariner.

Howell, Mordecai, of Tamworth, Co. of Warwick, gentleman.

Howell, Thomas, of Harelston, Co. of Stafford, yeoman.

Hoyland, Thomas, of Woodhouse, Parish of Handsworth, Co. of York.

Huckins, Roger, of Ford, Co. of Wilts, clothier.

Hudson, John, of London, cordwainer.

Huff, Peter, of the Parish of Christchurch, London, tailor, and wife Elianor.

Hughes, Wm., of the Parish of St. Paul Shadwell, Co. of Middlesex, cooper, and wife Deborah.

Hulines, William, of Cirencester, Co. of Gloucester, woolcomber.

Humphries, Walter, alias Powell, of Painswick, Co. of Gloucester, broadweaver.

Hunt, Joseph, of Stratford-upon-Avon, gentleman.

Hunt, Wm., of Radway, Co. of Warwick, yeoman.

Hunter, Richard, of Dublin, Ireland, tanner.

Hutcheson, George, of Sheffield, Co. of York, distiller.

Hutchinson, Thomas, of Beverley, Co. of York, yeoman.

Kent, William, of Bishopsgate Str., London.

Kinsey, John, of Great Hadam, Co. of Hertford, gentleman.

Knight, Nicholas, of Godmersham, Kent.

Lamb, Hugh, of St. Martins in the Fields, Co. of Middlesex, hosier.

Lambert, Tho., of Handsworth Woodhouse, Co. of York, tanner.

Land, Samuel, of the Parish of St. Martin's, Co. of Middlesex, tailor and wife Dorcas.

Lasswell, Wm., of Colchester, Co. of Essex, fellmonger.

Lefever, Hipolite, of St. Martins in the Fields, Middlesex, gentleman, and wife Mary.

Lucas, Nicholas, of Hertford, maltster.

Maddock, John, of the Parish of St. Sepulchres, Co. of Middlesex, chandler, and wife Elizabeth; also spelled Mattock.

Mainwaring, Thomas, of London, goldsmith.

Malster, Wm., of Westminster, gentleman, and wife Katharine Bowyer, who has sister Frances, of Iver, Buckingham, spinster.

Martin, John, of Stenning, Sussex Co., tailor.

Martin, Tho., of Lymehouse, Parish of Stepney alias Stebonheath, Co. of Middlesex, meatman.

Mathews, Edward, of St. Paul Shadwell, cooper.

Mathews, Richard, of London, factor.

Mathews, Wm., of Sheffield, currier.

Morgan, Richard, of St. Paul Shadwell, cooper.

Nettleship, Job, of the Parish of St. George Southwark, Surrey.

Nettleship, John, of Christchurch Parish, London.

Nettleship, Vicessimus, of London, salter.

Newbold, Godfrey, of Handsworth Woodhouse, Parish of Handsworth, Co. of York, yeoman.

Newbold, Michael, of Sheffield Park, Co. of York, husbandman.

Nicholson, George, of Burton Stather, Co. of Lincoln, yeoman.

Nicolson (Nicholdson), Samuel, of Wiseton, Co. of Nottingham, husbandman, and wife Anne.

Noble, Richard, of the Parish of St. Buttolph without Aldgate, Co. of Middlesex, surveyor, and wife Judith.

Norris, Samuel, of Watling Str., London.

Ollive, Tho., of Wellingborough, Co. of Northampton, haberdasher.

Padley, Benjamin, of North Carr, Co. of York, baker.

Park, Roger, of Hexham, Co. of Northumberland, yeoman.

Parkes, Richard, of Hook Norton, Co. of Oxon, ironmonger.

Peachee, Wm., of Martins le Grand, London, haberdasher.

Pearson, Francis, of Dringhoe, Holderness, Co. of York, yeoman.

Pearson, Tho., of Bonwick, Co. of York, yeoman.

Pedrick, Roger, of St. Paul Shadwell, lighterman, and wife Rebecca.

Pell, John, of Great Harroden, Northampton Co., grazier.

Penford, John, of Kerbymuckle, Co. of Leicester, grazier.

Perry, John, of Knocklofty, Tipperary Co., Ireland, gentleman.

Petty, Wm., of Cirencester, Co. of Gloucester, woolcomber.

Pike, John, of Widdingstone, Tipperary Co., Ireland, gentleman.

Pledger, John, of Portsmouth, shipcarpenter, and wife Elizabeth.

Pope, John, of Akebury, Co. of Wilts, yeoman.

Pope, Joseph, of Burton Stather, Co. of Lincoln, yeoman.

Porter, Geo., of Kelk, Co. of York, silkweaver.

Powell, see Humphries.

Reeve, John, of East Barnett, Herts, gentleman.

Richardson, Joseph, of Gramford Briggs, Co. of Lincoln, woolen-draper.

Rickston, Richard, of London, draper.

Ridges, John, of London, skinner.

Roberts, Roger, of Dublin, Ireland, innkeeper.

Robinson, John, of Beverley, Co. of York, gentleman.

Roydon, Wm., of Parish of Christchurch, Surrey Co., brewer.

Rudyard, Tho., of George Yard, Lombard Str., London.

Sadler, Thomas, of Lincoln's Inn, Middlesex Co., gentleman.

Scott, Benj. and John, of Widdington, Co. of Essex.

Scrase, John, of Patcham, Sussex Co., husbandman.

Searson, Edward, of the White Leay, Derbyshire, yeoman.

Sharp, Anthony (merchant), Thomas (woolcomber), both of Dublin, Ireland.

Skene, John, of Aberdeen, Scotland.

Slocum, Peleg, of Dartmouth, Co. of Bristol, yeoman.

Smith, George, of Farnsfield, Co. of Nottingham.

Smith, John, of Worshepp, Co. of Nottingham, meatman.

Snowden, Christr, of Kuckney, Co. of Nottingham, yeoman.

Snowden, Wm., of Edwinsboro, Co. of Nottingham, yeoman.

Stacy, Henry, of Peeter's Alley, Cornhill, London.

Stacy, Henry, of Stepney, merchant.

Stacy, Mahlon, of Dorehouse, Co. of York, tanner.

Stanton, Thomas, of Upton, Co. of Berks, maltster.

Starkey, Tho., of Abbey Lace, Queens Co., Ireland, gentleman.

Steele, Wm., of Cork, Ireland, merchant.

Taylor, Edward, of Brigghouse, Co. of York, gentleman.

Taylor, Wm., of Dore, Co. of Derby, husbandman.

Tideman, Edmond, of Redrith, Co. of Surrey, mariner.

Tompkins, Edmund, and wife Jane, of Radway, Co. of Warwick.

Towle, John, of London, baker.

Townsend, John, of Worcester, blacksmith, and wife Mary.

Townsend, Roger, of Tetbury, Co. of Gloucester, woolcomber.

Trent, Maurice, of Leith, Scotland, merchant.

Tucker, Richard, of Waymouth and Melcomb Regis, Co. of Dorset, merchant.

Turner, Robert, of Dublin, Ireland, linendraper.

Vaughan, Wm., of Clonwell, Tipperary Co., Ireland, merchant.

Wade, Edward, of London, clothworker, and wife Prudence.

Wade, Robert, of London, carpenter.

Waite, Daniel, of Westminster, Co. of Middlesex, *bodismaker*.

Walton, Wm., of Oxhite, Co. of Warwick, yeoman.

Warcupp, Richard, of Waymouth, Melcomb Regis, Co. of Dorset, mariner.

Warner, Edmond, of London, poulterer.

Wasse, James, of London, surgeon.

Watkins, John, of Twinflet, Co. of York.

Watson, William, of Farnsfield, Nottingham Co., husbandman.

Welch, Wm., of London.

Welsh, Robert, of Uffculmnae, Co. of Devon, gentleman.

White, Christopher, of the Parish of Stepney, Middlesex, carpenter, and wife Hester.

Wilkins, John, of Gussington, Co. of Leicester, laborer.

Wilkins, John, of Kegham, Co. of Leicester, husbandman.

Willis, John, of Chalow, Berks Co.

Willis, alias Westbrook, John, of Wantage, Co. of Berks, yeoman.

Wills, Daniel, of Northampton, chemist.

Wood, Constantin, Henry, Jeremiah, John, all of Bury, Co. of Lancaster, yeomen.

Wood, John, of Attercliff, Sheffield Parish, husbandman.

Wood, Jonathan, of Ewes, Parish of Maltby, Co. of York, husbandman.

Wright, Joshua, of Ashford in the Water, Co. of Derby, yeoman.

LISTS OF GERMANS FROM THE PALATINATE WHO CAME TO ENGLAND IN 1709.

The following lists are copied from the original documents preserved in the British Museum Library, London, England, and should be of the greatest genealogical interest to those families in the States of New York, New Jersey, Pennsylvania and elsewhere, which claim descent from the so-called Palatine settlers. These lists have never before been printed to the knowledge of the Editor, and it should be noted that the word "son" or "sons" and "dau." or "daus." followed by figures denote that the heads of the family had as many sons or daughters, as there are figures, and that these sons and daughters were of the respective ages denoted by the figures. The word "wife" indicates that the head of the family was married and that the wife was living. The abbreviations "Ref.," "Luth.," "Bap." and "Cath.," mean that the family belonged to the Reformed, Lutheran, Baptist or Catholic Churches.

BOARD OF TRADE MISCELLANEOUS. VOL. 2 D. 57.

A list of all the poor Germans lately come over from the Palatinate into this kingdom taken in St. Catharine's the sixth May, 1709.

FIRST ARRIVALS.

NAME	AGE	WIFE	SONS	DAUS.	CHURCH
Turch, Caspar, student of Divinity..................	25	sing.			Ref.
Machtig, Jacob, Schoolmaster	40	wife	11, 6	13, 12	"
HUSBANDMEN & VINEDRESSERS					
Meningen, John............	40	wife	5, 2		Ref.
Faubell, John..............	30	"		1½	Luth.
Leibengut, John Wendell...	53	none	28		Ref.
Ends, Matthew	50	wife	20		"
Engelsbruecher, Nicol......	57	"		15	"
Hirtzbach, Anton..........	36	"	10, 8, 5	4	"
Rohrbach, Christian........	34	"		¼	"
Hubmacher, Niclas........	33	"	6	4, 1	"
Bollon, Cristoff............	26	"	4	2, ½	"
Meyer, Henry.............	41	"		8, ½	"
Hobler, Abraham (he is also a tailor).................	32	"	6	1	"
Dixion, David (Englishman)	40	"	10		"
Kaff, Bazar...............	38	"	14, 12, ¼		Cath.
Lauber, Jacob.............	37	"		7, 6, 2	Ref.
Garrinot, Peter............	37	"			Cath.
Haun, Andrew.............	50	"	17, 11, 11, 8, 4	19, 14	Luth.
Kliein, Michael............	28	"		6, ½	"
Presler, Valentine..........	40	"	6, 4, 1½	10, 8	Cath.
Mey, David................	24	"			Ref.
Wagner, John..............	43	"	10, 8	12, 5, 3	"
Hornigh, John George......	38	"	8, 2	12, 10	"

84

NAME	AGE	WIFE	SONS	DAUS.	CHURCH
Albrecht, James............	26	wife			Luth.
Erkel, Bernhard............	33	"			Ref.
Hirzeach, Martin...	56	"	24, 14	21, 18	"
Bahr, John.................	38	"	8, 6, 3		"
Shwartz, Matthias....... ..	33	"	11, 4	8	Luth.
Durk, John Adam..........	36	"	10	12, 2	Cath.
Shonweiss, John............	48	"	1½	14, 12	Ref.
Ebert, Hartman............	30	"			"
Herman, Valentine.........	34	"	7½		Luth.
Helffert, Peter.............	49	"			Ref.
Gnaedi, Benedict...........	60	"	24	25	"
Gerhard, John George......	41	"	12, 2	16, 14, 8, 6	"
Kueffer, John..............	36	"		3, 1	"
Smith, John................	47	"	7, 5, 3, 1	24, 17, 15, 13, 11, 9	Luth.
Frey, Conrad..............	61	"	17, 14	25, 19	"
Shwa, Peter (also a cooper).	33	"	1	1½	Luth.
Seibert, Conrad............	31	"	4	1½	Ref.
Wenig, Peter..............	26	"		1½	Luth.
am Thor, Conrad...........	30	"		1½	Ref.
Daun, George.............	35	"		2	"
Reuling, Jacob.............	28	"		1	Luth.
Schneider, John Michael....	24	"	10	1½	"
Vogt, Abraham.............	50	"	12	16, 9, 7, 4	Ref.
Schneider, Philip...........	36	"	10, 3	¼	Cath.
Geisell, George.............	42	"	6, 1		"
Klein, Peter...............	42	"	2½	¼	"
Smith, Jacob..............	51	"	14, 10	4	Luth.
Trombauer, Niclas.........	33	"	6	3, ¾	Cath.
Werner, Christoff..........	33	"	1		Luth.
Huebner, Anton............	30	"	5, ¾	2½	"
Heidman, Peter............	30	"		6, 2½, ¼	"
Thevoux, Daniel...........	44	"	6	8	Ref.
Nagel, John................	40	"		9	"
Rath (Bath), John..........	29	"	2	6 da.	"
Schmitzer, John Martin.....	26	"	1		Cath.
Berg, Frederick............	32	"	3	1	Luth.
Bolker, Charles............	25	"			Ref.
Herman, Peter.............	28	"	5, 2½	1 mo.	"
Glaents, John..............	46	"	18		"
Klein, John Jacob..........	25	"	4		"
Messer, Sylvester...........	45	"	14, 5	23, 7	"
Schaeffer, Joseph..........	38	"	10, 3	14, 12, 8, 5	"
Meyer, Hartman...........	38	"	9	7, 4	"
Zeber, John................	46	"	18, 4	11, 8	"
Daninger, Jacob............	35	"	6, 1	10, 4	Luth.
Seibert, Martin............	35	"	2	4	Ref.
Bekell, Philip..............	53	"	10	12, 8, 6, 6, 1½	
Haas, John................	52	"	16, 11	9, 3	Ref.
Klein, John................	55	"	14, 6		Cath.
Wayner, Henry.............	40	"	8, 4	12	Luth.
Weitzell, John.............	29	"	1½, ¼		Luth.
Schwengel, John...........	40	"	12	4, 2, 1	"
Klug, George..............	37	"	1½		Ref.
Zeisler, Lorentz............	40	"	6, 3	1	"
Klaemer, Ludwig..........	37	"	¾	6, 4	Luth.
Spuehler, Jacob............	30	"	1		Ref.
am Rheine, John...........	30	"			Cath.
Closterbeker, John.........	31	"	6	4, 1	Luth.
Emichen, Ernst............	55	"	9, 6, 5, 1½		"

NAME	AGE	WIFE	SONS	DAUS.	CHURCH
Shwartze, John..............	32	wife	1¾	7	Ref.
Hahrlaender, Conrad.......	30	"	4½, 3		Cath.
Kaldauer, Valentine........	34	"	6, 1	14, 9, 3	"
Kuhner, Jacob.............	36	"	10, 8, 6	2	Luth.
Blesinger, Daniel...........	27	"		4, 1¼	
Lang, Philip...............	35	"	13	3	Cath.
Sheuer, John Adam........	35	"	8, 5	2	Ref.
Obender, Samuel...........	33	"		2	"
Hoffart, John Adam.......	27	"			Luth.
Weinrich, Balzar...........	40	"	7, 5, 3	15	"
Fuhrman, Jacob...........	34	none		7, 5	Ref.
Hesse, John...............	40	wife		7, 4	"
Schletzer, Jeremy..........	53	"	7, 5	12, 9, ¼	Luth.
Drechsler, John Peter......	28	"	1		"
Herman, Daniel............	28	"	2	4	Ref.
am Ende, John Philip......	35	"	¾	3	Luth.
Vogt, John................	25	"	2		Ref.
Berstler, Adam.............	30	"	8, 4	1	Luth.
Kolb, Henry...............	30	"		6, 3, ½	Bap.
Clemens, Gerhard (also a linen cloth weaver........	28	"	5, 1½		"
Volweider, Jacob...........	27	"			"
Baumann, Michael.........	37	"		8	Ref.
Herman, Jacob.............	26	sing.			Luth.
Schaeffer, John Conrad.....	23	"			Ref.
Mueller, Valentine.........	23	"			"
Hassmer, John.............	25	"			"
Bretschi, Lorentz..........	26	"			"
Hermann, Niclas...........	52	"			"
Rausch, George............	24	"			Luth.
Rudolff, John..............	24	"			"
Kolb, Arnold..............	22	"			Bap.
Hocky, Peter..............	26	"			Ref.
Hocky, Andrew............	22	"			"
THESE ARE ONLY HUSBANDMEN					
Goebell, Paul..............	59	wife	23	25	Luth.
Gring, Jacob...............	26	"		1	Ref.
Jocobi, John Thomas.......	38	"	13, 9	1	Luth.
Zitel, Jacob................	25	"			Ref.
Kinfeller, Frederick........	37	"	5	12	"
Becker, Gerhard (also a joiner)..................	38	"	½	5	"
Notzel, Rudolf.............	38	"		8, 7, 2	"
duBois, Abraham (tobacco planter).................	38	"	13, 9, 3	7	"
Durbecker, John Adam.....	26	"		2	"
Jalathe, John Wm..........	38	"	6, ½	12	"
Hartman, John George.....	40	"	9		Cath.
Buff, George..............	28	"		1	Luth.
Thomas, John George......	50	"	7, 2	5	"
Wismar, Jacob (also a tailor).	50	"	20	22	Bap.
Pfeiffer, John Jacob........	42	"	8	3	Ref.
Schuetz, John..............	46	"		6, 4, 3, 1½	"
Hubscher, Andrew.........	50	"	22	13, 9, 8, 5	Bap.
Trumph, John Michael.....	48	none	18		Ref.
le Dee, John...............	47	"		20, 16	"
le Fevre, Abram...........	50	wife	7	20	"
Schrager, Andrew..........	53	"		23, 20	Bap.
Oberholtzer, Mark..........	45	"	10, 8, 3	6, 1	"

NAME	AGE	WIFE	SONS	DAUS.	CHURCH
Fodder, John...............	38	wife	9, 4	1	Ref.
Staehler, Peter.............	24	sing.			"
Hermann, Niclas...........	52	"			"
Moor, John................	25	"			"
Moor, Austin..............	22	"			"
Moor, John Wm...........	18				"
Pelle, Peter................	24	"			"
Wentzen, Peter...	25	"			"
Hagder, John..............	27	"			"
Kuhlwein, Philip..........	26	"			"
HERDSMEN					
Beller, Jacob...............	28	wife	1 ½		Cath.
Zinkhan, Conrad...........	37	"	1 ¼	1 ¼, 4	Ref.
Schlingluff, John..........	30	"	20, 15, 11		"
WHEELWRIGHT					
Eyeach, John Valentine.....	22	sing.			Ref.
SMITHS					
Keyser, Geo. Frederick.....	40	wife		7, 5	Ref.
Zimmerman, John Wolff....	53	"	20, 16	22,18,11,9	Luth.
Willich, Peter..............	30	"		5, 2	Ref.
Leucht, Lewis..............	54	"	22		Luth.
Andrew, Benedict..........	40	"	1 ½		"
Hebenstreit, John Jas. (lock-smith)...................	30	"			Ref.
Degen, Felix..............	23	sing.			"
Heffen, Bartin.............	30	"			"
Zeitz John Peter...........	30	"			"
Bauer, George.............	40	"			Luth.
Gruendner, Matthew.......	33	"			Ref.
SADDLER					
Dieterich, John.............	44	wife	2		Cath.
MILLERS					
Lup, Henry................	28	wife	11, 9, 6	8	Ref.
Guth, Henry..............	30	sing.			"
Rebell, Jacob..............	30	"			"
Escherich, John............	37	"			Luth.
Anke, Joseph..............	28	"			Ref.
BAKERS					
Muller, Daniel.............	50	sing.			Ref.
Penning, Daniel............	22	"			Luth.
BREWER					
Truat, John................	40	wife	10, 6		Ref.
BUTCHERS					
de Rochefort, Peter.........	38	wife	12, 10	15, 3	Ref.
Smith, Henry..............	53	"	22,19,12, 6	15	Luth.
Buehler, John..............	48	"		16, 12, 11	"
CLOTH & LINEN WEAVERS					
Walter, John George.......	45	wife	12, 9, ½	17, 7	Ref.
Rider, Niclas..............	38	"			"
Lucas, Francis.............	46	"	17, 11	19,8,6,3,3	"
Bruchly, John Henry.......	32	"	4, 2		"
Adeler, Henry.............	41	"	12		"

NAME	AGE	WIFE	SONS	DAUS.	CHURCH
Hoherluth, George Adam...	45	wife	12, 9	17, 14	Bap.
Ziegler, Michael...........	25	sing.			Luth.
Bien, John................	24	"			Bap.
TAILORS					
Boos, John Henry..........	22	wife			Ref.
Riedell, John George.......	30	"	1	6	Luth.
Koenig, John Adam........	30	sing.			"
SHOEMAKER					
Mueller, John Jacob........	42	wife	13, 12, 10, 8, 6, 4	15	Ref.
Hohenstein, Christian......	37	"	4 , 1	6	Cath.
Schlottenhofer, Christof.....	38	"	6, 1		Ref.
Galathe, John Jacob........	32	"	12	6	"
Mendon, Jacob.............	22	sing.			"
STOCKING WEAVER					
Mason, Niclas.............	46	wife	17		Ref.
TANNER					
Bergleuchter, Anton........	24	sing.			Ref.
CARPENTERS					
Guthzeit, William..........	29	wife	3	2	Luth.
Neidhofer, John Quirinus...	42	"	8	20, 17	"
Gessienger, Henry.........	28	"		¼	"
Weber, John Engel.........	46	"		20, 18, 13, 8, 4	"
Weber, John Jacob.........	26	"			"
Schaeffer, John.............	44	"	14, 10, 2, 5 da.	8, 5	Ref.
Bauer, Christian...........	30	"	8, 6	10, 4, 1	"
Galathe, Jacob.............	75	sing.			"
JOINERS					
Heyde, Peter..............	28	wife	1½		Ref.
Hagenbeck, frederick......	30	"	6, 3		Cath.
Kirchofen, Francis Ludwig..	37	sing.			Ref.
MASONS					
Schaeffer, John.............	26	wife	1		Ref.
Hakl, John George.........	30	"	1	9, 5, 4	Cath.
COOPERS					
Stutz, John Eberhard.......	44	wife	7, 2	5	Luth.
Henrich, Lorentz...........	48	"	2½	1¼	Ref.
Reiser, John Peter..........	40	"	14, 12, 8, 6, 1½		Cath.
BOOKBINDER					
Hoffstaetter, Philip.........	19	sing.			Ref.
MINER					
la Forge, John Wm..... ...	50	wife			Ref.
UNMARRIED PERSONS, WIDOWS, ETC.					
Rose, Anna................	53		9	17, 4	Ref.
Rose, Catherine............	24			1½	"
Bettinger, Anna Christina...	60				"

NAME	AGE	WIFE	SONS	DAUS.	CHURCH
Tanner, Cathrina...........	35			6	Cath.
Schoen, Maria Cathrina.....	38		10, 8, 4	1½	"
Winter, Maria Cathrina.....	50			20	"
Raths, Jane................	50				Ref.
Schwaegerin, Apollonia.....	50				"
Martins, Gertrud...........	42		9		"
Eschelmanns, Anna........	37		16		Bap.
George Riedel's mother-in-law....................	50				Luth.
Warambour, Mary.........	56		24, 23, 19, 17	22	Ref.
UNMARRIED					
Sister of Henry Meyers.....	42				Ref.
Sister-in-law of Michael Klein	20				"
Cathrina, Servant maid.....	36				"
Friede, Cathrina...........	30				"
Wagner, Mary Elizabeth...	24				"
Bauer, Christina............	23				Bap.

SUCH AS ENTERED THEIR NAMES LAST.

NO. OF THE FAMILY	NAME
4	Lang, Johan
5	Stutz, Eberhard
4	Pens, Benedict
1	Bohm, Johannes
1	Denias, Philip
1	Albenz, Christoph
1	Lichtneggar, Gottlob August
1	Graeff, Jacob, whose parents live in Pennsylvania, a boy 10 years of age
1	George Klug, his sister's son, a boy 15 years of age

19 Persons who entered their names last

ALL PAGES SUMMED UP.

Husbandmen & Vinedressers....	115	Tailors........................	3
Only Husbandmen.............	32	Shoemakers....................	5
Herdsmen.....................	3	Stocking Weaver..............	1
Wheelwright..................	1	Tanner........................	1
Smiths........................	11	Carpenters....................	8
Saddler.......................	1	Joiners	3
Millers.......................	5	Masons........................	2
Bakers........................	2	Coopers	3
Brewer........................	1	Bookbinder........	1
Butchers......................	3	Miner	1
Cloth & Linen Weavers.........	8		

The whole sum of men, wives and children, lately come over from the Palatinate into this Kingdom makes out 852.

JOHN TRIBBEKO,
Chaplain to his late Royal Highness Prince George of Denmark.

GEORGE ANDREW RUPERTI,
Minister of the German Lutheran Church in the Savoye.

Endorsed: Miscellaneous. Account of the number, conditions and trades of the poor German come over from the Palatinate.

Referred to in mem. from the Lutheran minister.

Received and read 12th May, 1709, D.57 Entered A folio 401.

LISTS OF GERMANS FROM THE PALATINATE WHO CAME TO ENGLAND IN 1709.

The following lists are copied from the original documents preserved in the British Museum Library, London, England, and should be of the greatest genealogical interest to those families in the States of New York, New Jersey, Pennsylvania and elsewhere, which claim descent from the so-called Palatine settlers. These lists have never before been printed to the knowledge of the Editor, and it should be noted that the word "son" or "sons" and "dau." or "daus." followed by figures denote that the heads of the family had as many sons or daughters, as there are figures, and that these sons and daughters were of the respective ages denoted by the figures. The word "wife" indicates that the head of the family was married and that the wife was living. The abbreviations "Ref.," "Luth.," "Bap." and "Cath.," mean that the family belonged to the Reformed, Lutheran, Baptist or Catholic Churches.

BOARD OF TRADE MISCELLANEOUS. VOL. 2 D. 64.

The second list of 1193 Palatines lately come over from Germany into this kingdom taken at Walworth, 27th of May, 1709, by Mr. John Tribbeko and Mr. Ruperti, German Ministers.

SECOND ARRIVALS.

NAME	AGE	WIFE	SONS	DAUS.	CHURCH
SCHOOLMASTERS.					
Schenne, Justus............	34	wife	4, 1¼		Luth.
Moritz, John Philip.........	50	"		25, 27	Ref.
Rinner, Hans Henrich......	45	"	20, 4	14, 11, 9, 5	"
HUSBANDMEN & VINEDRESSERS					
Hodell, Michael............	34	wife		6, 3	Ref.
Schmidt, John George......	30	"	4	2	"
Hach, John Peter...........	60	"	20		"
Hach, John.	30	wife	14		"
Schmidt, Frederick.........	30	"	4		Luth.
Conradt, Martin............	45	"	9, 5	13, 3	"
Richardt, John.............	46	"	14, 3	19, 12, 9, 6	Ref.
Bertram, Peter.............	21	sing.			"
Korn, George..............	50	wife		7	Luth.
Dietrich, John Peter........	36	"	8	5, 1¼	"
Hertzog, Jacob Andreas.....	38	"	14, 10, 8	6, 4	"
Shwygart, Frederick........	34	"	6, 3, 1½	7, 4	"
Lutz, John George..........	49	"	3	14, 10, 8	Ref.
Meyer, John George........	25	"			Cath.
Weibel, John Jacob.........	36	"	8	10, 6, 3, 1¼	Luth.
Vogel, John (also a carpenter).....................	47	"	6	7, 3	"
Muller, Valentine..........	32	"	6		"
Emmich, Paulus............	30	"			"
Fuhrer, John..............	40	"	13, 6	8, 1	Cath.
Cunitz, John...............	33	"	15, 5	1	"
Holzer, John (also a hunter).	40	"	3		"

NAME	AGE	WIFE	SONS	DAUS.	CHURCH
Caselman, Christin.........	37	wife	2		Luth.
Hertzog, Casper....	34	"	7, 4		Ref.
Geiger, David..............	50	"	23, 10	5, 4	"
Jacob, Christian............	34	"	8, 5, 2		"
Ade, John.................	36	"	17, 5	15, 5	Luth.
Stauch, John Peter.........	44	"	12, 9, 2	5	Ref.
Mattern, William..........	30	"	4		Luth.
Kopf, Henrich.............	38	"	12	10, 7, 3	Ref.
Kroen, John George........	36	"		2	"
Henckel, John George......	38	"			Cath.
Klaus, Henrich............	36	"		7, 2	
Mattern, John George......	40	"	14, 4, 1	20, 17, 8	Luth.
Otzenberger, John Peter....	40	"		1	Cath.
Keller, John................	28	"	2		"
Heidman, Gerhard.........	20	sing.			Ref.
Becker, Frederick..........	23	"			Luth.
Eckart, Balzar.............	23	wife	2		Cath.
Sternberger, John Jacob....	29	"	10, 7, 4	9	Luth.
Zeiter, John George........	38	"	8	12	"
Ritweil, Frederick.........	32	"	2		"
Ritweil, Jacob..............	22	sing.			"
Peter, John................	38	wife		2	
Misemer, Daniel...........	28	"	3	5, 1½	Luth.
Misemer, Valentine.........	23	"	3, 1		"
Baltz, John Philip..........	18	sing.			"
Keller, Nicol..............	24	wife			Ref.
Roth, John................	24	sing.			Luth.
Werbel, John Wilhelm.....	23	"			"
Crammer, Christian........	24	"			"
Peters, Henrich............	24	"			Ref.
Tiel, Bernard..............	40	wife	13, 10, 2	18, 11, 6, 4	Ref.
Diestel, Peter Daube......	24	sing.			"
Friel, William..............	50	wife	9	13	Luth.
Buehler, John..............	53	"		20, 14, 1	Ref.
Jordan, Conrad.............	21	sing.			"
Meurer, John Quirinus......	53	wife	23, 17	26, 24	Luth.
Schneider, Bernard.........	48	"	18, 16	11	"
Schmidt, John William.....	54	"	4, 3	8, 6	"
Meyer, John Joseph........	24	"	1		Ref.
Eberhard, John............	30	"	16, 14, 12	6	Cath.
Bach, John (also gardner)...	38	"	7	13, 11	"
Muller, Henrich............	48	"	24, 16, 12	18, 9	"
Hartbeck, Matthew.........	30	"			"
Eckstedt, John George......	22				"
Langbein, Cristoph.........	25				Luth.
Keller, John Jacob.........	24	wife	3		"
Gerby, John Michael........	29	"	7	3	Ref.
Hust, Jacob................	52	"	18		"
Beuhman (B e u k m a n ?), Michael.................	24				"
Lang, John................	49	wife	17, 12, 6	18, 6	
Harnish, John..............	24	"	2		Ref.
Frick, Henrich.............	30	"			Luth.
Bonus, Julius..............	31	"	15, 6, 2		Ref.
Ziegler, Henrich...........	50	"	¾		"
Imberger, Andreas.........	22				Luth.
Hahn, Johann Martin.......	30	wife			Cath.
Martin, Matthew...........	50	"	11, 5	18, 12	"
Klein, Jacob...............	24				Luth.
Oberitter, John Georg.......	37	wife	5	10, 2	Cath.
Bush, Christian.............	16				Luth.

NAME	AGE	WIFE	SONS	DAUS.	CHURCH
Bush, Philip................	26	wife	15, 10	8, 3, ½	Luth.
Sprosser, Anton............	23	"			Cath.
Spanheimer, George........	45	"		11, 9, 7, 1	Ref.
Rauch, John Just...........	49	"	8	18	Luth.
Bonden, John..............	34	"		5, 3, 1	
Stoppelbein, Peter..........	24	"	5, 2 m.		Ref.
Lorentz, Peter.............	50	"	10	16, 14, 11	Luth.
Scherz, Jacob..............	25	"	5	2	Ref.
Kuehn, Matthew...........	34	"	2		Cath.
Bauer, Christian...........	28	"	1		Ref.
Crass, Philip..............	50	"	12	18, 13, 7, 2	Cath.
Lutz (Lut), John Peter......	29	"	11	3, ½	Luth.
Lut, Anton................	28				Cath.
Keyser, Matthew...........	38	wife		12	Ref.
Venus, John Jacob (also a mason)..................	45	"	14, 12, 8, 7	11	Luth.
Lescher, Sebastian.........	40	"	20, 14, 10, 8, 6	15, 12, 6, 4, 1	"
Vreel, John Nicol..........	29	"		3	Ref.
Stambach, John Jacob......	28	"			"
Weber, John George.......	34	"	1		"
Hepman, Melchior.........	53	"		17, 12, 8	Luth.
Werner, Michael...........	50	"		14	"
Neubauer, Andrew.........	37	"	19	6, 4	"
Fusz, John................	30	"	½	6, 3	Ref.
Bogenman, Jacob..........	30	"	2, 1 ½		"
Lorentz, John..............	39	"	2	14, 12, 10, 5, 5	"
Seitz, John Dietrich........	36	"	14	10, 3	"
Krems, John...............	29	"	4		Cath.
Wilmar, Ulric..............	53	"	16		Ref.
Spinlar, Caspar............	41	"	11, 3	18, 3	Cath.
Helwig, Henrich...........	27	"	3		Ref.
Krebs, Peter...............	35	"	4, 2		Luth.
Lickel, Daniel..............	24				Ref.
Arm, David................	52	wife	21, 13, 8	17, 6, 2	"
Buco, Jacob...............	28	"	5	3, 1	"
Kennel, Samuel............	25	"	1 ¼		"
Bason, Nicol...............	34	"	6, 4		"
Richard, Peter.............	34	"	13, 1	5, 3	
Thal, Philip...............	45	"	20, 3	10, 7, 3	Ref.
Schwegars, John Heinrich..	38	"	6, 1		Luth.
Balmus, Nicol..............	28	"	3	2	"
Herber, John Jacob...........	18				"
Lash, Jacob................	46	wife		23, 18	"
Schreckenberg, John Henrich...................	28	"		3	Cath.
Waldman, Leonhard.......	36	"	5	3, 1 ½	Luth.
Schombert, John Jacob.....	36	"	3		"
Keyser, John Michel........	46	"	14, 6	11, 3	
Port, Justus...............	30	"		8, 2	Ref.
Eyler, John Conradt........	30				"
Kraut, John George........	28	wife			"
Kieser, John Adam.........	29	"			"
Erhardt, John Simon........	46	"	6, 3	8	"
Helm, John Adam..........	44	"			Cath.
Dunger, John..............	20				"
Fisher, Simon..............	30	wife			"
Casselman, John...........	49	"	10, 3	19, 13, ½	Luth.
Pfadheucher, Marcel.......	52			30, 22	"
Pfadheucher, Hans Henrich	27	wife	10, 3	4	"

NAME	AGE	WIFE	SONS	DAUS.	CHURCH
Riesenbucher, Mattheus....	27	wife	4, 2	7	Luth.
Richter, John Andreas......	46	"	14	17, 7, 3	"
Shaeffer, Andreas (also a carpenter)...............	42	"	13	15, 7	Ref.
Umbach, John George......	35	"		7, 5	"
Depper, Lobonus..........	41	"	16, 1½	12, 4	Cath.
Duerr, Peter (also a carpenter).................	37	"	4	8, 2	Ref.
Rose, John Christoph.......	45	"	16, 12, 9, 7, 3, 1 d.	2	Luth.
Lambert, John.............	65	"	11, 8	13, 9	Cath.
Blaum, Herman............	50	"	6	12	Ref.
Fink, Andreas.............	34	"	9		"
Lutz, John (also a carpenter)	35	"	8, 6, 3	¼	Cath.
Wille, Henrich George.....	36	"	9, 7	2	Luth.
Holtzschuch, John Jacob....	31	"		16, 4	"
Fischbach, John...........	35	"	10, 1	3	"
Wentz, John George........	30	"	4	6	"
Mueller, Peter........	36	"	3	10	"
Gemelk, Michel............	30	"	1		"
Tuebell, Anton.............	40	"	12	9, 4	"
Graeff, Henry.............	44	"	4	12, 6	"
Schaeffer, Henry...........	43	"	20, 17	14	Ref.
Bernard, John George (also a carpenter)..............	36	"	5, 1	3	Luth.
Klingelstein, Nicol.........	36	"	7, 3	5, 1	Ref.
Roth, John Peter...........	29	"	3, 1½		Luth.
Brunn, John Tiel...........	35	"		¼	Cath.
Moor, Cleman..............	33	"	6, 2	8, 4	Ref.
Koerner, Wolf.............	30	"	4, 2		Luth.
Wordman, John............	40	"	10, 5	13, ½	Ref.
Wollhand, Engelhard......	26	"			"
Habig, Conrad.............	50	"	24, 21	16	Luth.
Shmidt, Caspar....	58	"	16, 14, 6, 3	27, 24, 10, 7	Cath.
Busch, Caspar (also a hunter)	22	"		2	Luth.
Minglen, Kilian............	36	"	9	11, 7	Ref.
Muntrian, Paul.............	38	"	8, 6, 4		Cath.
Rendel, John Peter........	43	"		2	Luth.
Oster, Arnd...............	24	"			Cath.
Debald, Francis............	30	"	7, 5, 3		Ref.
Debald, Conrad............	27	"	2	8, 5, 4	"
Rufenacht, Benedict........	46	"	9	13, 11, 6, ¼	"
Daul, John Michael.........	22	"			Luth.
Boehm, John Martin........	30	"			"
Riet, John George..........	50	"	20, 18, 16, 14, 7	22, 12, 10	"
Schaefer, Just Henry.......	35	"	9	4	Ref.
Fuhrman, John Michel.....	47	"		13, 7, 4	Luth.
Fuss, Andreas..............	34	"	9, 6	11, 3	Ref.
Kennleiter, John...........	38	"	6, 2	4	Luth.
Heischer, John (also a linen-weaver),.................	30	"	5, ¼	6	"
Ludorf, Conrad............	19				Ref.
Ruehl, John Peter..........	20				Luth.
Kuehn, Conrad.............	40	wife	14, 11, 8, 2		Ref.
Boltz, George.............	50	"	13, 7, 4		"
Beck, John Jacob....	50	"	18	20, 13, 10, 8, 6	Luth.
Bergman, Abraham........	46	"	10	19, 16, 14, 7	"
Zwick, Matthew............	35	"	11, 6, 5	13	"
Moret, Jacob..............	45	"		18, 13, 11	Ref.

NAME	AGE	WIFE	SONS	DAUS.	CHURCH
Bash, Daniel...............	45	wife		18	Ref.
Mutin, Peter...............	30	"	5	20	"
Duester, John..............	34	"	9, 3, ½	6	"
Schnell, Matthew...........	48				Cath.
WHEELWRIGHTS					
Kuntze, Nicol..............	33	wife	8, 7, 4	½	Ref.
Korman, Peter Jacob.......	50	"	20	19	Luth.
Kortner, Peter.............	46	"	11, 8, 6		Ref.
von dem Sabelgaul, John Leonhardt................	28	"		2	Cath.
Lutz, John Adam...........	22				Luth.
SMITHS					
Weber, John Adolf.........	18				Ref.
Bauer, Elias...............	23				"
Seyfried, John Jacob........	23				Luth.
Herman, Sebastian.........	23				"
Muller, John Ludiger.......	22				Ref.
Kopf, John.................	30				Cath.
Unstat, Valentin............	22				Luth.
Weber, John Philip.........	18				"
Wolf, John Michel..........	27				"
TAILORS					
Paular, Andreas Jacob......	20				Ref.
Ludwig, John..............	35	wife	10, 1	5	"
Frederik, Wendel..........	50	"	8	18, 4, ½	Luth.
Siegler, John Conrad........	20				Ref.
Wentzel, John Georg.......	20				Luth.
Petri, Henry...............	20				Ref.
Ulrich, Cristof.............	30	wife	2	7, 3	Luth.
——, Daniel................	24				Ref.
Fink, John Godfried........	44		18, 10		Luth.
Liebhan, John..............	36		12		Cath.
Stoll, John.................	16				"
Aman, John.................	27	wife			Ref.
Kleus, John................	24	"		½	"
Shaefer, Georg.............	18				"
Deibolt, John Georg	20				"
Schretz, Michael...........	18				Cath.
Kleus, Carl................	16				Ref.
Muschel, Jacob.............	25	wife	½		Luth.
Barrabam, John Wolf.......	34	"		4, 2	Ref.
LINEN WEAVERS					
Jacky, Ulrich..............	31				Ref.
Eck, Velentin..............	50	wife	16, 10, 7	12, 5	Cath.
Shaar, Daniel..............	24				Ref.
Cauer, Jacob Mitter........	40	wife	5, 3	1	Luth.
Becke, Ephraim............	32	"	4, 3		"
Haber, Barthel.............	29	"	¾	11, 6, 4	"
Frauch, Georg.............	30	"	5, 2		Ref.
Bastian, Andreas...........	21				Cath.
Ludolph, John.............	31	wife	5, 3	7, ½	Ref.
WOOLEN WEAVERS					
Dufin, Peter...............	53				Ref.
Hero, Henrich.............	33	wife	8	5	"
Schwartz, Christian.........	36				"

NAME	AGE	WIFE	SONS	DAUS.	CHURCH
Jung, Abraham (a shoe-maker)..................	18				Ref.
Kless, Henry (a shoemaker).	37	wife	6, 1	10, 8, 4	Luth.
Kauffer, Daniel (also a shoe-maker)................	27				"
BAKERS					
Martin, Thomas............	24				Luth.
Kling, John Conrad.........	22				"
Sigmund, John Michel......	27	wife	1		Ref.
Kornman, John Peter.......	37	"	5	1	"
Marx, Matthew............	23				Cath.
Schmotzer, John Jacob......	33	wife	4	12	Luth.
Windeberger, John Jacob. .	35	"	12, 3	10, 5	"
Weber, John Caspar........	20				Ref.
Hartwig, Caspar...........	38	wife	5, 4	7	"
Muller, John Jacob.........	30	"	1	1	"
MASONS AND STONE CUTTERS					
Kremmeln, Salomon........	23				Ref.
Meister, Jacob.............	24				"
Philip, George Thomas.....	40	wife			Luth.
Hernichel, Henrich.........	46	"	5	9, 2	Ref.
Vogelsperger, Joachim.....	30				Cath.
Winhofer, John Georg......	28				"
Stephen, John..............	36	wife	2		"
Bishop, Ludwig............	19				Luth.
Garter, John (Englishman)..	40				Ref.
CARPENTERS					
Frey, Henrich..............	27	wife		½	Ref.
John, Cristoph..............	33				Luth.
Flegler, Zacharra...........	36	wife	8, 4	1	"
Semter, John...............	38	"	2		Ref.
Dalem, Lambert...........	27	"		5	Cath.
Codd, John.................	26				Luth.
Riesenburn, Jacob..........	37				Cath.
Wambach, Nicol...........	36	wife	12, 8, 5, 2		"
Mueller, John Nicol........	22				"
Mueller, Jacob.............	37	wife	14, 10, 4	6, 3	"
Fuehrer, John Jacob........	26				"
Hartung, Caspar...........	25				Luth.
Schueler, Franciscus.......	42				Cath.
Dietz, John Peter...........	26				"
BUTCHERS					
Jung, John.................	28	wife			Ref.
Trep, John Jacob...........	28	"			"
Clanenberg, Conrad........	38	"		1	Luth.
MILLERS					
Selner, John Adam.........	51	wife		5, 2	Luth.
Schuch, John Peter.........	32	"		12, 10	Cath.
Stein, John.................	44	"			"
Muller, John...............	24				Luth.
COOPERS AND BREWERS					
Baehr, Tobias..............	45	wife	11, 9, 6, 3	14	Ref.
Matthew, John.............	37	"	8, 5	11	Cath.
Hartman, John Georg......	28	"	1		Luth.

NAME	AGE	WIFE	SONS	DAUS.	CHURCH
Milbert, John Martin.......	40	wife	13	11, 2	Luth.
Lutz, Cristoph..............	36				Ref.
Bruder, Valentin...........	25	wife			"
Mehder, John Henry........	28				"
JOINERS					
Tibold, Isaac...............	48	wife			Ref.
Schultheis, John...........	26	"	½	2	Luth.
Ellenberger, George........	45	"	15		Ref.
Crukot, Arnold.............	42	"	2	8	"
Dinant, Peter..............	39	"	11, 9, 7, 5	3	"
TURNERS					
Mueckel, Ulrich............	36	wife	3, 1		Ref.
Teske, Jacob...............	50	"	20, 16		Luth.
Hofman, Gabriel...........	40				Ref.
Hatteman, Ulrich..........	40	wife	10, 4	9, 5, 2	Mennon.
SADDLER					
Rudolf, John...............	20				Ref.
LABOURERS					
Wagner, Andreas..........	37	wife	6, 3		Cath.
Helm, Peter...............	30	"	15,11,9,6, 4, ¼	7	Ref.
SILVERSMITHS					
Reinhold, John Georg......	27				Luth.
Schmiedel, Siegmund.......	24				Ref.
TANNERS					
Jung, Jacob................	25				Ref.
Jacob, John (apothecary)....	21				Luth.
Beck, John (merchant's apprentice)	22				"
WIDOWS					
Bieco, Mary Lucas.........	52		25, 14	18, 11, 8	Ref.
Rockeln, Elizabeth.........	77				Luth.
Lichtnerin, Margaret.......	50				Ref.
Lichtnerin, Anna Maria.....	30		2		
Dinkelin, Appolonia........	80				Luth.
Plazerin, Sarah.............	36		2	10	"
Schultheis, Esther Susanna.	46		20, 9	11, 6, 4	"
Jungin, Elizabeth...........	49		24, 12	19, 16	Luth.
Mutten, Anna Maria..	50				Ref.
Bingerin, Elizabeth.........	24			2	"
Emmoch, Anna Eve........	44		21, 18		"
Kleinsin, Gertrud..........	48		14	11, 8	"
Mushelin, Anne Marg......	50		16		"
Steigerin, Cristina..........	60				"
Schaker, Susanne..........	70				"
Krebsin, Salome............	50				"
UNMARRIED WOMEN					
Weiss, Mary...............	34				Ref.
Weiss, Magdalena..........	30				"
Barrabam, Anna Clara......	23				"
Dresin, Gerdrut............	30				Cath.
Weritzen, Anne Catherine..	27				"
Kellerin, Barbara..........	21				Ref.
Schutmegenn, Charlotta....	26				Cath.

NAME	AGE	WIFE	SONS	DAUS.	CHURCH
Kiesenn, Anne Catherine...	18				Cath.
Woberin, Eva..............	22				Ref.
Barba, Anna...............	18				Cath.
Klessin, Maria.............	24				Luth.
Melkin, Anna Margaretha..	22				"
Guthman, Maria Barbara...	22				Cath.
Reichardin, Anna Barba....	20				"
Welkin, Maria.............	30				Ref.
Koernerin, Maria...........	24				"
Obermullerin, Mary Catherine....................	30				"
Hartwegin, Anne Elizabeth.	22				Luth.
Margareth, Elizabeth.......	20				"
Wunderlich, Christina......	21				Cath,
Bessenn, Dorethea.........	25				Luth.

THE WHOLE SUM:

```
Men.............................. 311
Women ........................... 263
Sons ............................ 323
Daughters........................ 296
                                 ────
                                 1193
```

(ENDORSED)

A second list of 1193 Palatines lately arrived from Germany, distinguishing their Professions, Ages, etc.

LISTS OF GERMANS FROM THE PALATINATE WHO CAME TO ENGLAND IN 1709.

The following lists are copied from the original documents preserved in the British Museum Library, London, England, and should be of the greatest genealogical interest to those families in the States of New York, New Jersey, Pennsylvania and elsewhere, which claim descent from the so-called Palatine settlers. These lists have never before been printed to the knowledge of the Editor, and it should be noted that the word "son" or "sons" and "dau." or "daus." followed by figures denote that the heads of the family had as many sons or daughters, as there are figures, and that these sons and daughters were of the respective ages denoted by the figures. The word "wife" indicates that the head of the family was married and that the wife was living. The abbreviations "Ref.," "Luth.," "Bap." and "Cath.," mean that the family belonged to the Reformed, Lutheran, Baptist or Catholic Churches.

BOARD OF TRADE MISCELLANEOUS. VOL. 2. NO. D 68.

PUBLIC RECORD OFFICE, LONDON.

List of the poor Palatines that are arrived in St. Cathrin's, the 2nd of June, 1709.

THIRD ARRIVALS.

NAME	AGE	WIFE	SONS	DAUS.	CHURCH
HUSBANDMEN & VINEDRESSERS					
Kuehlman, John..........	50	wife		20, 12, 9, 7, 2	Ref.
Reckhart, Justus..........	53	"			Luth.
Weber, Martin............	34	"		3, ¾	
Glass, Valentine..........	25	"			Cath.
Molendueck, Herman......	50	"		19, 12	Ref.
Stuetz, Johan.............	35	"	13, 6	11, 3	Cath.
Luetz, John George........	30	"		2	Ref.
Lutz, Peter...............	40	"	7, 2	10	"
Hildebrand, Johan........	50	"	11	15	Luth.
Heumacher, John Jacob.....	30	"	3, 2		Cath.
Schweitzer, Michael........	28	"	2, ½		Luth.
Schneider. Johan George....	38	"	11	6	"
Fechter, Martin...........	40	"	6	18, 15, 10, 3, 1½	"
Hartman, Conrad..........	45	"		4	"
Mohr, Christoph...........	40	"			"
Schiefer, Johan...........	42	"	9, 5, 3	1½	"
Beydelman, Johan Michel..	40	"	7, 5	9	
Lemp, Conrad.............	36	"	7	3	Ref.
Igelsbach, Wendal.........	45	"	4, 2	6, ½	"
Wegman, Mattheus........	35	"	11, 9, ½	13, 7, 6, 3	"
Graf, Philip Leonhardt.....	48	"	15	18, 12, 9, 4	"
Lehrers, Johan Philip.......	30	"		13	"
Thomas, Matheus..........	42	"	4	11, 8, ¼	"

NAME	AGE	WIFE	SONS	DAUS.	CHURCH
Meyer, Henrich............	43	wife	11	13	Luth.
Brandlin, Caspar..........	42	"	4	½	Cath.
Schlosser, John............	54	"		14, 8	"
Anweiler, John............	27	"	1		"
Stieb, John Reinhard.......	48	"	12, 9	23, 18	Luth.
Stieb, John Peter..........	45	"	5, 3	¾	"
Helfer, Cristop............	40	"	8, 2	6	"
Muller, George Philip......	36	"	11, 6	8, 5, 1	"
Lobwasser, Anton..........	41	"	7		Cath.
Tag, Francis Hendrich....	47	"	9	11	Luth.
Meyer, Jacob..............	32	"	2		"
Schnidt, John Jacob........	25	"	¾		"
Nakhan, William...........	38	"		5, ½	Ref.
Bunderskeil, Andreas.......	40	"	14, 7	15, 7	Cath.
Herman, Schweikhart......	40	"	19, 6	4	"
——, Matheus..............	23	"	1		"
Neumeyer, John August....	35	"	3	12, 8, 6	"
Quint, Anton..............	36	"	4, 3	3	"
Weber, Philip.............	60	"	20		"
Hunold, Seyfart...........	38	"	16, 14, 12, 3, ½	9, 5	Luth.
Craemer, Philip............	35	"			Cath.
Thomas, Francis...........	28	"	2		"
Gross, William.............	24	"	4	1½	Ref.
Ritz, John.................	40	"	10	6, 1½	Cath.
Weimar, Simon............	40	"	10, 8	5	Luth.
Conrads, Conrad...........	36	"		10, 1	Cath.
Charton, Hendrick.........	32	"		19, 6, 4, 1½	"
Wilmart, John Martin......	35	"	10, 5	13, 8, 5	"
Kolbe, Francis.............	36	"	20, 14, 10, 7	15	"
Beckart, Conrad...........	30	"	10, 1½	4	"
Fink, John Adam..........	24(?)	"	16(?)	1	"
Kast, John George.........	30	"	8	6, 4, 2	Luth.
Westhofer, Johan Jacob.....	30	"	2		Ref.
Paul, John Daniel.........	59	"		36, 33, 30, 20	"
Paul, John, Clother........	46	"	18, 7	9, 4	Luth.
Wrikedy, Philip............	30	"	7	1	Cath.
Hayn, John................	40	"	16	12, 7, 1½	"
Musier, John Jacob........	54	"	24, 12, 9, 3	21, 18	Ref.
Schwing, John.............	23	"			"
Sex, Philip................	53	"	20, 5	16, 13, 1½	Luth.
Weber, Henrik............	32	"	13, 10, 1	7	Ref.
Hammerleim, John Jacob...	45	"	13	11, 7, 2	"
Egelman, John Adam......	37	"	2	8, 6	Luth.
Cays, John B r i l l (a shoe-maker	45	"	18, 17	15, 11	Ref.
Braun, John Debauld.......	58	"	¼		"
Gedel, John Peter..........	27	"	¾		"
Dorn, Lazarus.............	48	"	14, 7	10, 9, 6, 1½, ¼	"
Schaefer, John Andreas.....	42	"	11, 7, 1	12, 4, 4	Luth.
Zwinger, George Peter......	40	"	21, 2		Cath.
Seip, John Peter...........	27	"		2	Ref.
Muench, Christoph.........	26	"	1		Luth.
Hillig, Andreas............	26	"	2		"
Hop, Christian.............	35	"			"
Straub, John...............	26	"		¼	"
Reisenberger, Lorentz......	46	"		9, 6	Ref.
Brummer, Johan...........	40	"	7, 1		Cath.
Knaub, Johan Christoph....	30	"	2	1	Ref.

NAME	AGE	WIFE	SONS	DAUS.	CHURCH
Rautebusch, Johan.........	30	wife		3	Luth.
Geschwind, Johan..........	35	"	7	5, 3, 1	Cath.
Gusman, Peter.............	40	"	8, 7, 1		"
Kraut, John Peter..........	38	"	1	10, 7, 4	Ref.
Mey, Christoph............	35	"		3	"
Hoechst, Burckard.........	27	"	5, ¼		Luth.
Ortminger, Nicol...........	34	"	7, 5	3, 1	Cath.
Emmerich, Peter..........	36	"		5	Ref.
Eyler, Johann..............	50	"	15, 3, 3 m.	12, 10, 8, 4	"
von der Muehler, Philip....	51	"	19, 1½	22, 17, 14, 13, 11, 7	"
Weber, Henry.............	52	"	16, 8, 6	2, ½	"
Neuman, Ludwig...........	37	"	12, 9, 6	9, 6	"
Appel, Christian...........	37	"		6, 3	Cath.
Reinhard, Henry...........	28	"	2		Luth.
Baehr, Frederick..........	29	"	4, 2		Cath.
Lentz, Henry..............	40	"	11, 9, 2		"
Schaeffer, Gerhard.........	30	"	6, 3, 1		"
Rhode, Johan Juste.........	28	"	3, 1	5	Ref.
Rup, Johan................	52	"		23, 20	Luth.
Dolmetsch, Johan..........	30	"	12, 9, 6	2, ½	"
Hecht, Caspar.............	50	"	24, 11, 9, 7, 2	27, 18	"
Beker, Michel.............	32	"	6	4	Ref.
Flor, Johan................	46	"	23	25	"
Mentz, Anton..............	28	"	8	6	Cath.
Henrich, Johan James......	23	"			Luth.
Falck, Arnold.............	32	"	6, 2		Cath.
Muster, Lambert...........	50	"	25	15	"
Strauch, Johan.............	30	"	2		Luth.
Hill, John William.........	40	"	1	5, 4	Ref.
Hill, Johan.	90	"			"
Nuentzeberger, Dieterich...	51	wife	17, 13, 10, 8, 4	19, 15	Cath.
Madler, Michel............	38	"	11, 7, 4	18	Luth.
Streit, Ludwig.............	42	"	8, 6	5, 3, ½	Cath.
Dungel, Matthey...........	33				"
Derding, Conrad...........	30				Luth.
Gross, Frederick..........	36	wife	3	1	"
Eckhard, Balzar............	60	"		21, 18	Cath.
Kuml, Johan Peter.........	40	"	20, 16, 12, 10, 5	18	"
Schenkelberger, Johan Jacob	36	"	3	21, 18, 16, 1	"
Bungart, Jacob.............	51	"	15		"
Bohne, Francis.............	39		10, 9	5	"
Bungart, Matthew..........	24	"		4, 1	"
Bungart, William..........	26	"	4, 2		"
Cleman, Bastian...........	44	"	21, 16, 7	10, 8	Ref.
Cleman, Valentine.........	20	"	1½		"
Stock, Johan Henrich......	33	"			Luth.
Eckard, Johan Jacob.......	24	"			Ref.
Buchebuerger, Johan Nicol.	53	"	11, 9, 5, ¾	9	Luth.
Wagner, Wendel...........	36	"	11, 4	9, 1 m.	"
Bishhoff, George Henrich...	28	"		6, 2	"
Plsch, Benedict	55	"	3	6, 2	Cath.
Wagner, Ernst Ludwig.....	40	"	16, 13, 10, 6, 3	10	Luth.
Shmith, Philip.............	42	"	13, 8	11, ¾	Ref.
Weigel, Valentine..........	43	"	11, 4	7, 6	Cath.
Hofferling, Henrich........	54	"	24	22, 21, 18	"
Engel, Johan Rupert.......	42	"	21, 17, 14	12	"

NAME	AGE	WIFE	SONS	DAUS.	CHURCH
Mey, Johan Peter..........	38	wife		7, 5	Cath.
Johan, Henry...............	36	"	11, 9	5, 3	"
Reisdorf, Johan............	34	"	1	4	"
Creylach, Urban............	50	"		18	Luth.
Apfel, Johan Jacob.........	21				Cath.
Petri, Nicol...............	38	wife	7	10, 1½	Luth.
Wagner, Valentine.........	48	"	7	13, 10	Cath.
Zentgraf, Johan Hendrich...	37	"	8, 2 m.	10, 6	Luth.
Simon, Philip..............	25	"			Ref.
Engel, Martin..............	36	"	13, 10, 2	5	Cath.
Schmif, Nicol..............	45	"	11, 6	3	"
Vogt, Daniel...............	46	"	7, 2	1	"
Tresanus, Johan............	45	"	20, 4	22, 16	"
Hermes, Johan.............	27	"		2	"
Klein, Johan Michael.......	40	"	11, 9, 7, 5	4	"
Puppelritter, Christian.....	43	"	5	20, 10, 12	"
Vogt, Johan...............	63	"	15, 8	10	Ref.
Zweller, Philip.............	44	"	12, 5	15	Cath.
Leinweber, Johan..........	36	"	14	9	Ref.
Boller, Philip.............	36	"	11, 9, 7	4, 2½	"
Gerhard, Valentine........	38	"		13, 11, 6, 4, 1	"
Penner, Henry.............	30	"	6, 4	¼	"
Erbs, Johan Henry.........	25	"	6, 4, ¼		"
Molsberger, Philip.........	30	"		4	"
Close, Peter...............	50	"	20, 11, 8	24, 13	"
Ramp, Nicol...............	37	"	13, 5	10, 2	
Dales, William.............	36	"	4, 1	6	Ref.
Schneider, Conrad..........	33	"		8, 5	"
Paul, Gerhard.............	52	"	24, 11	27, 18, 10, 8, 6	"
Abel, Michael.............	29	"	½	3	Cath.
Proebstel, George..........	40	"	7	11	"
Ruhl, John Caspar (also a linen weaver).............	25	"			Luth.
Freisen, John Riccas.......	27	"	2	3, ¼	Cath.
Hill, Balzar (also a carpenter).....................	45	"	16, 14, 10	18, 7	"
Merstallen, Henry..........	41	"	10, 5, 1	7, 6	Luth.
Rufel, John Nicol	49	"	17, 12, 5	21, 19, 7	"
Meyer, Nicol..............	33	"		10, 5, ½	Ref.
Fohrer, John (also a tanner).	60	"	20, 18		Cath.
Stork, John Henry..........	45	"	28, 18, 8, 6	12	Luth.
Fohrer, John...............	25	"		2	Cath.
Beisser, John..............	50	"	30, 20	18, 11	Ref.
Koerner, John Nicol........	50	"	6, 3	9, 4	"
Mandersel, John Peter......	24	"			Cath.
Seiffart, John..............	43	"	13	10, 8, 2	Luth.
Schaeffer, Matthew.........	40	"	8		Ref.
Kraus, John George........	62				"
Wolf, John George.........	37	wife	7, 2	10, 4	Luth.
Niedermeyer, Andrew......	43	"	6	11, 9, 5	Cath.
Benter, John Just..........	23	"	2		Luth.
Schmidt, Michel...........	50	"	18, 7	20, 14, 4	"
Diggart, Andreas...........	30	"	5		Ref.
Bode, John George.........	20	"			"
Wentzel, Lorentz..........	29	"		10, 8, 6, 4, 1	Luth.
Schaefer, John Peter.......	34	"			"
Walter, Adam.............	50	"	15, 12, 4	6	Cath.
Ruhl, Jacob...............	42	"	22, 12	17, 16, 10	"
Michel, Otto Henry........	30	"	1		"

NAME	AGE	WIFE	SONS	DAUS.	CHURCH
Schuch, Nicholas............	24	wife		4, 1½	Ref.
Koenig, Justis..............	36	"	7	12	"
Dorninger, Caspar.........	36	"	4	10	"
Spengeler, Frederick.......	53	"	20, 11		"
Strassberger, Frederick....	26	"	3		"
Emmel, John...............	36	"		4	
Braun, Sebastian...........	48	"	10	12, 5	Ref.
Spengler, Frantz...........	30	"			"
Lutz, Peter................	27	"	2	8, 5	"
Keselbach, John............	40	"	12	1, 5	Cath.
Heil, Matthew.............	30	"			Ref.
Christshiles, William.......	35	"		10, 8, 5, 2	Cath.
Christshiles, Dominic,.....	76	"	18		"
Schmaleberger, Cill........	26	"	2		"
Mehs, Paul................	24	"			"
Wehr, Christian............	54	"		22	Ref.
Bauer, Thomas............	40	"	14, 12, 10, 8, 7	19, 16, 13, 9	Cath.
Martin, Nicol..............	51	"	21		Ref.
Debald, Martin............	30	"	10	8, 2	"
Schum, John George.......	35	"			Luth.
Schrer, Ulrich.............	30	"	10, 8		Ref.
Schmidt, Andrew..........	47	wife	4	20, 14, 11, 7	Luth.
Bubeheiser, John Adam....	57	"	20, 15, 13, 12, 4	21, 19, 15, 12, 8	Ref.
Big, John..................	36	"	16, 8		Luth.
Titschke, John.............	30	"	4	1	Ref.
Braun, John...............	39	"	12, 9, 4, 1	7, 5, 3	Luth.
Graehl, Lorentz............	27	"	1		Ref.
Mick, John................	23	"			Ref.
Mick, Frederick............	65	"	23, 18	28, 26	Cath.
Mick, Henry...............	35	"	9, 5	12, 7	Ref.
Spiess, Werner............	50	"	11, 5	14, 9	"
Schmidt, Daniel............	33	"	2	4	"
Lesch, Balzar..............	38	"	14, 8, 2	9	Luth.
Walter, John Jacob.........	41	"	7	10	Ref.
Weitz, John................	35	"	6, 1	8	Luth.
Mathes, Henry.............	42	"	8, 6, 1	13, 10, 6	Ref.
Bredhauer, Israel..........	43	"	6, 1	9, 3	Luth.
Zeg, John..................	42	"	1, 6, ½		Cath.
Sprehd, Ignatius...........	28	"	3		"
Wagner, John..............	46	"	6, 2		"
Kuhn, Henry...............	53	"	8	10	Luth.
Koehler, John Simon.......	42	"	6	2, 2 m.	Ref.
Kuenstler, Henry..........	36	"	5	2	"
Eybach, Reinhard..........	50	"	20, 16	25	"
Maul, Johan Henry.........	48	"	8	13, 11, 4, ½	"
Haas, Nicol................	44	"	7, 4, 1	10	Luth.
Merich, George............	53	"	20, 15, 5		"
Muuer, Caspar.............	42	"	12, 10		Cath.
Walter, Philip.............	21	"	6, 3, 1		Ref.
Tiel, Johann...............	22	"			Cath.
Goerher, Sabastian........	23	"	1		Ref.
Mauer, John Jacob.........	22	"			Cath.
Geyer, Johan David........	34	"	4	12, 9, 2	Luth.
Hargart, Johan Nicol.......	30	"	14, ½	8	"
Reck, Jacob...............	50	"	20	16, 14	Cath.
Lipper, Johan Jacob........	30	"	13, 8	1	"
Rentel, Johan Nicol........	46	"	16, 12	5	Luth.
Brauch, Johan Valentine....	34	"	6, 5	1	"
Schmidt, Johan............	34	"	1	9	Ref.

NAME	AGE	WIFE	SONS	DAUS.	CHURCH
Schmidt, Caspar.......... ..	50	wife	18, 13, 11	20	Ref.
Lieborn, Ludwig...........	30	"		2	Luth.
Nacheigall, Johan Conrad...	26	"	2	5	"
Knut, Nicol...............	32	"	9		Cath.
Schleyer, Johan............	40	"		8, 4, ½	"
Feldnacht, Johan...........	37	"	3, ½		"
Land, Philip...............	24	"			"
Lauber, Johan.............	30	"		9, 6, 3	"
Becker, Hendrick..........	53	"	20, 19, 15, 11	22, 18, 16, 13	"
Guth, Johan...............	36	"	10, 6	11	"
Lorentz, Michel............	48		20, 18	15	"
Sarburger, Wenceslag......	43	wife	9, 7	13, 2	Ref.
Schnell, Matthew..........	43	"	17,13,10,5	7	Luth.
Sarburger, August.........	36	"	2	5	Ref.
Sarburger, Johan...........	25	"		3, 1	"
Herbener, Henrich.........	40	"	12	6, 3	Luth.
Hack, Conrad..............	80	"	16, 9		Ref.
Klein, Jacob..............	48	"	20		Luth.
Tielman, Johan............	30	"			Cath.
Geney, Jacob..............	50	"	22, 20	18, 16, 14, 11,7	"
Heins, Johan Valentine.....	33	"		10, 3	Luth.
Ebeling, Johan.............	35	"	14, 10	8, 1	Cath.
Winter, Henry.............	40	"	13, 6	14, 11	"
Leonhard, Johan Peter.....	24	"		½	"
Fuhrman, Johan Mathew...	32	"			Luth.
Schneider, Johan...........	30	"	7		"
Edian, Sebastian...........	32	"		2	"
Keller, Jacob..............	35	"	12,10,8,5	5, 2	Ref.
Ebrecht, John.............	40	"		5. 2	"
Seyfars, Johan Valentine....	44	"	17		"
Wickel, Johan.............	38	"			"
Zink, Rudolf..............	44	"	22, 17, 14	19	"
Hess, Jeremy..............	34	"	7, 5	2	Luth.
Kossing, Anthony..........	30	"			"
Rohn, Johan..............	45	"	20, 18, 16, 12, 8	14, 5, 2	"
Altvater, Johan Valentine...	24	"			Ref.
Weiler, Johan.............	32	"			"
Heyn, Paul...............	39	"	8, 3	11	Luth.
Kurtz, Johan..............	41	"	8	13	Cath.
Pliss, John...............	35	"	8, 3	11	Luth.
Boef, Johan...............	41	"	6, 2	4	Cath.
Petisht, Henry.............	50	"	14, 9, 12	6, 1	"
Petisht, Johan Dietrich.....	36	"		4	"
Kaul, Francis..............	36	"		2	Luth.
Hartman, Conrad..........	30	"	7	4, ½	Cath.
Bloss, Conrad.............	33	"	8, 6, 2	2 m.	Luth.
Heck, Bastian.............	40	"	6	8, 4	"
Graef, Johan..............	27	"			"
Mehser, Conrad............	54	"			"
Heinemann, Johan Henrich.	28	"	5	7, 1	Cath.
Kirshner, Philip...........	28	"	5, 2	2	Luth.
Schneider, John............	29	"	2 m.		"
Beckman, Michel..........	26	"	1	7	Cath.
Boef, William.............	70	"			"
Kraft, Valentin............	40	wife	6, 4	16, 9, 2	Luth.
Meyer, Johan..............	29	"	7, 3	4	"
Leyser, Christoph..........	56	"	24, 14, 11	20	"
Stiebel, Johann...........	36	"	6, 1 m.	8, 4, 2	"

NAME	AGE	WIFE	SONS	DAUS.	CHURCH
Reichard, Caspar..........	24	wife	3, 1		Cath.
Mathes, Johan............	33	"	15, 10	12	"
Sharnigk, Andrew..........	26	"	4	2	
Klitten, George...........	27	"	2		Cath.
Specht, Johan.............	31	"	5	4, ½	"
Stick, Horman............	40	"	14	8	"
Ourlea, Francis...........	50	"	8, 4, 3		"
Klein, Johan William......	42	"	18	24, 20	"
Mehrman, Johan Just.......	30	"			"
Jung, Johan...............	32	"	9	1	"
Freund, Johan.............	46	"	26, 24	19, 17, 14	Ref.
Holtzlaender, Albert.......	40	"	5, ¼	14, 9, 4	Cath.
Grosman, Johan............	26	"	2	8, 6	"
Mank, Jacob....	39	"		17, 9, 3	Ref.
Becker, Paulus............	42	"	14	14, 12	
Falkenburg, Valentin......	38	"	7, 2		Ref.
Valpert, Jacob............	40	"	8, 4	10	"
Boher, Andrew............	40	"			"
Ziegler, Nicol............	47	"	7	23, 15, 9	"
Petit, Johan Jacob.........	50				"
Busch, Herman............	54		4	24	Luth.
Schloemer, Mattheas.......	38	wife	¼	8, 3	Ref.
Flor, Johan................	36	"	8, 4	9	Cath.
Laurentz, Nicol............	40	"	15, 11, 5	8	Ref.
Boehm, Frantz............	44	"	12, 7, 3	20, 18, 5	"
Ludwig, Johan...........	54	"	20, 25	12, 10	"
Martin, Adam.............	36	"	3	7, 5	"
Boerwg, Michael...........	30	"	½		"
Holles, Henry.............	25	"			"
Tulges, Conrad............	36	"	8, 4	6, ½	Cath.
Teiss, Peter...............	25	"			Ref.
Wann, Francis.............	30	"	3	5	"
Hess, Friedrich............	42	"	2	11, 7	
Glass, William............	36	"	8, 5	3, ¼	Cath.
Otto, Johan...............	24	"			Ref.
Weiss, Johan..............	26	"	3	2	"
Feller, Johan..............	45	"	4, 2	12, 9	"
Bergman, Johan Just.......	32	"	4	8	Cath.
Berger, Veit..............	36	"	3	4	"
Hep (Hess?) Johan Jacob...	28	"		6, 4	Luth.
Braun Andrew............	26	"	3, 1½	5	Cath.
Villonger, Johan...........	30	"			Ref.
Schautz (Schantz), Johan....	63	"	7	20	"
Meyer, Thomas............	44	"	1	10	"
Schaefert Philip...........	36	"	10	2	Cath.
Knecht, Michael...........	50	"		21, 18, 15, 12	"
Becker, Anton............	30	"	5	7	"
Schmidt, Nicol............	30	"	2	4, 6 w.	"
Wiennegar, Ulrich.........	41	"	7	11, 14	"
Huber, Jacob..............	30	"	13	10, 7	Luth.
Mohr, Jonas..............	38	"	10		"
Weinmann, Andreas.......	30	"	2	10, 6	"
Wipf, Johan Jacob.........	27	"	½		"
Altheimer, Johan Georg....	40	"	13, 10, 8, 6, 4	11	"
Glaser Georg.............	47	"	5	9	"
Naser, Johan Michael.......	48	"	20, 12	18, 16	"
Medke, Daniel.............	41	"	15	14, 13, 3	"
Steinhauer, Christian.......	46	"	½	25, 22, 19, 16, 4	Cath.

NAME	AGE	WIFE	SONS	DAUS.	CHURCH
Nilius, Jonan	34	wife	12, 13	12, 6, ¼	Cath.
Schweitzer, Cristoph	23				Luth.
Hill, Johan	24				Cath.
Wezel, George	14				"
Wezel, John	12				"
Eshenbrender, Wolf	40				"
Ebelman, Jacob	36				Ref.
Meyer, Johan	25				Luth.
Zeber, Joseph	30				Cath.
von Rhein, Christian	23				Luth.
Burge, Arnold	24				Ref.
Paul, Johan	22				"
Gersner, Balzar	28				Luth.
Muench, Peter	24				"
Johan, Johan Michel	18				"
Meyfart, Jacob	12				Ref.
Hop, Michel	26				Luth.
Kuhn, Peter	24				Ref.
Reichard, Henry	25				"
Dungel, Matthew	33				Cath.
Belz, Leonhard	20				"
Koch, Martin	28				Luth.
Derding, Conrad	30				"
Jaeger, Peter	23				Cath.
Traut, Johan	20				"
Schreiner, Martin	20				"
Rup, Georg	18				Ref.
Gross, Joachim	25				Luth.
Claude, Francis	22				Ref.
Hoffman, Matthew	20				Cath.
Simon, Nicol	14				Ref.
Tiefenthaler, George	18				Luth.
Kesler, Johan Peter	21				"
Ternbach, Justus	18				Ref.
Wolfskeil, Georg	28				Luth.
Haub, Christoph	20				"
Henninger, Johan Adam	24				"
Fritzin, Johan	36				"
Gam, Jacob	24				Ref.
Kohl, Johan	24				"
Handwerker, Daniel	28				"
Handwerker, Peter	24				"
Zimmerman, Caspar	28				Luth.
Nick, Johan Jacob	15				"
Herman, Conrad	23				Ref.
Leperl, Matthew	24				"
Wolf, Johan	28				Luth.
Ulrich, Johan	25				Ref.
Lauer, Matthew	23				Luth.
Grien, Friedrick	22				Ref.
Hesper, Simon	30				Luth.
Hessel, William	22				Ref.
Werner, Henry	24				"
Koch, Johan	22				Luth.
Volker, Henry	32				"
Rosenthal, Johan	30				"
Heins, Adam	22				"
Loss, Jacob	25				"
Schmid, Bernhard	27				Cath.
Wentz, Balzar	24				Luth·
Clos, Peter	28				Cath.

106

LISTS OF GERMANS FROM THE PALATINATE WHO CAME TO ENGLAND IN 1709.

The following lists are copied from the original documents preserved in the British Museum Library, London, England, and should be of the greatest genealogical interest to those families in the States of New York, New Jersey, Pennsylvania and elsewhere, which claim descent from the so-called Palatine settlers. These lists have never before been printed to the knowledge of the Editor, and it should be noted that the word "son" or "sons" and "dau." or "daus." followed by figures denote that the heads of the family had as many sons or daughters, as there are figures, and that these sons and daughters were of the respective ages denoted by the figures. The word "wife" indicates that the head of the family was married and that the wife was living. The abbreviations "Ref.," "Luth.," "Bap." and "Cath.," mean that the family belonged to the Reformed, Lutheran, Baptist or Catholic Churches.

BOARD OF TRADE MISCELLANEOUS. VOL. 2. No. D 68.

PUBLIC RECORD OFFICE, LONDON.

List of the poor Palatines that are arrived in St. Cathrin's, the 2nd of June, 1709.

THIRD ARRIVALS—*Continued.*

NAME	AGE	WIFE	SONS	DAUS.	CHURCH
HUSBANDMEN & VINEDRESSERS					
Kuth, Peter................	26				Ref.
Sturteweg, Caspar..........	24				"
Schaffer, Lorentz..........	28				"
Homberg, Christian........	18				"
Drummer, Gerard..........	24				"
Becker, Peter..............	28				"
Klein, Ludwig.............	18				"
Bell, Johan Engel..........	27				"
Flor, Peter................	25				Cath.
Schreiber, Albert..........	26				Ref.
Wolf, Peter................	28				"
Thurdoerf, Friederich......	24				"
Rosbach, Peter.............	28				"
Eslich, Paul...............	21				"
Jung, Adam................	17				"
Jung, Johan...............	18				"
Knoehl, Herman...........	24				Cath.
Neuss, Andrew............	27				"
Schmids, Christian.........	22				Ref.
Burder, Johan.............	16				"
Noll, Daniell..............	22				"
Middler, William..........	12				"
Eyfel, Helkert.............	13				"
Huhn, Matthew...........	20				"
Rabenegger, Nicol.........	20				Cath.

NAME	AGE	WIFE	SONS	DAUS.	CHURCH
Scherer, Ebald............	20				Ref.
Loucks, Philip............	28				"
SCHOOLMASTERS					
Zinger, Nicol.............	40	wife	12, 6	9, 3	Ref.
Hirt, Stephen.............	42		13, 10, 7, 3		Luth.
Auckland, Arnold.........	42		11, 9, 5, ¾	9	"
Wendels, Johan Peter......	42		10	3	"
Frank, Johan Martin.......	27				"
CARPENTERS					
Koster, Henry............	51	wife	17, 13	10, 6	Luth.
Bertshy, Rudolph..........	24				Ref.
Gedert, Johan.............	26				Luth.
Wolfschlager, Melchoir.....	28				Cath.
Schmidt, Caspar...........	27				Luth.
Rottenflohr, John..........	36	wife	7	10	Cath.
Ehrenwein, John..........	30	"		2	"
Hafer, Peter..............	23				Luth.
Menges, John.............	35	wife	9, 3, ¼		Ref.
Dietrich, Bernhard........	24				Luth.
Eisen, Anton..............	30	wife		5	Cath.
Schlecht, John............	25	"		2	Ref.
Gnaedig, John............	40	"	11, 5	1	Cath.
Escheroeder, Hendrick.....	46	"	18		Luth.
Conrad, Matthew..........	21				Cath.
Port, John................	23				"
Lang, Christian...........	37	wife	5	11, 9, 2	"
Wickert, Melchoir.........	21				Luth.
Huper, Ludolf.............	24				Cath.
Schwarz, George..........	44	wife		13, 6, 3, 1 m.	Ref.
Knichel, John.............	27				Luth.
Metz, Andrew.............	40	wife	10, 5, 2	13	Ref.
Schlick, Martin...........	36	"			Cath.
Kniddelmeyer, Caspar......	25				"
Metz, Andrew.............	28	wife			Luth.
Dorry, Conrad............	36				Cath.
Spad, Ludwig.............	30				"
Rufner, Thomas...........	28				Luth.
Gerhard, Peter............	32	wife			Cath.
Wolf, Conrad.............	32	"	1		Ref.
Schneider, Conrad.........	30	"	½	3	Luth.
Volldrauer, Matthew.......	34	"	15, 9, 8	4, 1	Cath.
Kuntz, Philip.............	22				Ref.
Kegelman, Leonhard.......	35	wife	9	6	"
Graef, Georg..............	30	"	½	4	Luth.
Bergman, Andreas.........	32	"		3	"
Lineman, Justus...........	26				Ref.
Buss, John Jacob..........	25				Luth.
Vier, Jacob...............	26				"
Drap, Lorentz............	50	wife	13, 9, 3	10, 8, 4	Cath.
Noll, Bernhard............	47	"			Ref.
Habigt, John.............	50	"	9	6	Luth.
Black, Nicol..............	25	"			Ref.
Eydicker, John...........	23				Cath.
BAKERS					
Jacobi, John (will turn Protestant).................	45	wife	18, 12, 11, 6, 2	15, 8, ½	Cath.
Kraemer, John............	30	"		2	"

NAME	AGE	WIFE	SONS	DAUS.	CHURCH
Lanbegeier, Gottlieb.......	26				Luth.
Reif, John Peter............	64				Ref.
Hamel, John................	66	wife	26		"
Lesch, John................	25	"	10, 6, 4, 5 ds.		Luth.
Wollebe, John..............	33	"	8, 5	10, 4, 1	Ref.
Wickhart, Conrad..........	31	"	4, 2	2	Luth.
Kloetter, John..............	29	"	1		Ref.
Hamel, Jonas..............	24				"
Dienes, August.............	26	wife			Cath.
TAILORS					
Barrabam, Ezechias........	30	wife			Ref.
Beck, Conrad..............	53	"			Cath.
Zacharias, Lorentz.........	47	"	12, 10	23,21,14,3	Luth.
Corrier, Carl.	31	"			Cath.
Herber, Caspar............	48	"			Luth.
Warnon, Jacob.............	40	"	1	4	Cath.
Fisher, John...............	23	"	3		Luth.
Petri, Jacob...............	42	"	16, 10	19,15,12,5	"
Liebler, John..............	19				Cath.
Horst, Walter..............	39	wife	5	9, 3	Luth.
Spanknebel, Peter..........	19				Ref.
Umbauer, Adam...........	20				"
Wiesenegger, Caspar.......	24				Luth.
Conradt, Christoph.........	18				Ref.
Eydecker, Michel..........	16				Cath.
Weber, Valentin...........	31	wife	2		Ref.
Spader, Simon...	20				"
Alberts, Jacob..............	20				"
SHOEMAKERS					
Lichte, John...............	40	wife		5, 2	Ref.
Rab, Kilian................	47	"	10, 7, 2		"
Diel, Adolf................	32	"			"
Volk, Peter................	29	"	6, 5, 1		Luth.
Volk, Oswald..............	27				"
Mekes, Bartin.............	31				"
Meic, Andrew.............	30				"
LaMothe, Daniel...........	30	wife	4	9, 1	"
Lerner, Matthew...........	50	"	9	8	Ref.
Gaus, Nicol................	23				Luth.
Eich, Martin..............	29	wife	11	14,6,3,1	Cath.
Bay, Wendell..............	38	"	9, 4	13, 5, 3	Luth.
Kraft, Matthew............	37	"	12, 6	8, 2	Cath.
Weiler, Andrew............	45	"	7, 5, ½		Ref.
Weiss, Philip..............	44	"	20	18, 11, 9, 7, 4	Luth.
Schiler, Matthew..........	36	"	6, 4, 1	7	Cath.
Heisterbach, Nicol.........	52	"	3	7, 5	Ref.
Doettel, John..............	22				Cath.
Spielman, John.............	33				"
Roethgen, Nicol...........	20				Ref.
MASONS AND STONE CUTTERS					
Munkenast, Joseph.........	27	wife			Cath.
Trip, Matthew.............	30	"	2	4	"
Halgarde, Peter...........	24				"
Blank, Cassran.............	28				"
Waldman, Balzar..........	24				Luth.

NAME	AGE	WIFE	SONS	DAUS.	CHURCH
Egler, Christian	28	wife	2	8, 7, 4	Ref.
Tragsal, Jacob	43	"	15	13, 11, 3	Cath.
Glaser, Dietrich	26	"	4	6, ½	"
Master, Lambert	50	"	25	15	"
Los, Adam	21				Luth.
Los, John	40	wife	7	11	Cath.
Zick, Conrad	21				"
Roethgen, Peter	27	wife	1		Ref.
Krochner, John	40	"	18		Cath.
Schoepf, Thomas	40	"			"
Schmidt, Henry	48	"	19, 15, 6	21, 15	Ref.
Theis, Thomas	30	"	1		Cath.
Roeger, Dietrich	32				"
Lopp, Jacob	40	wife	7, 1 m.	5, 4	Luth.
Weimar, Simon	30				Cath.
Wolfee, Peter	30	wife			"
Mulleker, Francis	30	"	1		"
Trausch, John	18				Luth.
Isler, Nicholas	48	wife	15, 8, 6	5, 1	Ref.
MASONS					
Reideman, Martin	24				Cath.
Gerger, John	31				"
Mueller, Georg	26				Luth.
Lunch, Caspar	37	wife		7, 2	"
JOYNERS					
Zimmerman, Matthew	38	wife	9, 6		Ref.
Naegler, Jacob	30				"
Koster, Dietrich	36	wife	11	6, 3	Luth.
Rufer, Peter	19				Ref.
Ditmar, David	22				Luth.
Menges, John	32	wife			"
Weber, Michael	50	"	18, 13		Cath.
Scheman, Valentin	25				Ref.
HUNTERS					
Lambrecht, Georg	44	wife	20, 16, 14, 7	17, 9	Luth.
Bundersgell, John	36	"	4	9, 7, 2	Cath.
Goeddel, Jacob	60	"	20, 16, 14	10, 4, 2	Luth.
BUTCHERS					
Giees, Fridrik	42	wife	4	10, 2	Ref.
Andrus, Michel	30	"		2	"
Diess, John	30	"			Cath.
Marry, David	40	"	10, 2	8 days	Ref.
Munchofer, Philipp	36	"			Cath.
Ashenburg, William	40	"		3	Luth.
Schomberger, Georg	31	"			Ref.
du Bray, Peter	19				"
LINEN WEAVERS					
Slott, Ulrich	43	wife	17, 9	11	Cath.
Kern, Francis	30	"		6, 2	"
Miller, Philip	23				Ref.
Dietz, William	33	wife		1	"
Schnaeblin, Rudolf	30	"	3, ¾	6	"
Merket, Peter	38	"	4		"
Schafer, John	29	"	4, 2, ¼	5	Cath.
Rhode, Philip	34	"	2 m.	19, 14, 4	Ref.

NAME	AGE	WIFE	SONS	DAUS.	CHURCH
Hach, Peter...............	35	wife		2	Ref.
Hochappel, John...........	43	"	23, 16, 10	12, 4	"
Artus, Isac................	43	"			"
Heyd, Nicol...............	24				Cath.
Koehler, Jacob............	54	wife	16, 10, ½	18, 14, 12, 10, 4	Luth.
Wickhart, William.........	23				"
Mahler, Bastian...........	24	wife			Cath.
Land, Anton...............	26	"		1	"
Aldenuess, Philip.........	43	"	9, 4	7	Luth.
Kreisher, Ludwig..........	24				"
Ringer, John Thiel........	24				"
Hanson, Bernhard.........	32	wife	12, 4	9, 1	Cath.
Gesch, Godfried..........	37	"	3		Luth.
Schwan, John.............	25				"
Big, John.................	24				Ref.
Dietrich, Jacob...........	44	wife	18, 12, 2	15, 12, 10, 6	"
Walter, Rudolf............	28	"	15, 8		"
Scherer, Just.............	76				"
Rehm, Anton..............	41	wife	3	2	Cath.
COOPERS AND BREWERS					
Friedrik, Nicol...........	60	wife	25, 21	17, 15	Luth.
Alman, Simon.............	25				"
Reiser, Michel............	24				Ref.
Strickstheiser, Balzar.....	45	wife	9	13, 5	"
That, Bernhard...........	45	"	6	2	Luth.
Meyer, Jacob.............	20				"
Bruch, Michael...........	27				"
Frank, Michel............	20				Cath.
Frantz, Conrad...........	20				Ref.
Tanner, Urban............	33	wife		6, 4, 3, 1	
Kemmer, Peter...........	28	"			Luth.
Metzger, Philip...........	40	"	13, 10, 7, ¼	9, 4	"
Herman, Philip...........	25	"			"
Hardtz, John.............	30				Cath.
Behler, Henry............	30				Ref.
Zeller, John..............	23				Luth.
Kaul, Matthew...........	50	wife	16, 14, 10, 8	5, 2	Ref.
Braun, Lucas.............	32	"	1	6	"
Mara, Peter..............	24				Cath.
Kirches, Paul.............	23				"
Ehrlich, John.............	25				Ref.
Muller, Adam.............	36	wife	8	12, 6	"
Merden, Christoph........	40	"	8, ¼	12, 6	"
TURNERS					
Schneider, Joachim.......	41	wife		13, 11, 4	Ref.
Faber (Taber), Ebert......	20				Luth.
MILLERS					
Meier, Paul..............	43	wife	12, 7	13, 8, ½	Luth.
Schmidt, Matthew.........	30	"	5, 3		Cath.
Hofman, Henry...........	33	"		6, 3, 1	Luth.
Herling, Conrad..........	28				"
Christhiles, George.......	28	wife	¼		Cath.
Pfeifer, Peter............	57	"	19, 5		Luth.
Kraus, John Michel.......	50		24, 6		"
Mungesser, Philip........	27	wife	6	1 ¼	"
Weiss, George............	20				Ref.

NAME	AGE	WIFE	SONS	DAUS.	CHURCH
SMITHS					
Meiss, Henry..............	38	wife	3, ¼		Ref.
Wagner, Conrad...........	46	"	15,12,11,9	7, 5	Luth.
Schezinger, John...........	37	"	5		Cath.
Bauer, John...............	22				Luth.
Ruhl, Daniel..............	24				Ref.
Sherer, Peter..............	26				Luth.
Becker, Michel.............	24	wife			"
Shmidt, Nicol..............	46	"	18, 9	9, 12, 10	"
Giessiebel, John Michel,....	28	"		2	"
Fuchs, John Bernhard......	39	"	9, 5, 2	7	Cath.
Carp, John.................	50	"	14, 12	22, 17, 7	Luth.
Albert, John...............	23				Ref.
Scheur, Peter.............	22				Cath.
Bast, Nicol................	50	wife	23, 21, 2	18, 15, 13, 12, 8	Ref.
Steinbacher, Philip........	30	"	2		Luth.
WOOLEN WEAVERS					
Weichel, Frederick........	30	wife	2		Ref.
Hollander, Melchoir........	20				Luth.
STOCKING WEAVERS					
Schmidt, Peter.....	36	wife	8	12,10,3, ½	Ref.
Michel, Henry.............	38			6	Luth.
TANNERS					
Fohrer, John..............	60	wife	20, 18		Cath.
Hess, Andrew..............	24				Ref.
SADDLERS					
Winter, Melchior...........	42	wife	5		Cath.
Petri, Andrew..............	39	"		9, 6, 4	Ref.
WHEELWRIGHTS					
Schmidt, Michel...........	55		23, 21,12,8	25	Luth.
Philipps, Jacob.............	19				"
Henrich, Caspar...........	24				Cath.
Gresman, Henry...........	28				Luth.
Manke, George.............	20				Ref.
POTTERS					
Mehden, Martin...........	42	wife	10, 7, 4	14, 7	Cath.
Meyer, Egidy..............	22				"
Walter, Jacob..............	16				Ref.
TILE					
Wannenmacher, Henry.....	64	wife	20		Cath.
BRICKMAKERS					
Carten, John..............	46	wife	20, 14, 11	9, 6, 2	Luth.
du Bray, John..............	26	"	4, 2		Ref.
SURGEONS					
Bucholts, John.............	30				Luth.
Rhod, Jacob...............	44	wife	8	2	Cath.
FIGUREMAKER					
Legoli, John..............	26	wife	1		Ref.
LOCKSMITH					
Herbst, John..............	46	wife	5	3	Cath.

NAME	AGE	WIFE	SONS	DAUS.	CHURCH
HATTER					
Hopf, George..............	38	wife			Luth.
MINERS					
Pfiz, Joseph...............	33	wife	6, 2		Luth·
Pfiz, Jacob................	30				"
WIDOWS					
Zinckin, Elizabeth.........	26		2	6, 3	Luth.
Wenzelin, Anne............	47				Cath,
Mullerin, Mary............	30			8, 6	Ref.
Meyerin, Barbara..........	60			18	Luth.
Rosmanin, Catherin........	54			20	"
Finkin, Ursula.............	46		9	19	Cath.
Wellerin, Anna............	38		7, 2		Ref.
Mullerin, Mary............	30			8, 6	"
Meyerin, Barbara..........	60			18	Luth.
Seelingerin, Margretha.....	54				Ref.
Rutigin, Elizabeth.........	60				Cath.
Hay, Eva..................	30			1	Ref.
Andelsin, Catherin.........	50				Cath.
Keinin, Rose..............	50		19		Ref.
Ekern, Anna..............	44		9		Luth.
Schneiderin, Margretha.....	30			7	Ref.
Sonnenhofin, Mary........	60				"
Keyserin, Anna............	30				Cath.
Noset, Susana.............	60				"
Lescherin, Magdalen.......	34		18		Ref.
Mathesin, Anna............	53			23, 20, 18	"
Bodin, Mary...............	50			24, 22, 12	"
Wenzel, Anna Mary........	50				Luth.
Schuch, Anna Catherine....	64				Ref.
Schmid, Christine..........	60				"
Schaeferin, Eleanore.......	45				Luth.
Sickin, Cecelia.............	26		6		Ref.
Jaegerin, Elizabeth........	70				"
Nellesin, Anna Eve........	50		16	11	"
Huntin, Jane..............	60		30		Cath.
Meyschin, Jane............	36			2	Luth.
Schwart, Jane Jacob...			13, 9	7, 14, 2	Ref.
Jungin, Elizabeth..........	45				"
Schmid, Barbara...........	22		2		"
Kueferin, Eva.............	25		8	6	Cath.
Muellerin, Susanna.........	32				Ref.
Herzin, Margretha.........	50		16, 10	14, 7	Cath.
Engels, Anna Mary........	60				Ref.
Nonin, Elizabeth...........	60				"
Volpertin, Margretha.......	45			26	"
Slacyrin, Elizabeth.........	23			5	"
Hup, Margretha...........	30		8	11, 6, 4	"
Fischerin, Margretha.......	55				Cath.
Altheim, Anna.............	64				Luth.
Schellberger, Catherine.....	34		1	5	Ref.
Meyshin, Anna............	30			2	Luth.
Schwartz, Elizabeth........	40		13, 9	7, 2	"
UNMARRIED WOMEN					
Tauflin, Catherine..........	20				Ref.
Tagin, Catherine...........	30				Luth.
Forsterin, Anna............	20				Ref.
Fuchsin, Mary.............	22				Luth.
Fuchsin, Margareth........	18				"

NAME	AGE	WIFE	SONS	DAUS.	CHURCH
Bergin, Anna..............	25				Ref.
Weidmannin, Elizabeth....	21				"
Zeltnerin, Urzula..........	20				"
Ozeberger, Mary...........	18				Cath.
Hey, Anna................	18				Ref.
Durrin, Catherine.........	30				Cath.
Appelin, Elizabeth........	30				"
Rup, Margretha...........	16				Ref.
Jaegerin, Mary...........	18				Cath.
Meyerin, Elizabeth........	30				Luth.
Gott, Mary...............	38				Ref.
Huberin, Christina........	21				"
Manderset, Mary..........	26				Cath.
Schmidt, Eva Mary.......	17				"
Lutz, Anna Mary..........	20				"
Brugerin, Mary...........	19				Luth.
Muserin, Anna............	24				"
Lauer, Agnes.............	20				Cath.
Henzelin, Eva............	21				"
Henzelin, Mary...........	23				"
Margareth, Elizabeth......	18				"
Jahnin, Elizabeth.........	19				"
Volkerin, Margareth.......	20				Luth.
Closin, Mary.............	30				"
Margretha, Anna..........	15				"
Geldmacherin, Sabina.....	21				"
Hubnerin, Margaret.......	20				Cath.
Hoffman, Catherin........	24				"
Bellin, Mary.............	21				Ref.
Midler, Juliana...........	21				"
Eyfelin, Christina.........	20				Cath.
Witschlager, Magdalene....	25				"
Haas, Elizabeth..........	21				Ref.
Langin, Elizabeth.........	22				Cath.
Dales, Catherine..........	25				Ref.
Fishers, Margaretha.......	24				Cath.
Burder, Magdalena........	22				Ref.
Mullerin, Margaretha......	23				Cath.
Laurmannin, Eva..........	22				Ref.
Mallot, Catharina.........	20				Cath.
Kahl, Margaretha.........	31				Ref.
Fischerin, Margaretha.....	55				Cath.
Glasin, Margaretha........	21				"
Catherin, Anna...........	16				"
Dres, Catherine..........	19				"

LIST.

Schooolmasters	5	Turners	2
Husbandmen & Vinedressers ...	460	Millers.......................	9
Carpenters....................	45	Smiths........................	15
Bakers.......................	11	Wheelwrights..................	5
Tailors.......................	18	Woolen Weavers...............	2
Shoemakers	20	Stocking Weavers..............	2
Masons.......................	28	Tanners......................	2
Joiners.......................	8	Saddlers......................	2
Butchers..................	8	Hunters......................	3
Linenweavers	27	Potters.......................	3
Coopers	23	Brickmakers..................	3

Total, 590

(Endorsed) Miscellanies List of Poor Palatines arrived from Germany 2. June, 1709. Received from Mr. Rupert, 21 Juue, 1709. D. 68.

LISTS OF GERMANS FROM THE PALATINATE WHO CAME TO ENGLAND IN 1709.

The following lists are copied from the original documents preserved in the British Museum Library, London, England, and should be of the greatest genealogical interest to those families in the States of New York, New Jersey, Pennsylvania and else-where, which claim descent from the so-called Palatine settlers. These lists have never before been printed to the knowledge of the Editor, and it should be noted that the word "son" or "sons" and "dau." or "daus." followed by figures denote that the heads of the family had as many sons or daughters, as there are figures, and that these sons and daughters were of the respective ages denoted by the figures. The word "wife" indicates that the head of the family was married and that the wife was living. The abbreviations "Ref.," "Luth.,' "Bap." and "Cath.," mean that the family belonged to the Reformed, Lutheran, Baptist or Catholic Churches.

BOARD OF TRADE MISCELLANIES. VOL. 2. NOS. D 69 & D 70.

PUBLIC RECORD OFFICE, LONDON.

BOARD OF TRADE MISCELLANIES. VOL. 2, D 69.

List of poor Palatines who arrived at St. Cathrin's, June 11th, 1709, taken at St. Catherine's and Debtford, June 15.

NAME	AGE	WIFE	SONS	DAUS.	CHURCH
HUSBANDMEN & VINEDRESSERS					
Schnorr, Nicol.............	50	wife	12	22, 17	Luth.
Baehr, Nicol..............	52	"	18		Ref.
Keller, Jacob.............	58	"	4		"
Liris (Siris), Martin.........	40	"	¼	12,11,10, 4	Luth.
Mueller, Jacob.............	50	"	6	14	Ref.
Hank, Bleigart.............	46	"	7	4	"
Ledig, Nicol.......... ...	25	"	2 weeks	1½	"
Biederman, John..........	48	"			"
Zolker, Balzar.............	70	sing.			"
Helfrich, Henrich..........	50	wife	19, 16		"
Lechner, Michel..........	40	"	14, 3		Cath.
Wingart, John.............	46	"	18, 13, 11, 8, 6		Bapt.
Wiehelm, Mathes..........	40	"	23, 15, 11		Ref.
Rappell, John.............	32	"		4	
Leib, John................	43	"	10	14, ½	Ref.
Mess, Abraham............	34	"		14, 2	
Herzel, Adam.............	44	"		14	Luth.
Zerbst, Peter.............	50	"	24	28, 27, 25, 23, 14	Cath.
Resch, Adam.............	50	"	17, 11, 6	19, 18	
Maur, John...............	36	"	13,11,10, 3	½	
Kuehn, Herman...........	55	"	26	28, 18	Cath.
Peder, Nicol..............	40	"	16,15, 9, 2	8	"
Krutsch, John.............	40	"	2	8, 6, 4	"

NAME	AGE	WIFE	SONS	DAUS.	CHURCH
Bork, Henrich..............	50	wife		20, 12, 4	
Doenny, Martin............	44	"	6	16	Cath.
Herman, Justus............	41	"		14, 7	Luth.
Becker, John...............	30	"		3, 1	Cath.
Hofman, Philip............	30	"	1		Luth.
Bork, Matthes.............	40	"	13, 11, 2	10, 8, 5	Cath.
Tielman, Conrad...........	30	"	8, 6, 1½	9	"
Steiner, Michel............	50	"			"
Schutz, Martin.............	22	"	½		"
Metzger, John.............	32	"		1½	"
Graner, Jacob.............	60	sing.			Ref.
Buntz, Nicol..............	30	wife	16	14, 8	Cath.
Meyer, Paulus.............	18	"			"
Scheuer, John.............	35	"			"
Engel, William............	27	"			"
Mutz, Friederik............	22	"			"
Schueler, Peter............	46	"	7, 1	20, 14, 5	"
Sontag, Francis...........	36	"	5, 1	13, 5	"
Engler, Peter.............	30	"	5	2	"
Borr, Matthes.............	45	"	21	18	"
Schunger, Theobald........	38	"	13, 11, 5	2	"
Creutz, Matthes...........	40	"	18, 7, 6, 2	9, 4	"
Creutz, John..............	36	"	13	10, 7	"
Schmidt, Caspar...........	30	"	2		Ref.
Ludwig, Henry............	40	"	18, 10		Luth.
Keusel, Jacob.............	44	"	7, 1½	13, 11	"
Mueller, Martin...........	32	"	8, 6, 5	2	Ref.
Lang, Wolf...............	30	"	1	6, 3	Cath.
Schoepfer, George.........	32	"			Ref.
Ulrich, Elias.............	46	"	8	13, 2½	"
Rosbach, Peter............	40	"	12, 7		Luth.
Rennersbacher, Christian...	24	"			Ref.
Herman, Sebastian.........	26	"			"
Mansbeil, Caspar..........	33	"	5		Luth.
Kurtz, George.............	37	"	12		"
Fritz, Nicol..............	54	"	20, 14, 13, 9	15, 11, 2	Cath.
Reischardt, Christian.......	32	"	3	4	Ref.
Meyer, Adam.............	30	"			Cath.
Heibel, Bernhardt..........	40	"	8	14, 3, 1	Ref.
Gro, George..............	40	"	2	7, 5	Luth.
Gro, Philip...............	30	"	6, 5, 3, 1		"
Stengel, Philip............	54	sing.			"
Rink, Melchior............	42	wife	16	10	Ref.
Walter, Caspar...........	44	"	21, 16, 12, 8, 4	18, 14, 12, 6	Luth.
Schales, Peter.............	38	"		15, 12, 4	Ref.
Baum, Abraham.	34	"	14, 12, 3, 1	15	
Schmidt, Peter............	33	"	12, 10	14, 2	Ref.
Hodel, Isaac..............	36	"	¼		"
Eschweilen, Thomas.......	34	"		10, 6	"
Eschwein, Jacob...........	41	"	15	7, 1	"
Zepp, Leonhardt...........	44	"	20, 19, 8	17	"
Mengel, Wendel...........	27	"	3	5, 2 days	"
Brathecker, Justus.........	44			18, 11, 9, 3, 1	"
Schaefer, Zerben..........	40	wife	12		Cath.
Coblentzer, John..........	28	"	5	2	Ref.
Christman, John...........	41	"	7, 5	9, 2	Mennon
Kintig, John..............	45	"	12, 10	17, 16, 6	Ref.
Hedgen, Conrad..........	42	"	17	1	"
Krenig, John..............	40	"	6	11	"

NAME	AGE	WIFE	SONS	DAUS.	CHURCH
Batz, Friedrich.............	28	wife	5, 3	8	Luth.
Crabbecher, Peter..........	28	"	2		"
Tachfletter, George........	30	"	3		"
Seip (Leip), Michel........	23	"			"
Speicherman, Herman.... .	46	"	16	18	"
Boll, Caspar...............	40	"		4	"
Morheiser, Nicol...........	26	"	7	2	Cath.
Matthes, Lorentz...........	75		24		Luth.
Brunwasser, Herman.......	31	wife	1		"
Schwed, Jacob.............	42	"	18, 13, 8	10, 5, 4, ¼	Cath.
Binhammer, Barthel........	37	"	6, 1	10, 3	"
Lutz, John.................	33	"	10, 7, 3	14	Ref.
Peter, Jacob...............	22	"			"
Bachler, Michel............	47	"	5	12, 10, 7	"
Hupfer, David.............	30	"		12, 9	"
Hern, John................	37	"	7, 5	2	"
Weber, Dietrich...........	42	"	1	15	Cath.
Vorbeck, John.............	56	"		½	"
Eilen, Henry..............	38	"	12, 8, 3		"
Pommer, Bongraf..........	45	"	17	14	"
Stegen, Nicol.............	58	wife	7, 3	14, 12	Luth.
Schleicher, George........	40	"	3	19, 17, 1	"
Hagadorn, Peter...........	60	"	24, 22, 15	17, 11	"
Salbach, John.............	52	"		17, 14	"
Sahlbach, Edmund........	21	"			"
Fuchs, John...............	30	"	4, 1		"
Propfer, Justus............	30	"	7, 4	9	"
Balzar, Jacob.....	40	"	9, 6	15	Cath.
Thiel, John...............	50	"		18, 12	Luth.
Tiel, Herman..............	26	"		2	"
Ess, Jacob................	49	"		1	Cath.
Wend, Henry..............	38	"	15, 5, 2	10	Luth.
Bitter, Jacob..............	31	"	10, 5, ½		"
Bakus, Ferdinand..........	31	"	4	2	Cath.
Stott, Dietrich............	31	"		4	"
Dietrich, Nicol............	46	"	17, 10, 5, 2	18, 15, 7	"
Beyer, Thomas.............	28	"		6, 4, 2	Luth.
Fischer, Peter.............	36	"		5, 2	Ref.
Busch, Daniel.............	65	"			"
Meyer, Henry.............	43	"	4	6	"
Pulver, Wendel............	30	"	5, 2		Cath.
Wilmar, Anton............	40	"	13		Luth.
Eberhard, Michel..........	44	"	21, 12, 8	13	Ref.
Mueller, Henry............	34	"	4, 3	1	"
Kuhns, Conrad............	44	"	24	20	Luth.
Gesner, Conrad............	26	"	2, ½		"
Schaefer, Andreas.........	50	"	27, 24, 17	20	"
Sorg, Matthes.............	54	"	4	10, 7	Cath.
Paul, Henry...............	50	"	21, 7, 5	17, 14, 12, 9	Luth.
Sperling, Peter............	47	"	10, 8, 4	18, 16, 14	"
Kaefer, Casimir............	23	"			"
Schintzerling, John.........	41	"		12, 8, 4	Ref.
Rup, Peter................	42	"	20, 16	14, 12, 2	"
Berger, John..............	45	"	16, 14, 8	20, 10	"
Nuss, Ludwig.............	46	"		15, 12, 10	"
Oberdubbel, Jacob.........	35	"	4, 2	11	Cath.
Kesler, George............	40	"	14, 10, 6, 3		"
Wolpert, Nicol............	30	"	10	4	"
Engel, John...............	36	"		10, 6, 3	"
Borkes, Herman...........	25	"	1, ¼		"
Themer, John.............	36	"	15, 11, 8, 6	1	Luth.

NAME	AGE	WIFE	SONS	DAUS.	CHURCH
Ehresman, Michel.........	46	wife	20	22, 13, 7	Ref.
Johann, Nicol..............	32	"	13, 9, 7	6, 1	Luth.
Laekman, Isaac............	36	"	10	7, 4	Ref.
Schreiner, Simon...........	36	"	4, 2	12, 10, 8	Cath.
Lauer, John................	27	"		7, 6, 3	"
Daniel, Anton..............	40	"	17, 12, 6, 1	18, 8, 4	"
Mitwig, Germanus.........	54	"	18	14	"
Baum, Fridrik..............	45	"	14	21, 19, 15	"
Wind, Peter................	41	"	21, 8, 7, 2	18	"
Volks, Arnold..............	32	"	9, 1	13, 4	"
Schmidt, Nicol.............	36	"	12		Ref.
Froebus, George...........	39	"	18	20, 12	"
Schmidt, Nicol.............	19	"			"
Emmel, Christoph..........	27	"	7	3	"
Kesseler, Caspar...........	65		20	25	Cath.
Sottig, Herman.............	40	wife	11, 7	14, 9, 5	"
Bestel, Jacob........	33	"			"
Becker, John...............	26	"		1½	"
Lorentz, Dietrich..........	34	"	12, 3		"
(L?) Sinnenbaum, Peter....	50	"	20, 3, 1		"
Schneider, Ulrich..........	34(?)	"	24(?), 1		Ref.
Schmidt, Adam.............	36	"		13, 10, 8	Cath.
Hilles, Nicol..............	40	"	10	16, 13, 5	Ref.
Fuchs, George.............	40	"	12	17, 10, 8, 6	Cath.
Dressel, John..............	32	"		1	"
Schmidt, John..............	35	"	8	3, ¼	"
Lennebaum, Christoph.....	26	"		4, 2	"
Wicked, Bernhard.........	36	"	11, 5, ½	8	"
Staut, Grin.................	30	"			Ref.
Mohr, Augustin............	36	"	13, 4, 2	6	Cath.
Autlen, Paulus.............	39	"	17, 9, 6, 3	12	"
Roemer, John..............	26	"	1	3	"
Lerne, Matthes............	42	"	15, 12, 2	14, 8	"
Leophard, John............	38	"	7, 3	14, 12, 7	"
Guck, John................	35	"		3	"
Alten, John................	56	"		23, 22, 9, 4	"
Lenacker, Peter............	36	"	14, 9, 6	14, 12, 10, 7, 2	"
Leich, Simon...............	34	"	6	1½	Luth.
Heins, John Adam..........	33	"	6		"
Heins, Nicol.	24	"			"
Gross, Dietrich.............	27	"			Cath.
Getman, Caspar............	36	"	16, 14, 8, 5	6, 5, 2	Luth.
Gross, William.............	56	"	12, 9	5	
Valentins, Velten..........	20	"			Cath.
Kulpfaber, Jacob...........	26	"		4, 2	Ref.
Gebel, Henrich............	24	"	12, 10	14, 2	Luth.
Schmids, Henry............	60		15, 12		
Schenkel, John.............	44	wife	10	13, 8, 5	Ref.
Valentin, John.............	56	"	14, 3	16, 8	Cath.
Arnold, Philip..............	30	"		5, 3	"
Volhart, John..............	30	"	20, 18, 15	13, 12	Luth.
Schmidt, John..............	35	"	8	3, ¼	Cath.
Mueller, Peter.............	45	"	18, 6, 4		"
Fris, John..................	30	"	7, 2	8, 5	"
Metz, Sebastian........	36	"	18	15, 7	Luth.
Mumenthal, Jacob..........	48	"			Ref.
Schmidt, Arnd.............	30	"	10	3	"
Herich, Jost...............	50	"	16, 11, 7	18, 12, 5	Cath.
Braun, Nicol...............	60	"	20, 15, 11	17, 8, 1	Ref.

NAME	AGE	WIFE	SONS	DAUS.	CHURCH
Hauch, Lucas..............	31(?)	wife	22(?), 16, 13, 9, 3, 8 days	13, 12, 9	Ref.
Becker, John..............	28	"			Luth.
Mullen, Gerhard...........	35	"	7		Cath.
Ermitter, Francis..........	35	"	7	5, 2	"
Schumacher, Bartel........	41	"	11, 6	17, 14, 8	Luth.
Bellesheim, Peter..........	27	"	1		Cath.
Fehling, Henry............	24	"			Ref.
Krantz, Conrad............	23	"		1	"
Sherner, John Michel.......	39	"	7, 3	18,16,14, 4	Luth.
Schmidt, George...........	53	"	22, 20, 2	18,16,14, 8	"
Reuter, Ludwig............	32	"			Ref.
Zerbst, Martin.............	34	"	11, 8, 4, 2		Luth.
Mullen, Michael...........	26	"	2	1	"
Michel, Nichol............	30	"			"
Bartel, Henrich............	45	"	17, 14, 9	20, 6	"
Stoss, John...............	40	"	10, 1	16, 3	Cath.
Giss, Jost................	39	"	12, 10, 3	5	"
Saar, John................	50	"	20, 18, 5, 5, 2	14, 9	"
Huhn, Henry..............	48				Ref.
Faber, Adam..............	30				"
Kludy, George.............	22				"
Wilhelm, Paul.............	30				"
Son, Philip...............	30				"
Cleman, Peter.............	17				Luth.
Reichardt, Valentin........	18				Cath.
Friede, Nicol..............	21				Luth.
Biss, Nicol...............	20				Cath.
Stin, Titius...............	20				"
Baus, Nicol...............	24				"
Knauer, Zacharias.........	26				Ref.
Busch, Justus.............	24				Luth.
Schwab, Philip............	20				Ref.
Peters, John..............	19				Cath.
Seibel, Valentin...........	22				Ref.
Seibel, George............	20				"
Wilhelm, John............	40				"
Riegel, Christian..........	20				Cath.
Geibel, Peter.............	17				Luth.
Schnick, Michel...........	22				Ref.
Heller, Wolf..............	26				Luth.
Ehrenbach, Michel........	27				"
Valentin, Henry...........	20				Cath.
Burger, Caspar............	26				"
Dewick, Francis...........	22				"
Henning, Andreas.........	38				Ref.
Beckart, Christian.........	26				Cath.
Hohenfedd, Lorentz........	22				"
Durr, Philipp.............	27				"
Dudenbecker, John........	18				Luth.
Omes, Peter..............	21				Cath.
Reuter, Nicol.............	25				"
Christ, John..............	20				"
Reuter, Ludwig...........	14				"
Gamben, John............	24				"
Vogt, Henry..............	25				Ref.
Wenckel, Henry...........	23				Cath.
Drosel, William...........	36				Ref.
Hensel, Valentine.........	20				"

NAME	AGE	WIFE	SONS	DAUS.	CHURCH
Schuster, Peter..............	40				Cath.
Zerbst, Conrad..............	39				Ref.
COOPERS					
Tieffenbach, Conrad........	50	wife		11, 4, 1	Ref.
Leasch, Burchard..........	28	"			Luth.
Kirsch, Adam..............	28	"	6	2, ¼	Cath.
Leis, Matthes..............	38	"	12, ½	18, 16, 11, 8, 7	"
Tiel, Jacob.................	24				Luth.
Frantzberg, John...........	24				"
Ganter, Christian..........	50	wife	4	20, 1	Ref.
Heiden, Jacob..............	44	"	1		"
Schoemacher, Michel.......	24				Luth.
Ziegler, Andreas..........	40	wife		3, 1	Ref.
Baum, Friederich..........	45	"	14	21, 19, 15	Cath.
Buch, Henry...............	49	"	17	24, 16, 12, 3	"
CARPENTERS					
Klein, William.............	26	wife			Luth.
Margart, Peter.............	50	"	24		Cath.
Kless, John................	28	"		3	"
Rosing, Matthas...........	23				"
Weber, Sebastian..........	30				Ref.
Weber, Henry.............	24				"
Schummer, John...........	20				Cath.
Siffer, Bastian.............	21	wife			Ref.
Metz, Simon...............	33	"	4	7, 2	Cath.
Blatz, Andreas.............	32	"	2	5	Luth.
Buchsel, Augustin..........	50	"	25, 22, 20, 16, 12, 8, 1		Ref.
Schmidt, Peter.............	39	"	10	14, 5, 2	Cath.
Strosser, Daniel............	60	"	12		Ref.
Scheyer, John..............	30	"	3		"
Liset, Philip...............	24	"			"
Luich, Kostman............	36	"	22, 8		"
Wadenspfhul, Jacob........	32	"	3, 1		Luth.
Gerser, Henry.............	36	"	7, 4	13, 10	"
Thalheimer, Nicol..........	27	"		3, 1	"
Schezel, Jacob.............	39	"			"
Bauer, Christoph...........	21				"
Jung, Nicol................	21				"
MASONS					
Closs, Simon...............	26	wife		½	Cath.
Mauer, George.............	32				Luth.
Besler, Francis.............	46	wife	18, 16, 7		Cath.
Moor, David...............	36	"			Ref.
Beus, Jacob................	30	"	6, 1		Cath.
Carat, John	16				Ref.
Mey, John.................	36	wife	½	8, 6, 4	Cath.
JOINERS					
Son, Elias.................	21				Luth.
Pfhul, Peter...............	48	wife	10, 5, 1	12, 6	"
Gruber, Matthes...........	46	"	14, 12, 10, 4	1	Cath.
Julius, Henrich.............	21				Luth.
Koerner, John..............	33				"
WHEELWRIGHTS					
Tiel, Ananias..............	36	wife	5, 1		Luth.
Hoges, Michel.............	26				Cath.
Klein, Adam...............	28				Ref.

NAME	AGE	WIFE	SONS	DAUS.	CHURCH
SMITHS					
Deller, Jacob...............	22				Luth.
New, Wenceslag...........	20				Cath.
Meyer, George.............	19				Luth.
Schmidt, Christian.........	18				Ref.
Kerber, Nicol..............	50	wife	¼		Cath.
Stein, William.............	23				"
Klein, Philip...............	45	wife	9, 7	4	Ref.
Schmidt, Carl..............	36	"	10, 9, 7, 4	1	Luth.
Hohn, Michel..............	31	"	4	10, 4	"
Roll, Jost..................	26	"			Cath.
Schantz, Peter.............	20				Luth.
Michel, John...............	42	wife			Cath.
LINEN AND CLOTH WEAVERS					
Brill, Michell..............	21				Cath.
Waller, John...............	49	wife			"
Forster, George............	39	"		14, 10, 7, 5	Luth.
Kessler, Nicol.............	24	"			"
Muller, Anton.............	56	"			Ref.
Bless, Conrad.............	29	"			"
Wieser, Jacob..............	52	"	16		"
Boset, Daniel..............	59	"	14, 5	21, 19, 13, 11, 9, 1 m.	"
Herman, Sebastian.........	36				Cath.
Kolhaus, Lucas............	40	wife	3	11, 8	"
Barl, Henrich..............	54	"	22	18, 16, 14, 12	Ref.
Kuhn, Peter...............	24				Luth.
Maus, Michel..............	24				Cath,
Maus, Reinhard............	18				"
Bock, Jacob...............	40				Ref.
TAILORS					
Reichard, Henry...........	15				Cath.
Ludwig, Anton.............	28	wife	2	6	"
Brozis, Adam..............	33	"	1	4	"
Arlot, Francis.............	22				"
Ostwald, John.............	44	wife	14, 3	22, 6	Luth.
Heddesheimer, Henry......	22				Ref.
Walten, John..............	20				"
Leilling (Salling?), Francis.	16				Cath.
Erlenbach, George.........	53	wife	6	16, 8	Ref.
Wremmar, John...........	18				Cath.
Merzel, Jacob..............	30	wife			Luth.
Hag, Caspar...............	20				"
Forster, Nicol.............	22				Ref.
Schmidt, John Peter........	19				Luth.
Schmidt, Peter.............	19				"
Klein (Lang?), Moritz......	30	wife	8, 6	10, 4, 1	Cath.
SCHOOLMASTERS					
Regel, Matthes.............	40	wife	2		Cath.
Kummer, John.............	40		9, 1	8, 6	Ref.
Rasor, Frederick...........	29				Luth.
SHOEMAKERS					
Decker, John..............	29	wife	½		Cath.
Ferry, John C..............	23	"			"
Pfalzer, Henry.............	36	"	5, 2	10	"
Horsbach, Dietrich.........	36	"	6	1	"

NAME	AGE	WIFE	SONS	DAUS.	CHURCH
Nusbaum, John............	46	wife	13, 9, 6, 2	17, 13	Mennon
Hen, Henrich................	40	"	13, 11, 9, 6	2	Luth.
Albiger, William...........	34	"			"
Eckman, John,.............	36	"		4	
Munster, Peter............	30	"	9, 4	8, 6	Luth.
Adams, Jacob..............	24	"			"
Reid, Nicol................	34	"	13	10	"
Gibstein, Martin...........	33				Cath.
BRICKLAYERS					
Maus, Dietrich.............	30	wife	9, 6	¼	Cath.
Klepper, Conrad...........	33	"	9, 2	5	"
Horning, Gerhard..........	40	"		6, 2	Ref.
Hag, Henry................	26	"	3	1	Luth.
STOCKING WEAVERS					
Matthes, Mareus...........	88			24	Ref.
Matthas, George...........	32	wife	3		"
Michel, Henry.............	38	"	8, 5	10, 1	Luth.
BAKERS					
Schmidt, John..............	23	wife	3		Cath.
Brandau, William..........	30	"	3		Ref.
Schwab, Conrad............	20				Luth.
Kuhlbrunner, Caspar......	23				Ref.
Brenner (Bronner), Balzar..	20				Luth.
Ganglof, John..............	28	wife		4 mos.	"
Shoemaker, John...........	37				Ref.
Meyer, Barthol.....	50	wife		14, 3, 6, 5	Luth.
Buerger, John..............	55	"	12	20	Cath.
Lucerni, Abraham..........	27				Ref.
Roth, Andreas.............	24				Luth.
HUNTSMEN					
Reuter, Henry.............	34	wife		4, 2	Cath.
Gerlach, Conrad...........	49	"	7, 5	16, 11	Ref.
HATTERS					
Wegrauch, Valentin........	38	wife	7, 2	11, 9	Luth.
Andoit, Samuel............	44	"	20	13, 13	Ref.
GLAZIERS					
la Dour, John.....	18				Cath.
Rose, Christoph............	35				Luth.
Meiss, Barthol.............	26				"
BUTCHER					
Nutzberger, Matthes.......	56	wife	3	18, 12, 7	Luth.
SADDLER					
Weisgerber, John..........	45	wife			Cath.
FIGUREMAKER					
Zerbst, Philip..............	25				Luth.
LOCKSMITH					
Schoenwolf, John...........	23				Ref.
BRICKMAKERS					
Wirs, Frederick............	39	wife		8, 6, 2	Luth.
Meyer, Henry..............	43	"	4	6	Ref.
Pitty, Jacob................	50			18, 10	"

NAME	AGE	WIFE	SONS	DAUS.	CHURCH
HERDSMAN					
Meyer, Henry..............	31	wife	7, 4, 2		Cath.
SURGEON					
Gudi, Philip..............	40	wife		3, 1	Cath.
MILLERS					
Berchtold, Jacob..........	44	wife	18, 15, 12	4	Ref.
Mueller, Peter.............	45	"	15, 14, 7	19, 3	"
Jager, Carl................	36	"	7	4	"
Schnick, Michel...........	22				Luth.
Cobel, Jacob..............	27	wife	½		Cath.
Shaeflin, Henry...........	49	"	15		"
Walraf, William...........	23				"
Dunckel, Andreas.........	38	wife	3	8, 1	"
Dunckel, John.............	26				"
Martin, Peter.............	33	wife	1	7	"
WIDOWS					
Tieffenbach, Anna........	74				Ref.
Breien, Barba.............	40		18	12, 4	"
Sheffen, Elbot............	40		10	5	Luth.
Schmidin, Gertrud........	30			3	Cath.
Osevald, Adelia...........	28		8		"
Daubin, Barba.............	60				Luth.
Kochin, Elizabeth.........	55				"
Seibelin, Christina........	56				Ref.
Weisrockin, Catherine.....	47			18	"
Baum, Sarah...............	70				"
Crausin, Catherine........	52			24, 16	"
Blasig, Maria.............	46		26		Cath.
Segbin, Apollonia.........	50		24, 18, 9		"
Ganglof, Magdalena.......	60				Luth.
Creuzin, Elizabeth.........	48		16, 13	19,17,11,8	"
Hibig, Anne...............	50		29, 24, 22	26	Ref.
Vogt, Elizabeth...........	48				Cath.
Lisin, Eva.................	45		12	10	Ref.
Hilles, Catherine..........	28			2	"
Clossmannin, Margaretha...	40			19	Cath.
Albin, Engel..............	63				Luth.
Reichman, Anne..........	43		9	6, 3	Cath.
UNMARRIED WOMEN					
Khidy, Catherine..........	30				Ref.
Wilhelm, Jane.............	28				"
Krutsch, Margaretha.......	24				Cath.
Hausen, Eva...............	24				"
Bork, Elizabeth...........	20				"
Hofman, Sophia...........	18				Luth.
La Force, Barbara.........	20				Cath.
La Force, Anne...........	18				"
Bauman, Mary.............	30				Luth.
Singerin, Anne............	20				"
Schinkin, Christina........	24				"
Schaeds, Anne............	20				Ref.
Mussel, Barba.............	24				Luth.
Dumbacher, Catherine.....	20				Ref.
Schreibin, Margaretha.....	24				Cath.
Heins, Eva......	24				Luth.
Barbe, Anne..............	22				Ref.
Leich, Catherine.....	30				Luth.

NAME	AGE	WIFE	SONS	DAUS.	CHURCH
Schellin, Magdalene........	22				Ref.
Krinin, Mary..............	24				Luth.
Meyerin, Delia............	21				Cath.
Jakoettin, Mary...........	24				Ref.
Jackoettin, Anne..........	20				"
Mosenheim, Mary..........	23				Luth.
Meyerin, Margretha........	23				Ref.
Wagnerin, Catherine.......	20				Cath.
Haasin, Engel.............	22				"
Wiedmacher, Catherine....	24				Ref.

(Endorsed) Miscellanies List of Poor Palatines arrived from Germany the 11th June, 1709. Received from Mr. Ruperti, Juue 21, 1709. D. 69.

An abstract of the fourth list of 1745 Palatines that are arrived the 11th June, 1709.

Men................................	338
Wives..............................	331
Widows............................	16
Unmarried Men......................	92
Unmarried Women...................	29
Sons above 14 years...................	122
Daughters above 14 years.............	127
Sons under 14 years..................	351
Daughters under 14 years.............	339
	1745

An abstract of the three former lists of 4775 Poor Palatines that are come over from Germany from 1st of May to the 10th of June.

Men...............................	940
Wives.............................	903
Widows...........................	73
Unmarried Men.....................	292
Unmarried Women..................	77
Sons above 14 years.................	257
Sons under 14 years.................	1016
Daughters above 14 years............	247
Daughters under 14 years.....	970
	4775
The whole sum from 4th list...........	1745
All that are here now..................	6520

(Endorsed) Abstract of the lists of the poor German arrived here from the Palatinate from the 1st of May to 11th instant amounting in all to 6520.

Received from Mr. Tribbeko.

Received 16th June, read 21st. D. 70.

PERSONS NATURALIZED IN NEW JERSEY BETWEEN 1702 AND 1776.

BY DR. JOHN R. STEVENSON.

THE names of the persons naturalized by the Assembly of New Jersey between the union of the provinces of East and West Jersey in 1702 and the commencement of the Revolutionary struggle are collated from Allinson's "Acts of the General Assembly of the Province of New Jersey from the Surrender of the Government to Queen Anne on the 17th Day of April in the Year of our Lord 1702, to the 14th day of January 1776," a book published in Burlington, N. J., in 1776.

The work gives the full text of only a limited number of laws; the remainder are indicated by their titles. The reason for the naturalization of these citizens is given in the title to the law passed July 8, 1730, viz.: "An Act for the better enabling divers inhabitants of the Province of New Jersey to hold Land, and invest them with the privileges of natural born Subjects of the said Province."

Naturalization enactments of a private and personal character continued to be passed until September 16, 1772, when a general law was enacted for the reasons assigned in its preamble. This shows the status of foreigners born out of the jurisdiction of Great Britain, especially when taken in connection with the qualifications of electors under colonial régime. By the act passed April 4, 1709, no one could vote for members of the Assembly unless possessed of one hundred acres of land in his own right, or was worth £50 in real and personal estate. To be eligible to membership in the Assembly, one must own one thousand acres of land, or be worth £500 in real and personal property. These laws were in force up to the Revolution.

The enacting clause and preamble of the general law above referred to reads: "An Act to enable all Persons who are His Majesty's liege Subjects either by Birth or Naturalization, to inherit and hold Real Estates, notwithstanding any Defect of purchases, made before Naturalization within this Colony."

"Whereas divers foreign Protestants, born without the Liegeance of the Crown of Great Britain are settled within this Colony, who, being unacquainted with the Laws and Customs thereof have purchased Real Estates within the same before they were naturalized; and such Estates are now held and claimed under such Purchases by his Majesty's natural born Subjects, or such as are naturalized; and as the greater Number of these are poor Persons who will be utterly ruined if Advantage is taken of the Alienism of such Purchaser; in tender Commiseration of all Persons holding or claiming by such defective Title, and confiding in His Majesty's great Bounty, the General Assembly prays that it may be Enacted," &c.

This was confirmed by the King in Council, September 1, 1773.

NAMES.	DATE OF ACT.	NAMES.	DATE OF ACT.
Adam Agee	Aug. 20, 1755	Jacob Allright	June 3, 1763
Jacob Akeley	Dec. 6, 1769	John Allison	Feb. 23, 1761

Names.	Date of Act.	Names.	Date of Act.
Nicholas Angle	June 3, 1763	Adam Diels	Dec. 8, 1744
Jacob Arents and 3 children	Jan. 27, 1716/7	Hendrick Diels	" " "
Nicholas Arents.		Henry Diffidaffy	April 28, 1762
Mary Arents.		Hendrick Dirdorf	July 8, 1730
Margaret Arents.		Anthony Dirdorf and his 4 sons	" " "
Peter Bard, a native of France	Mar. 11, 1713/4	Christian Dirdorf.	
William Barwick	June 21, 1754	Anthony Dirdorf.	
Christian Beck	Aug. 20, 1755	John Dirdorf.	
George Beck	Mar. 10, 1762	Peter Dirdorf.	
Henry Bemer	Aug. 20, 1755	Johannes Doremus	June 21, 1754
John William Berg and his 3 sons.		Daniel Dorn	June 3, 1763
Johannes Berg.		Peter Dosgel	Dec. 8, 1744
John Berg.		Charles Duran	Mar. 15, 1738/9
Peter Berg.		William Ecker	Aug. 20, 1755
John Diel Berg	Dec. 8, 1744	Jacob Eigh	July 8, 1730
William Bellesfelt.	July 8, 1730	Christiana Elsington, widow	" " "
Adam Bellesfelt	Dec. 8, 1744	Jacob Engle	" " "
Peter Bellesfelt	" " "	William Engle	" " "
Johan William Bellesfelt	" " "	Valentine Ent.	Aug. 20, 1755
Johannes Belesvelt	May 19, 1756	William Evalman	Oct. 23, 1751
John Beulesheimer	Aug. 20, 1755	Laurence Eykeinier	Oct. 27, 1770
Hendrick Beus	June 21, 1754	Jacob Faish	June —, 1766
Hendrick Beus, Jr.	" " "	*John GeorgeFelthausen	Sept. 26, 1772
Joseph Behringer	Feb. 23, 1764	Cornelius Ferberg	June 3, 1763
Francis Bickle	Aug. 20, 1755	Pieter Fisher	July 8, 1730
Christopher Bishop	Dec. 6, 1769	Marton Fisher and his 2 sons	" " "
John Blom	Mar. 15, 1738	Jacob Fisher.	
Perter Bodine	July 8, 1730	Phillip Fisher.	
John Bohn	Dec. 6, 1769	Henry Fisher	March 15,1738/9
John Bower	Oct. 27, 1770	Johannes Fisher	June 6, 1751
John Boshart and wife Anna Boshart and their children	Feb. 10, 1732	Pacel Flag	July 8, 1730
		Jacob Foofman	March 15,1738/9
Christopher Boshart		Leonard Fox	April 28, 1762
Dorothy Boshart.		Peter Franberg	March 15,1738/9
Hendrick Bost	July 8, 1730	John Martin Fulkemer.	Dec. 6, 1769
Joseph Bost	" " "	Justus Gans	Aug. 20, 1755
Jacob Brown	Aug. 20, 1755	George Geeser	" " "
Peter Brown	Dec. 6, 1769	Jacob Gerhart	July 8, 1730
Nicholas Bud	Mar. 15, 1738/9	Johannes Giddeman and his son	" " "
Pe er Case	Aug. 20, 1755	HendrickGiddeman	
Tunis Case	" " "	Peter Goeglets	Dec. 16, 1748
Stephen Chalmes	Mar. 17, 1713/4	Caspar Grim	April 28, 1762
Peter Coens	Aug. 20, 1755	Willem Guise	July 8, 1730
Peter Colsher	May 10, 1768	John Haas	May 10, 1768
Henry Cook	April 28, 1762	Anthony Habback	July 8, 1730
Andrew Congle	Dec. 6, 1769	Ann Hagg	" " "
John Cosman	Dec. 6, 1769	William Han	" " "
Christian Cornelius	July 8, 1730	Ludwig Hadn	Dec. 8, 1764
Henry Croo	June, 6, 1751	Adam Hag	Aug. 20, 1755
Adam Cuncle	Feb. 23, 1764	Thomas Hall	" " "
Nicholas Dahlberg	Mar. 15, 1738/9	Henry Harter	" " "
John Deilar	Dec. 7, 1763	Michael Hammer	April 7, 1761
Peter Demond of Monmouth Co.	Aug. 16, 1733	John Hartman	Dec. —, 1769
John De Witt	Mar. 15, 1738		

* Disallowed September 1, 1773.

NAMES.	DATE OF ACT.	NAMES.	DATE OF ACT.
Johan Balthazar Harff..	Dec. 6, 1769	Peter Lame	Dec. 6, 1769
Frederick Hayn.......	May 10, 1768	Henry Landis.........	Aug. 20, 1755
Christian Hasell.......	July 8, 1730	Henry Lashie.........	" " "
Christian Hassen......	Aug. 20, 1755	Johannes Laux	July 8, 1730
Kornraet Henerigh.....	July 8, 1730	John Lewis of Hunter-	
Johannes Heyler.......	June 3, 1763	don Co.	Nov. 30, 1723
John Herbergs........	June 20, 1765	Henry Lishman	Dec. 6, 1769
Rudolph Hesley.......	July 8, 1730	Peter Louderbouch and	
Jacob Hertel..........	June —, 1766	his three daughters...	June 19, 1747/8
Carel Hierlegh........	July 8, 1730	Catharine Louder-	
George Hinns	Dec. 7, 1763	bouch.	
Henry Hoffman........	Aug. 20, 1755	Barbara Louder-	
Johannes Hoffman. ..	Dec. 8, 1744	bouch.	
Peter Hoffman	June 21, 1754	Elizabeth Louder-	
William Hoffman......	" " "	bouch.	
Johannes Hofses.......	Dec. 6, 1769	John Louterman	May 10, 1768
Adam Homer..........	July 8, 1730	Peter Lupp	Oct. 27, 1770
Herbert Homer.......	" " "	Henry Lutz..........	April 7, 1761
Adam Hoeshield.......	Dec. 8, 1744	Michael Maps........	April 28, 1762
Matthias Houshilt......	" " "	Carel Maret.....	July 8, 1730
Jacob Houselt........	July 8, 1730	Philip Marks........	April 28, 1762
Johan Housilt........	" " "	John Marlin........ ..	Dec. 6, 1769
John Howze..........	June 20, 1765	Henry Marshon of Hun-	
Joseph Hupple........	June 3, 1763	terdon Co...........	Aug. 16, 1733
Christopher Huson....	April 28, 1762	Matthew Marton......	Dec. 6, 1769
Gabriel Hymer	June 3, 1763	Johannes Mayer.......	May 10, 1768
Hieronymus Ilorin.....	July 8, 1730	Bartholomeus Melsbagh.	July 8, 1730
John Immell..........	Aug. 20, 1755	Johannes Meyer.......	June 21, 1754
John Irick...........	Oct. 27, 1770	Johan Gerig Miller...	July 8, 1730
Mattys Kaelfelt.......	July 8, 1730	Hans Michael Milner ..	Dec. 8, 1744
Johan Phillip Kaes.....	" " "	John Morkel..........	Feb. 23, 1764
Willem Kaes.........	" " "	Jacob Moor...........	July 8, 1730
Johannes Kank........	Dec. 7, 1763	John Moor..........	" " "
Johannes Kase........	June 21, 1754	Peter Neyzard.	Aug. 20, 1755
Matthias Kase........	" " "	Leonard Nimaster	Oct. 27, 1770
Christian Kaul	" " "	George Obert..........	" " "
Christian Kaul	Aug. 20, 1755	Peter Obert...........	" " "
Kornraet Keiel........	July 8, 1730	Frederick Outgelt......	" " "
William Kelin........	Aug. 20, 1755	Cornelius Parent.......	June 21, 1754
Jacob Kemper.........	June 6, 1751	Jacob Peer...........	July 8, 1730
John Kemper.... ...	Aug. 20, 1755	Godfrey Peters..... ...	" " "
Bastiyan Kes..........	Dec. 8, 1744	John Pheger.	Aug. 20, 1755
George Kesler........	Dec. 7, 1763	Nicholas Philips.......	April 28, 1762
Hieroninus Keyser.....	July 8, 1730	Adam Pocke	Aug. 20, 1755
Michael Kiney........	Aug. 20, 1755	John William Pollman.	June 20, 1765
Peter Knott of Mon-		Albertus Poppledorf....	Aug. 20, 1755
mouth County, Planter	Aug. 16, 1733	Hans Jacob Prettiker...	April 28, 1762
Paul Kole............	July 8, 1730	Francis Ralph........	Dec. 6, 1769
Johannes Casparus Koch		John Raker..........	Aug. 20, 1755
" his wife Katherine		Justus Rangal........	" " "
and their three sons".	Mar. 15, 1738/9	Andrew Redick..... .	" " "
Anthony Koch.		Hantil Rester........	June 21, 1754
Jacobus Koch.		Johan Ludowick Right-	
Joseph Koch.		mier................	July 8, 1730
Hareborn Koch	June 21, 1754	Martin Roan	April 28, 1762
Hendrick Koch........	" " "	Johan Peter Rockefelter	
Christian Kule	" " "	and his two sons ..	July 8, 1730
Peter Kurtz..........	June 20, 1765	Johannes Rockefelter.	
John Lame	Dec. 6, 1769	Peter Rockefelter.	

NAMES.	DATE OF ACT.	NAMES.	DATE OF ACT.
Susanna Roeters	July 8, 1730	William Stodder	May 10, 1768
Johannes Ross.	June 21, 1754	Jacob Stucky	April 28, 1762
Christopher Rob	Dec. 6, 1769	Martin Swortwelder	Feb. 23, 1764
John Rouse	April 28, 1762	Michael Tilheaver	Dec. 8, 1744
Peter Romeur, a native		Johannes Trimmer	" " "
of France	Mar. 17, 1713/4	Matthias Trimmer	" " "
George Sawiback	Dec. 6, 1769	Andrew Trinmer	Aug. 20, 1755
Jacob Sartor and his 2		Jacob Urtz	Dec. 8, 1744
sons	July 8, 1730	Peter Vanallen	May 19, 1756
Johannes Sartor.		George William Van-	
Hendrick Sartor.		bagh	Aug. 20, 1755
John Senting	Aug. 20, 1755	John Vandreson	March 15, 1738/9
Henry Sevinck	April 28, 1762	Johannes Martinus Van	
Gasper Shepperd	Feb. 23, 1764	Harlingen	July 31, 1740
Martin Shipley	June 21, 1754	Jacob Vogt	Aug. 20, 1755
Matthias Sharpentin	Dec. 8, 1744	Walton Vokes	Feby. 23, 1764
Michael Shuatterly	June 6, 1751	Johannes Vos	June 3, 1763
Nicholas Signe	July 8, 1730	Andrew Wagoner	Feb. 23, 1764
David Slayback	April 7, 1761	Harman Wagoner	Aug. 20, 1755
Peter Slim	Dec. 6, 1769	Henry Warner	" " "
Frederick Smith	" " "	Christian Wertchen	" " "
Johan Chris. Smith, Jr.	Dec. 8, 1744	William Wertchen	" " "
Matteys Smith	July 8, 1730	Peter Werts	" " "
Filleep Sneider	Dec. 8, 1744	John Philip Weiker	Feby. 23, 1764
Christopher Snider	July 8, 1730	George Windemude	" " "
Hendrick Snock	" " "	Jacob Winnacker	June 6, 1751
Johan Willem Snock	" " "	Casper Wister	March 15,1738/9
John Henry Snoffer	Feb. 23, 1764	Thomas Whisler	Dec. 6, 1769
John Snoffer	Feby. 23, 1764	Gerhart Winter	" " "
Adam Snook	Aug. 20, 1755	Walter Wob	" " "
John Snook	May 10, 1768	Johannes Yagar	July 8, 1730
Henry Snug	Dec. 8, 1744	Johannes Peter Yagar	" " "
John Snyder	June 23, 1763	Peter Yagar	Aug. 20, 1755
Frederick Tendle Spick.	Dec. 8, 1744	Benedict Yare	June 3, 1763
Joseph Staneman	Aug. 20, 1755	Jacob Young	Aug. 20, 1755
Martin Streetman	" " "	Tunis Young	" " "
John Hendrick Stree-		Pieter Young	July 8, 1730
pers	June 20, 1764	John Peter Zenger	March 15,1738/9
Henry Stricklan	Dec. 6, 1769		

SOME EMIGRANTS TO AMERICA FROM THE LUDWIGSBURG DISTRICT, WURTTEMBERG, GERMANY, 1738-1750

CONTRIBUTED BY PAUL W. PRINDLE

This contributor, in a co-operative effort with others under the leadership of Commander Howard Carlyle Wagar, U.S. Naval Reserve, engaged Herr Egon Oertel, Oehringen, Kernstrasse 10, Wurttemberg, Germany, a genealogist of note who has made many contributions of German extensions to American pedigrees, to seek records of the Wagar-Wager-Waeger families who emigrated in 1738 and thereafter from the Ludwigsburg district, Wurttemberg, to the Dutchess-Rensselaer area of New York State.

The result was successful beyond expectations. One custom most helpful to the search was that citizens of that area of Germany, desiring to emigrate to America, were then required to declare their intentions by signing renunciations or waivers of their citizenship. Such records are a fertile field for genealogists endeavoring to connect emigrants to their homes in the old world.

During the course of his search in the archives of the City Council of Poppenweiler, Ludwigsburg district, Herr Oertel came across the following renunciations which will doubtless provide hitherto unknown European origins of the respective American families. The reader is to understand that an expressed intention to emigrate to Pennsylvania is not necessarily significant; the emigrant may well have settled in New York State. Thus, although the Poppenweiler records show that Johann Jacob Weger and his family emigrated to Pennsylvania in May 1753, he had, by 1755, settled in Rhinebeck Precinct, Dutchess County, New York.

Melchior Betz*, former resident-citizen and vintner, signed a renunciation on April 2, 1738, announcing his intention of emigrating "to America

---

* Herr Oertel states that there is a book of 453 pages available, at a price of $2.00 entitled *Interesting Persons and Events in Beihingen-on-the-Neckar,* by Albert Ritz, printed in German in 1939. In a chapter devoted to emigrants, mention is made of Melchior Betz who, in 1747, was a "Royal English citizen of Pennsylvania," and married to Maria Catharina Walter, daughter of Johann Jakob Walter.

or the new world," together with his wife Agnes and their two children, Elizabeth and Barbara.

Johannes Berner Weber, son of the late Joseph Berner, former resident-citizen, went to New York many years ago. He brought his inherited fortune over March 31, 1750.

Jacob Brust, aged 23 years, son of the late Jerg Brusten (or George Brust), former resident-citizen and vintner, left April 13, 1750, to go to his aunt, Barbara Netter(in), his mother's sister in Pennsylvania, "because she was without heirs."

[Barbara was the widow of the late Jacob Mayer, resident-citizen and blacksmith of Poppenweiler, when she left in 1738 as a member of the family of her brother-in-law, Johann Leonard Weger. His renunciation, for the purpose of moving into "strange lands" with his wife Catharina, nee Netherin [sic] and their two children, Paul and Eleanor, was signed Feb. 13, 1738. They are believed to have arrived at the port of New York Oct. 12, 1738, on the ship *Amsterdam* or on the *Anne* the following day. Leonard and his family settled in Rhinebeck, Dutchess County, N. Y.].

Matheus Klopfer, wife Rosina, and four children. George (aged 8 years), Elizabeth (6 years), Johannes (3 years), and Michael (1 year). Presumably May 8, 1750.

Daniel Machleyd, wife Rosina, and four children. Margaret (aged 10 years), Adam Frederick (5 years), Jacob (2 years), and Anna (1 year). Presumably May 8, 1750.

Ulrich Mayer, wife Catherina, and their two children. Carol (aged 2 years), and Michael (aged 8 weeks), to Pennsylvania May 8, 1750.

Jerg [George] Michael Schmid, former resident-citizen and vintner, to Pennsylvania April 30, 1750, with his wife and children.

Johann Jacob Schmid, son of the late Hans Jerg Schmidt [sic], resident-citizen and farmer, to Pennsylvania May 8, 1750.

Jacob Walter [referred to in the preceding footnote], resident-citizen and blacksmith, and his wife Maria Catharina, to Pennsylvania April 23, 1749.

Anna Catharina Wolff, daughter of the late Hans Adam Wolff, resident-citizen and linen weaver, to Pennsylvania May 8, 1750.

Andreas Zitzer, former resident-citizen and linen weaver, with his wife Elizabeth and their still unmarried daughter Veronica, from her [Elizabeth's] first marriage to Johannes Closs. To America April 2, 1738.

Johan Martin Zitzer, resident and linen weaver, and brother of Andreas [just above], with his wife Salome "and the children from the first and second marriages": Johann Friedrich, Andreas, Jacob, Regina, and Maria Catharina. To America April 2, 1738.

THE COLONIAL NATURALIZATION ACT OF 1740
WITH A LIST OF PERSONS NATURALIZED IN NEW YORK COLONY, 1740-1769

CONTRIBUTED BY RICHARD J. WOLFE

During the first seventy-five years of British sovereignty over the Colony of New York it was impossible for a foreigner living there to acquire the rights and privileges of a natural-born Englishman except through an arbitrary exercise by the Governor of the royal prerogative of denization or through a special act of naturalization passed by the Colonial Legislature.[1] It followed that rights thus granted were considered local in nature and could not be exercised outside of the local jurisdiction of the Colony, much less in the mother country, for Parliament alone had the power to bestow naturalization so that the recipient of it should become a denizen of the empire. And while such local actions remedied some of the disadvantages attached to the alien status—allowing foreigners ownership, transfer, and inheritance of land within the Colony, for example—they did little to repair the feeling of separation from the mother country which arose after the colonies began to acquire strength. The immigrations of 1709-1711 and afterwards had brought a great multitude of foreigners into the various colonies and their numbers were increasing steadily, and it seemed to the Government of George II to be in the best interests of promoting colonization, trade, and agriculture to attach these permanently by granting them full civil and political privileges.

By the provisions of 13 George II, c. 7 (1740), entitled "An Act for Naturalizing such foreign Protestants, and others therein mentioned, as are settled or shall settle in any of His Majesty's Colonies in America," the status of a natural-born Englishman was conferred upon foreign Protestants and others residing seven years in America who should take the oath of abjuration, make the declaration of fidelity, and receive the sacrament. (The only limitation imposed was the concluding proviso that no such persons could be of the Privy Council or of Parliament or could hold an office of trust in Great Britain or Ireland or receive grants of land therein from the Crown, the usual proviso in such 17th and 18th century British acts.) Neither special act of Parliament nor attendance in London was required. To acquire naturalization a person simply went before the Chief Judge or another judge of the Colony and took the prescribed oaths and proved through the testimony of two witnesses and a certificate from his minister that he had received the sacrament within the previous three months, though Quakers and Jews were exempted from this requirement.

In return for these proofs and a record fee of two shillings the petitioner received a certificate which served as a complete naturalization paper.[2] This law remained in force in the colonies up to the time of their revolt, and subsequent legislation on the subject merely modified its administration or broadened its scope. In 1747, by Statute 20 George II, c. 44, the benefits of the Act were extended to Moravian Brethren and in 1761, by 2 George III, c. 25, officers and soldiers who had served in the Royal-American Regiment or as engineers in America for two years became entitled to naturalization.

According to the Act of 1740, all naturalizations were to be recorded in a book kept by the court for that purpose and re-entered into a master copy maintained in the office of the Secretary of the Colony. The latter was charged with transmitting to the office of the Commissioners for Trade and Plantations in London at the end of each year a true and perfect list of all persons naturalized under the Act. The names on these annual returns were then to be transferred by the Commissioners into a book or books kept for that purpose in their office and these were to be made available for public inspection upon request.

It was the information contained in two such books—transcribed therein from lists forwarded to the Commissioners by the Secretaries of the Colonies of South Carolina, Virginia, Maryland, New York, Pennsylvania, and the West Indies—which furnished the source material for M. S. Giuseppi's *Naturalizations of Foreign Protestants in the American and West Indian Colonies (Pursuant to Statute 13 George II, c. 7)*, published by The Huguenot Society of London in 1921. These had been previously located among the records of the Commissioners which are now classed with the records of the Colonial Office in the Public Record Office, London.[3] Concerning the publication of this information in the Giuseppi volume only a few words need be said. First, the information contained in the original lists sent from the various colonies was not uniform, and indeed the Act required only that a list of names be forwarded to the Commissioners, though more complete information was to be recorded in the court where naturalization took place and in the office of the Secretary of the Colony. (Of all the returns from the several colonies only the New York lists contained the names of witnesses, but only in about half the cases, and information provided on these returns was usually restricted to name, place of abode, and date, though in the case of New York again religion and profession were also frequently given.) And secondly, no mention is made of the existence of the original books from which these returns were prepared, and it is to be assumed that none was known to the compiler.

Recently, in the course of work on a new edition of Harold Lancour's *Passenger Lists of Ships Coming to North America, 1607-1825*, a bibliography originally published by The New York Public Library in 1937 and to

be reissued in a revised and enlarged form this spring, there came to my
attention the original record book of naturalizations maintained by the
Secretary of the Colony of New York between 1740 and 1769. This is a
folio volume contained in the Manuscript Division of The New York
Public Library, having been among the 2,500 miscellaneous items accom-
panying the Emmet Collection upon its presentation to the Library in
1896. Because the information recorded in the original is so much more
complete and obviously more correct than the transcriptions printed in
the Giuseppi volume, it is published here.

The book in The New York Public Library consists of twelve sheets of
crown paper folded once over so as to make twenty-four pages which are
now enclosed within a red cloth library binding. The 1740-1769 material
covers only seventeen of the twenty-four pages, the remainder being blank
or given over to a seven page list of naturalizations in New York State
between 1802 and 1814 which was later added to the volume.[4] Entries
within run across the length of the page, from bottom to top, and pages
have been ruled off in parallel columns so that entries continue through
all inside pages, one under the other. The first page is titled "The Severall
Persons hereafter named took the Oaths made, repeated the Declaration
as directed by an Act of Parliament made in the thirteenth Year of the
Reign of King George the Second Entituled 'An Act for naturalizing such
foreign Protestants, and others therein mentioned, as are settled or shall
settle in any of His Majesty's Colonies in America'," and the columns
following are headed:

> Names of the Persons Naturalized
> Their Religious Profession
> Their Temporall Profession and Place of Abode
> Minister Certifying Receiving the Sacrament
> The Witnesses Names to the Certificate
> The Day of the Month

That this must have been the book kept in the office of the Secretary of
the Colony seems obvious, for cumulations from 1740 through 1744 are
followed by the notations "So far Sent Home in May 1741 according to
the Statute," "So far sent Home in December 1742 According to the
Statute," etc. (The Secretary later grew lax in this respect, transmitting
cumulations for several years at one time; and it is evident that the passing
of years caused officials in London to become equally careless in making
entries into the official books, for a great many errors of transcription—and
some of omission—are shown through a comparison of The New York
Public Library list with the returns published in the Giuseppi volume.)
It is hoped that the present publication of this document will identify
many persons—especially those named as witnesses—previously unknown
in New York at this time. And it seems likely that the religious affiliations
and professions supplied by the individuals themselves upon subscribing

to the oaths will prove valuable for supplementing the scant records we have of many of them. A number of aliens named here can undoubtedly be traced to their original foreign origins through the aid of some of the ship and immigrant lists recorded in the Lancour bibliography.

In transcribing the 1740-1769 list for publication here I have not given the contents of each column verbatim but, for reasons of brevity, have recorded the essential information only in digested form. However, the sequence of the original has been retained throughout, as have the six columnar divisions noted before. And the spelling of all names has been faithfully followed. In a few cases, the names of witnesses are lacking from entries which contain the name of a certifying minister. When this occurs I have inserted the letter M in parentheses " (M) " after the minister's name so as to remove any ambiguity. The full name of a minister is given only upon its initial occurrence below, except in cases where wide variation exists in the spelling of Christian names.

[*page 1*]

The Severall Persons hereafter named took the Oaths made, [and] repeated the Declaration as directed by an Act of Parliament made in the thirteenth Year of the Reign of King George the Second Entituled "An Act for naturalizing such foreign Protestants, and others therein mentioned, as are settled or shall settle in any of His Majesty's Colonies in America"

Miller, Johannes
Miller, Philip
Christee, Johannes
Sensiback, Frederick
Sensibach, John Christ
Felton, Girronimus
Becker, Zacharias; Dutch Reformed; Ulster County farmer; Georgus Wilhelmus Mancius; Matis Marckel, Conrd Myer; Oct., 1740.
Snider, Martinus; Dutch Reformed; Ulster County farmer; G. W. Mancius; Matis Marckel, Conrd Myer; Oct., 1740.
Rightmeyer, Coenradt; Dutch Reformed; Ulster County farmer; G. W. Mancius; Martin Snyder, Zacharias Becker; Oct., 1740.
Marckell, Martinus; Dutch Reformed; Ulster County farmer; G. W. Mancius; Martin Snyder, Zacharias Becker; Oct. 1740.
DeLancey, Stephen; Church of England; New York City merchant; William Vesey; Richard Charlton, Anthony Duane.
(11)
[*page 2*]

Faviere, James; French Church; New York City merchant; Lewis Rou; Jeremiah Lattouch, Peter Vergereau.
Bringier, Marie; French Church; New York City; Lewis Rou; James Faviere, Samuel Bourdet.
Emar, Jean; French Church; New York City yeoman; Lewis Rou; Peter Vergereau, Jerem^h Latouch; Oct., 1740.
Roge, John; Church of England; New York City merchant; William Vesey; Thomas Duncan, James Lyno; Jan. 24, 1740 [1741].

Auboyneau, John

Gomez, David; Jew; New York City merchant

Gomez, Mordecai; Jew; New York City

Gomez, Daniel; Jew; New York City

Ferro, Jacob, Jr.; Jew; New York City

Levy, Samuel; Jew; New York City

Cohen, Samuel Myers; Jew; New York City

Cohen, Abraham Myers; Jew; New York City

Isaacs, Abraham; Jew; New York City

Levy, Isaac; Jew; New York City

Myers, Solomon; Jew; New York City

Simson, Joseph; Jew; New York City

Nare, Solomon; Jew

Hay, David; Jew

DeRivera, Ab^m Rodrigues; Jew

Vinera, Da^u Rodrigues; Jew

Lopez, Moses; Jew

Hay, Judah; Jew; New York City merchant

Samuel, Levy; Jew; New York City; Apr. 27, 1741

Hart, Solomon, Jr.; Jew; New York City; Apr. 27, 1741

(35)   So far Sent Home in May 1741 according to the Statute
   [*page 3*]

Gombauld, Moses; French Church; New York City merchant; L. Rou; James Faviere, Jeremiah Lattouch; July 28, 1741

Bontecou, Daniel; French Church; New York City merchant; L. Rou; John Hastier, Alexander Allaire; July 31, 1741

Buvelot, James; French Church; New York City brasier; L. Rou; John Hastier, Alexander Allaire; July 31, 1741

Kurts, Johannes; Lutheran; Albany County shoemaker; Michael Christian Knoll; Jn° David Wolf, Gustaph Martin Ruck; Oct. 20, 1741.

Gillot, Samuel; French Reformed; Westchester County merchant; L. Rou; James Buvelot, Alexander Alaire; Oct. 21, 1741.

Spach, Jonas; French Reformed; L. Rou; James Buvelot, Alexander Alaire; Oct. 21, 1741.

Sornberger, George Jacob; Lutheran; G. W. Mancius; Johannes Weber, Henrick Berringer; Oct. 23, 1741.

Weber, Johannes; Lutheran; G. W. Mancius; Geo. Jacob Sornberger, Henrich Berringer; Oct. 23, 1741.

Sneider, Christopher; Lutheran; G. W. Mancius; Johannes Weber, Henrick Berringer; Oct. 23, 1741.

Betser, Adam; Lutheran; G. W. Mancius; Wilhelm Schneider, Teunis Schneider; Oct. 23, 1741.

Henriques, Isaac Nunes; Jew

DeLeas, Abraham; Jew

Favieres, Charlotte Bouyer; French Church; New York City married woman; L. Rou; Moise Gombauld, Samuel Bourdett; Apr. 27, 1742.

Lawrence, William; Dutch Reformed; New York City gardener; Gaultherus DuBois; Hermanus Rutgers, Jn° Roosevelt; Oct. 25, 1742.

(49)   So far sent Home in December 1742 According to the Statute
   [*page 4*]

Levy, Moses; Jew; New York City merchant; Apr. 19, 1743.

Huntziger, Johannes; Lutheran; Dutchess county blacksmith; M. C. Knoll; John Phafer, Laurens Van Boskerck; Apr. 25, 1743.

Oel, John Jacob; Lutheran; Albany County clerk; Henry Barclay; Jacob Glen, Jacob H. Ten Eyck; July 28, 1743.

Diel, Laurentz; Lutheran; Dutchess County yeoman; M. C. Knoll; E. Christian Hoyer, Hendrick Beringer; Oct. 19, 1743.

Gernreich, Johan Peter; Lutheran; Dutchess County yeoman; M. C. Knoll; Johan Valentine Schefter, Andrios Widerwax; Oct. 24, 1743.

So far Sent home in Decr 1743

Peterson, George; Lutheran; New York City sugarbaker; M. C. Knoll; Charles Beekman, Johan David Wolf; Apr. 17, 1744.

Coleck, Jonas N.; New York City baker; M. C. Knoll; Hans Pfefter, Henrick Behr; Apr. 23, 1744.

Heder, Henrik; Dutch Reformed; New York City carman; G. DuBois; Abraham Lott, Johannes Lott; Aug. 7, 1744.

Schultz, Casparus; Lutheran; Dutchess County farmer; G. M. Weiss; Johannis Snue, Teunis Snyder; Oct. 17, 1744.

Klyn, Johannes Peter; Lutheran; Dutchess County farmer; G. M. Weiss; Johannis Snue, Frederick Beringen; Oct. 17, 1744.

Staats, Johannes; Lutheran; Dutchess County farmer; G. M. Weiss; Johannis Snue, Frederick Beringen; Oct. 17, 1744.

Dieter, Hendrick; Lutheran; Dutchess County farmer; G. M. Weiss; Johannis Snue, Frederick Beringen; Oct. 17, 1744.

Fritz, Christophell; Lutheran; Dutchess County farmer; G. M. Weiss; Johannis Snue, Teunis Snyder; Oct. 17, 1744.

Weys, Andrew; Lutheran; Dutchess County carpenter; M. C. Knoll; Joh^s Snyder, Christian Haver; Oct. 18, 1744.

So far sent home in Decr 1744

Van Dalsem, Willem; Lutheran; New York City schoolmaster; Johannes Ritzema; Elbert Haring, Ahasuercus Turck; Aug. 1, 1745.

Will, John Michel; Lutheran; New York City cordwainer; M. C. Knoll; Jacob Boss, Jacob Foerster, Jeronimus Reigler; Oct. 31, 1745.

Debele, John George; Lutheran; New York City gardener; M. C. Knoll; Jacob Boss, Jacob Foerster, Jeronimus Riegler; Oct. 31, 1745.

Seixas, Isaac; Jew; New York City merchant; Nov. 4, 1745.

Reber, Andreas; Lutheran; New York City shopkeeper; M. C. Knoll (M) ; Nov. 5, 1745.

Hertz, Casparus; Lutheran; New York City cartman; M. C. Knoll; Johan Frederick Harman, Jonas Melick; Apr. 17, 1746.

Hoyer, Erich Christian; Lutheran; New York City schoolmaster; M. C. Knoll; Johann David Wolf, Jacob Christop^r Foerster; July 29, 1746.

(70)

[*page 5*]

Helms, Emus; Church of England; New York City mariner; Richard Charlton; Cornelis Tiebout, Christian Hertell; Aug. 4, 1746.

Revera, Jacob Rodrigues; Jew; New York City merchant; Jan. 21, 1746 [1747].

Huber, Hans Jacob; Dutch Reformed; New York City yeoman; G. DuBois; Apr. 23, 1747.

Meyer, Christopher; Lutheran; New York City cartman; M. C. Knoll; Fredericus Oesterman, Casparus Hertz; July 30, 1747.

Sinseback, Johan Teunis; Dutch Reformed; Ulster County yeoman; G. W. Mancius; Daniel Schneider, Johannes Schneider; Oct. 20, 1747

Schneider, Daniel; Dutch Reformed; Ulster County yeoman; G. W. Mancius; Johan Teunis Sinseback, Johannes Schneider; Oct. 20, 1747

Kool, Johannes; Dutch Reformed; New York City Cordwainer; G. DuBois; William

Crelus, Christian Stouber; Oct. 23, 1747

Michell, Andries; Dutch Reformed; New York City labourer; J. Ritzema; Johannes Myer, Daniel Smith; Apr. 21, 1748

Smith, Daniel; Dutch Reformed; New York City; J. Ritzema; Johannes Douebach, Andries Michell; Apr. 21, 1748

Hays, Isaac; Jew; New York City tallow chandler; Apr. 26, 1748.

Creutz, Christopher Godlieb; Lutheran; New York City baker; M. C. Knoll; Henricus Schrifter, Casparus Hertz; Aug. 1, 1748

Franks, Moses Benjamin; Jew; New York City; Oct. 18, 1748

Steenbagh, Anthony; Dutch Reformed; New York City baker; G. DuBois; Henry Heder, William Laurens; Oct. 19, 1748

Hering, John Andrew; Lutheran; New York City weaver; M. C. Knoll; Charles Beekman, Jr., John Michael Wille; Oct. 25, 1748

> Hitherto Sent Home pursuant to Act of Parliament

Lewis, John; Church of England; New York City mariner; H. Barclay; Coenradt Ten Eyck, Abraham Ten Eyck; Jan. 18, 1748 [1749]

Goetschius, John Henry; Dutch Reformed; Hackinsack, New Jersey, minister of the Gospel; U. Van Sinderen; Abraham Lott, Barent Vandewenter; Jan. 19, 1748 [1749]

(86)

[*page 6*]

Goetschius, John Mauritzius; Dutch Reformed; Hackinsack, New Jersey, chirurgeon; Jn° Henricus Goetschius; Abraham Lott, Barent Vandewenter; Jan. 19, 1748 [1749]

Pypper, David; Lutheran; New York City taylor; M. C. Knoll; Johan George Windlinger, Valentine Lambert; Apr. 18, 1749

Giselbreecht, Gottfried; Lutheran; Dutchess County physician; M. C. Knoll; Casper Hertz, Henricus Schefter; Apr. 24, 1749

Bowman, Mathew; Lutheran; New York City yeoman; M. C. Knoll; Leendert Riegeler, John Michael Will; July 28, 1749

Tenni, Jacob; Dutch Reformed; New York City cartman; Joan. [sic] Ritzema; Willem Crolius, Willem Lounrens; Oct. 17, 1749

Speder, Daniel; Dutch Reformed; New York City; Joan. Ritzema; George Pettersson, Dirck Amerman; Oct. 18, 1749

Sneyder, Henderick; Dutch Reformed; New York City; G. DuBois; Willem Corcilius, Willem Crolius; Apr. 17, 1750

Metsiger, Jacob; Dutch Reformed; New York City; G. DuBois; Willem Corcilius, Willem Crolius; Apr. 17, 1750

Zuerigher, Johannes; Dutch Reformed; New York City; G. DuBois; Evert Pels, Willem Corcilius; Apr. 17, 1750

Rynlander, Bernard; Church of England; Westchester County tanner; P. Stouppe; Isaac Varian, Willem Rhinlander; Apr. 21, 1750

Shoals, John; Church of England; New York City mariner; H. Barclay; Tho⁸ Grigg, Jr., Jos. Hildreth; July 31, 1750

Knecht, Mattys; Lutheran; New York City mason; M. C. Knoll; Johan Leonhard Weiland, Christoffer Meyer; Aug. 1, 1750

Schaff, Philip; Lutheran; New York City brassfounder; Jean Frideric Ries; Peter Grim, John Ebert; Aug. 1, 1750

Grim, Jacob; Lutheran; New York City feltmaker; J. F. Ries; Peter Grim, John Ebert; Aug. 1, 1750

Mildenbergen, Johan Adam; Lutheran; New York City husbandman; M. C. Knoll; Matthys Knecht, Willem Bauman; Aug. 2, 1750

Sax, Johan Peter; Dutch Reformed; Albany County farmer; G. W. Mancius; Corneles

Kneckerbaker, John West; Aug. 2, 1750

Axson, Elizabeth; Dutch Reformed; New York City widow; J. Ritzema; Aeltye Binmer, Mary Wentworth; Oct. 18, 1750

Witeman, Hendrick; Dutch Reformed; New York City brass button maker; G. Du-Bois; Jacob Boshart, Hannes Huber; Oct. 18, 1750

Melsbach, Nicholas; Dutch Reformed; Ulster County farmer; G. W. Mancius; William Smith, Christian Rockefeller; Oct. 18, 1750

Binder, Hans Ulrich; Dutch Reformed; Ulster County husbandman; G. W. Mancius; William Smith, Philip Sinseback; Oct. 18, 1750

(106)

[*page 7*]

Rokkenfelder, Christian; Dutch Reformed; Ulster County blacksmith; G. W. Mancius; Nicholas Milsbach, Phillipus Zinsebach; Oct. 18, 1750

Sensebach, Phillipus; Dutch Reformed; Ulster County farmer; G. W. Mancius; Nicholas Milsbach, Hans Ulrich Binder; Oct. 18, 1750

Cyffer, William; Dutch Reformed; Dutchess County farmer; Benj^m Meynerd; John Brinckerhoff, Johannes Schurri; Oct. 18, 1750

Schurri, Johannes; Dutch Reformed; Dutchess County blacksmith; B. Meynerd; John Brinckerhoff, William Cyffer; Oct. 18, 1750

Smith, William; Dutch Reformed; Ulster County blacksmith; G. W. Mancius; Hans Ulrich Binder, Christ^n Rockefeller; Oct. 18, 1750

Ute, John; Lutheran; New York City butcher; J. F. Ries; Peter Grim, Mark Phaffar; Oct. 18, 1750

Steinbrinner, Jacob; Lutheran; New York City blacksmith; J. F. Ries; Peter Grim, Mark Phaffar; Oct. 18, 1750

Busch, Johann Henrich; Lutheran; Ulster County blacksmith; Wm Ch^r Berkenmeyer; Charles Beekman, George Pettersson; Oct. 22, 1750

Van den Ham, Henry; Church of England; New York City vintner; H. Barclay; Joseph Hildreth, Joseph Greswold; Jan. 15, 1750 [1751]

Jacobi, Christopher; Lutheran; Germantown, Pennsylvania, stocking weaver; J. F. Ries; Peter Grim, John Eberts; Jan. 15, 1750 [1751]

Oesterman, John Fred^k; Lutheran; New York City labourer; J. F. Ries; Philips Grim, Jacob Grim; Apr. 16, 1751

Heroy, James; Church of England; New York City cartman; P. Stouppe; Aman Guion Elder, Isaac Coutant; Jan. 21, 1752

Heroy, Charles; Church of England; Westchester County weaver; P. Stouppe; Aman Guion Elder, Isaac Coutant; Jan. 21, 1752

Crane, Josiah; Church of England; New York City merchant; Saml Auchmuty; Peter Ewetse, James Wells; Apr. 21, 1752

Boshart, Jacob; Dutch Reformed; New York City stone cutter; Lambertus DeRonde; Hans Zurigher, Casper Gester; Apr. 21, 1752

Brown, William; Dutch Reformed; Schohary, Albany County wheelwright; Johannes Schuyler; Johann Willem Dietz, Johann Jacob Werth; July 29, 1752

(122)

[*page 8*]

Werth, Johann Jacob; Dutch Reformed; Schohary, Albany County doctor of physick; J. Schuyler; Johan Willem Dietz, Willim Brown; July 29, 1752

Dietz, Johan Willem; Dutch Reformed; Schohary, Albany County shoemaker; J. Schuyler; Johan Jacob Werth, William Brown; July 29, 1752

Graaf, Johannes Jacob; Dutch Reformed; Kings County farmer; L. DeRonde; Willem Creilus, Willem Lawrens; July 29, 1752

Ranck, Hans George; Dutch Reformed; Ulster County shoemaker; J. H. Goetschius; Lawrence Alsdorf, Hans George Neits; July 29, 1752

Alsdorf, Lawrence; Dutch Reformed; Ulster County farmer; J. H. Goetschius; Hans George Ranck, Hans George Neits; July 29, 1752

Niets, Hans George; Dutch Reformed; Ulster County farmer; J. H. Goetschius; Lawrence Alsdorf, Hans George Ranck; July 29, 1752

Thus far sent home

Risler, Tunis; Dutch Reformed; New York City baker; L. DeRonde; William Crolius, William Crolius, Jr.; Jan. 17, 1753.

Funck, Jacob; Lutheran; New York City baker; Philippus Stenrious; John Debele, John George Cook; Oct. 17, 1753

Sax, Johannes Michael; Lutheran; New York City baker; P. Stenrious; John Debele, John George Cook; Oct. 17, 1753

Melsback, Peter; Dutch Reformed; Ulster County farmer; B. Vrooman; Johannes Krans, Johan Philip Spies; Oct. 17, 1753

Minema, Benjamin; Dutch Reformed; Dutchess County clerk; Benjamin Minema; John Alsop, Bartholomew Crannel; Oct. 24, 1753

Haaghort, Gerardus; Dutch Reformed; Essex County, New Jersey clerk; Gerardus Haaghort; Francis Wouterse, Hendrick Bruyn, Jr.; Oct. 24, 1753

Beaudovin, Jeremiah; French Protestant; New York City staymaker; Mayor; Daniel Mesnard, Francis Blanchard; Jan. 17, 1754

Veldtman, John; Church of England; Richmond County farmer; R. Charlton; Richd Lawrence, Andr^w Puckitt, Thos Price; July 31, 1754

Roos, Lodowick; July 31, 1754

Rhinelander, William; Church of England; New York City yeoman; H. Barclay; John Ellis, William Ustick; July 31, 1754

Clement, Moses; Church of England; New York City cabinet maker; H. Barclay; Joseph Hildreth, Thos Grigg, Jr.; Apr. 16, 1755

Winthrop, Balthazar; Lutheran; New York City mariner; John Albert Weygand; Sam^{11} Beeckman, George Petterson; Oct. 23, 1755

Smith, Mathias; Oct. 24, 1755

Casper, Casper; Oct. 24, 1755

Smith, Christopher; Oct. 24, 1755

Fritz, Elias; Lutheran; New York City yeoman; J. A. Weygand; Charles Luyfferditz, Lodwick Roose; Apr. 21, 1757

Fry, Jacob; Church of England; Westchester County yeoman; P. Stouppe; John Durham, Wm Baldwin, Isaac Guion; Oct. 24, 1757

(145)

[*page 9*]

Brown, John Hendrick; Dutch Reformed; New York City baker; James Ritzema; Marselus Gorbrandts, Henry Swart; July 25, 1758

Adolphus, Isaac; Jew; New York City trader; July 27, 1750

Streit, Godfried; Lutheran; New York City cordwainer; J. A. Weygand; Johan Casper Linche, Joh. Matth. Rudolph; Oct. 20, 1750

Myers, Hyam; Jew; New York City butcher; Jan. 16, 1759

Myers, Manuel; Jew; New York City trader; Jan. 16, 1759

Ritter, Henry; Lutheran; New York City cordwainer; J. A. Weygand; John Goodpertel, Alex^{dr} Augspurger; Apr. 19, 1759

Ritter, Michael; Lutheran; New York City taylor; J. A. Weygand; John Goodpertel, Alex^{dr} Augspurger; Apr. 19, 1759

Goodpertel, John; Lutheran; New York City taylor; J. A. Weygand; Henry Ritter, Alex^{dr} Augspurger; Apr. 19, 1759

Frederick, Andrew; Lutheran; New York City baker; J. A. Weygand; John Balthus Daesch, Joh. Matth. Rudolph; Apr. 17, 1760

Painter, John; Lutheran; New York City shopkeeper; J. A. Weygand; Charles Beekman, Jr., George Gorgus; July 31, 1760

Lorilland, John and George; French Protestants; New York City yeomen; Jean Carle; Peter Vallade, Jaque Desbrosses; Oct. 27, 1760

Hoyer, Mathew; Lutheran; New York City baker; J. A. Weygand; John Balthus Dalsen, Jan Godfrid Muller; Oct. 28, 1760

Keyser, George Michael; Lutheran; New York City labourer; J. A. Weygand; John Balthus Dasch, Michael Nestil; Jan. 21, 1761

Mellow, David Henry; Lutheran; New York City mariner; J. A. Weygand; Jacob Funck, John George Sheffield; Jan. 21, 1761

Blanchard, James; French Protestant; New York City cooper; J. Carle; Peter Vallade, Jaᵉ Desbrosses, Daniel Bonet; Apr. 22, 1761

Chappelle, John Peter; French Protestant; New York City labourer; J. Carle; Peter Vallade, Jaᵉ Desbrosses, Daniel Bonet; Apr. 22, 1761

Morrell, Mathew; French Protestant; New York City labourer; J. Carle; Peter Vallade, Jaᵉ Desbrosses, Daniel Bonet; Apr. 22, 1761

Tiers, John Henry; French Protestant; New York City labourer; J. Carle; Peter Vallade, Jaᵉ Desbrosses, Daniel Bonet; Apr. 22, 1761

Epply, Jacob; Lutheran; New York City carman; J. A. Weygand; John Balthus Dasch; Apr. 22, 1761

(164)

[*page 10*]

Ladner, Andrew; Lutheran; New York City baker; J. A. Weygand; John Balthus Dasch, Charles Beekman, George Gorgus; Apr. 22, 1761

Linder, Benjamin; Lutheran; New York City practitioner in physick; J. A. Weygand; David Fairley, Jacob Epply; July 29, 1761

Muller, John; Lutheran; New York City labourer; J. A. Weygand; John George Auch, Jacob Epply; July 29, 1761

Gans, Bernard; Reformed German Church; New York City vintner; Frederick Rothenbuhler; Johannes Myer, Abraham Young; July 29, 1761

Heitz, Jacob; Lutheran; New York City carman; J. A. Weygand; David Fairley, Johan George Auch; July 29, 1761

Kuyper, Cornelius; Unitas Fratrum; New York City house painter; Thomas Yarrell; Jacobus Montanije, Wᵐ Pearson; July 29, 1761

Armpriester, John Christophel; Reformed German Church; F. Rothenbuhler; Johannes Myer, Abraham Young; Oct. 21, 1761

Will, Philip; Reformed German Church; New York City pewterer; F. Rothenbuhler; Hendrick Schwatz, Abraham Young; Oct. 21, 1761

Will, Henry; Reformed German Church; New York City pewterer; F. Rothenbuhler; Frederick Schwatz, Johannes Myers; Oct. 21, 1761

Spies, John Philip; Reformed German Church; New York City cordwainer; F. Rothenbuhler; Abraham Young, Johannes Myers; Oct. 21, 1761

Remmy, John; Reformed German Church; New York City potter; F. Rothenbuhler; Jnᵒ Christʳ Armpriester, Hendrick Schwatz; Oct. 21, 1761

Leonard, George; Lutheran; New York City butcher; J. A. Weygand; Casper Reisper, Henry Datliff; Oct. 21, 1761

Resler, Jacob; Lutheran; New York City tallow chandler; J. A. Weygand; David Fairley, Henry Datliff; Oct. 21, 1761

Moore, Blazey; Lutheran; New York City inholder; J. A. Weygand; David Fairley, Henry Price; Oct. 21, 1761

Rokheffeller, Johannes Petrus; Reformed Dutch Church; Albany County farmer; G. W. Mancius; Tiels Rokhefeller, Simon Rokhefeller; Oct. 21, 1761

Rokheffeller, Simon; Reformed Dutch Church; Albany County farmer; G. W. Mancius; Tiels Rokhefeller, Michael Blass; Oct. 21, 1761

Mulledaller, John; Reformed German Church; New York City cordwainer; F. Rothenbuhler; John Remmy, John Philip Spies; Oct. 21, 1761
Thus far sent home
Tiers, Daniel; French Protestant; New York City labourer; J. Carle; Jacques Desbrosses, Pierre Vallade; Jan. 21, 1762
Tiers, Mathew; French Protestant; New York City blacksmith; J. Carle; Jacques Desbrosses, Pierre Vallade; Jan. 21, 1762
Tiers, Magdalen; French Protestant; New York City spinster; J. Carle; Jacques Desbrosses, Pierre Vallade; Jan. 21, 1762
Tobias, Christopher; Quaker; Queens County yeoman; Jan. 23, 1762
Hess, John; Lutheran; New York City tallow chandler; J. W. Weygand; Jacob Reyslar, Daniel Wiedershyne; Apr. 21, 1762
(186)
[page 11]
Ritman, David; Lutheran; New York City carpenter; J. A. Weygand; Henry Keysler, Jacob Reysler; Apr. 21, 1762
Boos, Wendell; Lutheran; New York City baker; J. A. Weygand; William Mucklevain, Henry Ustick; Apr. 21, 1762
Pontius, Christian; Lutheran; New York City taylor; J. A. Weygand; William Mucklevain, Henry Ustick; Apr. 21, 1762
Regler, Andreas; Lutheran; New York City butcher; John Nicholas Kurts; Peter Grimm, Philip Lydig, John Ekbert; Apr. 21, 1762
Oxbury, Alexander; Church of England; New York City cordwainer; H. Barclay; William Mucklevain, Henry Ustick; Apr. 21, 1762
Croob, Nicholas; Lutheran; New York City cordwainer; J. M. Kurts; Philip Lydig, John Ebert; Apr. 21, 1762
Vallade, Peter; French Protestant; New York City merchant; J. Carle; James Desbrosses, Daniel Bonet; Apr. 21, 1762
Louillard, Peter; French Protestant; New York City stocking weaver; J. Carle; Daniel Bonet, Peter Vallade; Apr. 21, 1762
Tetard, John Peter; French Protestant; New York City clerk; J. Carle; James Desbrosses, Daniel Bonet; Apr. 21, 1762
Carle, John; French Protestant; New York City clerk; John Peter Tetard; James Desbrosses, Daniel Bonet; Apr. 21, 1762
Rougeon, Peter; French Protestant; New York City ship carpenter; J. Carle; Peter Vallade, Daniel Bonet; Apr. 21, 1762
Anthony, Joseph; French Protestant; Westchester County merchant; Michael Houdin; Isaac Guion, Moses De La Croix; Apr. 22, 1762
Andrews, Abraham; Jew; New York City shopkeeper; Apr. 22, 1762
Panet, Johannes; Dutch Reformed; New York City gentleman; James Ritzema; Adrianus Van Dersman, Jacobus Van Antwerp; July 29, 1762
Durand, Peter; French Protestant; New York City taylor; J. Carle; Peter Vallade, Daniel Bonet; July 29, 1762
Habener, Andrew; Lutheran; New York City cordwainer; J. A. Weygand; Michael Nestel, Johannes Schnous; July 29, 1762
(202)
[page 12]
Gress, Michael; Lutheran; New York City sadler; J. A. Weygand; Frederick Wise, Lodowick Cocks; July 29, 1762
Ranzier, Frederick; Lutheran; New York City cooper; J. A. Weygand; Frederick Wise, Michael Nestel; July 29, 1762
Gasner, John; Lutheran; New York City glazier; J. A. Weygand; Frederick Wise, Lodowick Cocks; July 29, 1762

Hoertse, Jacob; Lutheran; New York City mason; J. A. Weygand; David Ritman, Henry Pries; July 29, 1762

Rhinehart, Valentine; Lutheran; New York City inholder; John Siegfrid Gerock; John Ebert, George Wachtel; July 29, 1762

Deetz, Frederick; Lutheran; New York City taylor; J. S. Gerock; John Ebert, Samuel Falkenham; July 29, 1762

Workhard, George; Lutheran; New York City baker; J. A. Weygand; John Snows, John George Kaup; Oct. 21, 1762

Muller, Jacob; Dutch Reformed; Manor Cortlandt farmer; James Ritzema; William Mucklevain, Wendell Boos; Oct. 29, 1762

Parisien, Otho; French Protestant; New York City silversmith; J. Carle; Elisha Gallaudet, Jon Sebastian Stephani; Jan. 18, 1763

Wonderly, Egydius; Lutheran; New York City joyner; J. A. Weygand; John Michael Wille; Apr. 20, 1763

Ritman, Michael; Lutheran; New York City weaver; J. A. Weygand; Daniel Ritman; Apr. 20, 1763

Ruger, Frederick; Lutheran; New York City carman; J. A. Weygand; Jacob Risler; Apr. 20, 1763

Croskop, John George; Lutheran; New York City baker; J. A. Weygand; Jacob Risler; Apr. 20, 1763

Server, Tobias; Lutheran; Orange County husbandman; J. A. Weygand; Daniel Ritman; Apr. 20, 1763

Mannel, John; Lutheran; Orange County husbandman; Apr. 20, 1763

Frolick, Christian; Unitas Fratrum; New York City sugar baker; T. Yarrell; James Arden, Jarvis Robuck; Apr. 21, 1763

Elizer, Isaac; Jew; Rhode Island merchant; July 23, 1763

Lentz, Frederick Sigism^d; Lutheran; New York City gentleman; J. A. Weygand; Benjamin Lindner, Jn° Matt^w Rudolph; Oct. 18, 1763

Vogel, John; Lutheran; New York City vintner; J. A. Weygand; Fred^k Sigismund Lentz, Jn° Balthus Dasch; Oct. 19, 1763

Barnes, Coenrad; Lutheran; New York City hatter; J. A. Weygand; Jacob Risler, George Hibner; Oct. 19, 1763

Muller, Adam; Dutch Reformed; Manor Cortlandt farmer; James Ritzema; Daniel Clements; Oct. 19, 1763

(223)

[*page 13*]

Muller, Andries; Dutch Reformed; Manor Cortlandt farmer; Johanes Ritzema; Daniel Clements; Oct. 19, 1763

Voss, Jurian; Dutch Reformed; Manor Cortlandt farmer; Johanes Ritzema; Daniel Clements; Oct. 19, 1763

Swartz, Peter; Dutch Reformed; Manor Cortlandt farmer; Johanes Ritzema; Daniel Clements; Oct. 19, 1763

Hart, Levy; Jew; New York Colony merchant; Oct. 27, 1763

Solomons, Jonas; Jew; New York Colony merchant; Oct. 27, 1763

Thus far sent home

Toulon, Nicholas; French Protestant; Westchester County mariner; Michael Houdin; Jacobus Bleecker, Moses De La Croix; Jan. 18, 1764

Meyer, Napthaly Hart; Jew; New York City merchant; Apr. 27, 1764

George, John; Dutch Reformed; Orange County farmer; B. Van der Linde; Cornelius Meyer, [   ] Muller; July 31, 1764

Bell, William; Dutch Reformed; New York City cooper; Samuel Vesbryck; Johannes Haring, David Fowler; Oct. 17, 1764

Strebell, John; Lutheran; Albany County farmer; J. A. Weygand; Philip Kauterman, Henry Johghan; Oct. 26, 1764

Blattner, Jacob; Lutheran; Albany County miller and millwright; J. A. Weygand; Martin Shylr, Melcher Hoefnagel; Apr. 23, 1765

Henderer, Jacob; Lutheran; Albany County cordwainer; J. A. Weygand; Martin Shylr, Melcher Hoefnagel; Apr. 23, 1765

Wolhaupter, David; Lutheran; New York City turner; J. A. Weygand; Michael Crass, Melcher Hoefnagel; Apr. 23, 1765

Klinck, Jacob; New York City carman; J. A. Weygand; Michael Crass, Melcher Hoefnagel; Apr. 23, 1765

Tueter, Daniel; Unitas Fratrum; New York City silversmith; T. Yarrell; Jacob Reed, Henry Clopper; July 31, 1765

Kilman, Nicholas; Lutheran; New York City inholder; J. A. Weygand; David Fairley, Frederick Ranseer; Aug. 2, 1765

Fryenmoet, Rev. John Caspar; Dutch Reformed; Albany County minister; Gerhard Daniel Cock; Rud⁸ Ritzema, Garrit Rapalje; Oct. 15, 1765

[*page 14*]

Kous, John Thys; Dutch Reformed; Dutchess County farmer; G. D. Cock; Rud⁸ Ritzema, Garrit Rapalje; Oct. 15, 1765

Rose, Johan Peter; Dutch Reformed; Albany County shoemaker; G. D. Cock; Rud⁸ Ritzema, Garrit Rapalje; Oct. 15, 1765

Hartesteim, Michael; Lutheran; New York City labourer; George Bager; John Ebert; Oct. 15, 1765

Fach, George; Lutheran; New York City baker

Lodz, Reynold; French Protestant; Oyster Bay, Queens County gardener; J. P. Tetard, Past.; Ja⁸ Desbros, Fra⁸ Blachard, Isaac Noble, John Lorrilliard, Peter Lorrilliard; Oct. 13, 1765

Muller, John; Reformed German Church; New York City doctor of physick; J. Michael Kern; Henry Will, Wendel Boos; Oct. 15, 1765

Kline, John; Reformed German Church; New York City baker; J. M. Kern; Henry Will, Wendel Boos; Oct. 15, 1765

Gartner, David; Reformed German Church; New York City taylor; G. Bager; Michael Crass, David Wolhaupter; Oct. 15, 1765

Schonneret, Frederick; Lutheran; New York City shopkeeper; G. Bager; Andrew Merrell, Peter Grim; Oct. 18, 1765

Fink, Alexander, Jr.; Lutheran; New York City butcher; G. Bager; Philip Lydig; Oct. 18, 1765

Ott, Jacob; Lutheran; New York City butcher; G. Bager; Philip Lydig, Peter Grim; Oct. 18, 1765

Fach, Henry; Lutheran; New York City shoemaker; G. Bager; Philip Lydig, Peter Grim; Oct. 18, 1765

Lucam, George; Lutheran; New York City butcher; G. Bager; Philip Lydig, Peter Grim; Oct. 18, 1765

Menold, Martin; Lutheran; New York City shoemaker; G. Bager; Philip Lydig, Peter Grim; Oct. 18, 1765

Leonhard, Wilhelm; Reformed German Church; New York City baker; J. M. Kern; Joh. Philip Spiess, Josony Micsellhogg; Oct. 21, 1765

Kopp, Michael; Reformed German Church; New York City cooper; J. M. Kern; H. Billyneur Znuserort, Joh. Philip Spiess; Oct. 21, 1765

Horneffer, Henrich; Reformed German Church; New York City baker; J. M. Kern; Christian Smith, Sonring Ishand; Oct. 21, 1765

Oertly, Henrick; Reformed German Church; New York City yeoman; J. M. Kern; Christian Smith, Sonring Ishand; Oct. 21, 1765

Fischer, John; Lutheran; New York City tanner; G. Bager; Philip Lydig, John Vogel; Oct. 21, 1765

Zimmerman, Henry; Lutheran; New York City carpenter; G. Bager; Philip Lydig, John Vogel; Oct. 21, 1765

Cammerdinger, Ludewig; Lutheran; New York City taylor; G. Bager; Philip Lydig, John Vogel; Oct. 21, 1765

[*page 15*]

Klein, John; Lutheran; New York City nailsmith; G. Bager; Philip Lydig, John Vogel; Oct. 21, 1765

Ekert, Philip; Lutheran; New York City carpenter; J. A. Weygand; Oct. 21, 1765

Schel, Christoph; Lutheran; New York City cartman; J. A. Weygand; Philip Lydig, John Vogel; Oct. 21, 1765

Brugman, Godfried; Lutheran; New York City mason; J. A. Weygand; Morris Goebel, George Worckhartt; Oct. 21, 1765

Klein, George; Lutheran; New York City baker; J. A. Weygand; Morris Goebel, George Worckhartt; Oct. 21, 1765

Poyshert, Peter; Lutheran; New York City blacksmith; J. A. Weygand (M) ; Oct. 21, 1765

Gobel, David; Lutheran; New York City baker; J. A. Weygand; Morris Goebel, George Worckhartt; Oct. 21, 1765

Weber, Michael; Lutheran; New York City shoemaker; J. A. Weygand; Morris Goebel, George Worckhartt; Oct. 21, 1765

Mannhard, Philip; Lutheran; New York City house carpenter; G. Bager; Philip Lydig, Jacob Ropblor; Oct. 23, 1765

Schenerhinger, Mathew; Lutheran; New York City hatter; G. Bager; Philip Lydig, Jacob Ropblor; Oct. 23, 1765

Egle, Martin; Lutheran; New York City carpenter; G. Bager; Philip Lydig, Jacob Ropblor; Oct. 23, 1765

Herbert, John; Lutheran; New York City butcher; G. Bager; Philip Lydig, Jacob Ropblor; Oct. 23, 1765

Stubarare, Peter; Lutheran; New York City stocking weaver; G. Bager; Philip Lydig, Jacob Ropblor; Oct. 23, 1765

Wiedershein, John Daniel; Lutheran; New York City butcher; J. A. Weygand; Nicholas Killman; Oct. 23, 1765

Voshee, Daniel; Lutheran; New York City tobacco cutter; J. A. Weygand; Nicholas Killman; Oct. 23, 1765

Pinto, Joseph Jesurum; Jew; New York City minister of Jewish Congregation; Jan. 22, 1766

Hitherto List sent to the Board [of] Trade

Phenus, Philip; Lutheran; Queens County taylor; J. A. Weygand; Friedrick Ransier, Michael Cross; July 31, 1766

[*page 16*]

Heght, Frederic W^m; Church of England; New York City gentleman; S. Auchmuty; Jos. Hildreth, Wm Butler; Aug. 1, 1766

Weygand, John Albert; Lutheran; New York City minister of the Gospel; John Christ^r Hartwick; Jacob Kemper, Dederick Heyer; Apr. 21, 1767

Britt, William; Reformed Protestant Dutch Church; Westchester County farmer; Johannes Ritzema; Rinier Skaats, Moses Sherwood; Apr. 24, 1767

Enters, John; Reformed Protestant Dutch Church; Westchester County farmer; Johannes Ritzema; Ranier Skaats, Moses Sherwood; Apr. 24, 1767

Detloff, Henry; Lutheran; New York City cartman; J. A. Weygand; Jacob Kemper, Johan Baltus Dasch &c.; Apr. 24, 1767

Stuber, George; Lutheran; New York City taylor; J. A. Weygand; Jacob Kemper, Johan Baltus Dasch &c. Apr. 24, 1767

Man, George; Lutheran; Orange County farmer; J. A. Weygand; Jacob Kemper, Johan Baltus Dasch &c.; Apr. 24, 1767

De Joncourt, Jane; Church of England; New York City widow; John Ogilvie; Isaac Noble; Jan. 20, 1768

Dealing, John; Unitas Fratrum; New York City shopkeeper; George Neisser; Lawrence Kilbrunn, Jacob Reed; Apr. 20, 1768

Kilbrunn, Lawrence; Unitas Fratrum; New York City merchant; G. Neisser; John Dealing, Jacob Reed; Apr. 20, 1768

Johnson, Christopher; Lutheran; New York City tavern keeper; J. S. Gerock; John Ufancie, William Scott; Apr. 20, 1768

Smith, Barend; Reformed Protestant Dutch Church; New York City taylor; L. De-Ronde; Nicholas Welp, Jacob Durye; July 27, 1768

Jouch, John; Lutheran; New York City shingle shaver; J. A. Weygand; John Balthers Dash, John Gassnar; Oct. 18, 1768

Luneman, Carl; Lutheran; New York City carpenter; J. A. Weygand; John Balthers Dash, John Gassnar; Oct. 18, 1768

Lorentz, John Peter; Reformed Protestant Dutch Church; Rhinebeck, Dutchess County yeoman; G. D. Cock; Joseph McKenie, Evert Heermase; Oct. 22, 1768

De Noyelles, John; Church of England; Orange County gentleman; S. Auchmuty; John Strafford Jones, John L. C. Roome; Jan. 18, 1769

Hitherto List sent to the B^d of Trade

Grim, David; German Evangelical Church; New York City vintner; J. S. Gerock; Peter Grim, John Young; Apr. 18, 1769

Heerbenk, John; German Reformed Congregation; New York City tanner; J. M. Kern; Antson Appel, Jasarm Gill; Apr. 20, 1769

Rossel, Henry; German Reformed Congregation; New York City tanner; J. M. Kern; John Harbenk, Antson Appel; Apr. 20, 1769

Appel, Anston; German Reformed Congregation; New York City baker; J. M. Kern; Josorm Hill, John Harbenk; Apr. 20, 1769

Hill, John; German Reformed Church; New York City labourer; J. M. Kern; John Harbenk, Antson Appel; Apr. 20, 1769

Chappelle, Peter, Jr.; French Protestant; New York City stocking weaver; Abraham Keteltas; Mathieu Morel, Pieter Tier; Apr. 20, 1769

Tier, Daniel; French Protestant; New York City cartman; Abraham Keteltas; Mathieu Morel, Pieter Tier; Apr. 20, 1769

Ries, John; Lutheran; outward of New York City farmer; J. A. Weygand; Apr. 20, 1769

Krauskop, Ludewyk; Lutheran; outward of New York City farmer; J. A. Weygand; Apr. 20, 1769

[*page 17*]

All, Adam; Lutheran; New York City yeoman; J. S. Gerock; Peter Grim, John Young; Apr. 19, 1769

Heyer, Dietrick; Lutheran; New York City sugar boyler; J. A. Weygand; Daniel Forsche, Joh. Jacob Stapell; Apr. 19, 1769

Moore, Jacob; Lutheran; outward of New York City farmer; J. S. Gerock; Apr. 20, 1769

Fagh, John; Lutheran; New York City cartman; J. S. Gerock; Apr. 20, 1769

Deybertsyer, George; Lutheran; New York City chimney sweeper; J. S. Gerock; George Wachtel; Apr. 20, 1769

Snyder, Hendrick; Reformed Protestant Dutch Church; Orange County farmer; Cornelius Blaun; Peter T. Haring, Hendrick Snyder, Jr.; Apr. 21, 1769

Bell, Christopher; Reformed Protestant Dutch Church; Orange County farmer; C. Blaun; Peter T. Haring, Hendrick Snyder, Jr.; Apr. 21, 1769

Trumper, Harmanus; Reformed Protestant Dutch Church; Orange County farmer; C. Blaun; Peter T. Haring, Hendrick Snyder, Jr.; Apr. 21, 1769

Kiers, Edward William; Reformed Protestant Dutch Church; Orange County merchant; Joh. Casp. Rubel; George Briks, Henry Depue; July 25, 1769

Breytigam, Frederick; Lutheran; New York City baker; J. S. Gerock; Michael Nestel, George Deybertseyer; July 26, 1769

Randeker, John; Lutheran; New York City cartman; J. G. Weygand; Michael Nestel, George Deybertseyer; July 26, 1769

Westermeyer, John; Lutheran; New York City baker; J. G. Weygand; Michael Nestel, George Deybertseyer; July 26, 1769

Will, Christian; German Reformed Congregation; New York City pewterer; J. M. Kern; Philip Oswald, D^d Grim; Oct. 18, 1769

Eckart, Jonathan; Lutheran; New York City trader; J. S. Gerock; Philip Oswald, D^d Grim; Oct. 18, 1769

Hitherto list sent to the Board of Trade 2d July 1770

NOTES

[1] Of course, New York aliens could be (and infrequently were, it has been said) naturalized by special act of Parliament. A report of the Attorney General of the Kingdom made in late 1699 resulted in an order in Council issued January 18, 1700 laying down the principle that the method of granting denizations in the plantations be by acts of Assembly and that the governors desist from granting letters of denization unless expressly authorized to do so by their commissions. Several contemporary legal interpretations of arbitrary assumptions of this prerogative by various governors previously are discussed in William A. Shaw's *Letters of Denization and Acts of Naturalization for Aliens in England and Ireland, 1603-1700* (Lymington, The Huguenot Society of London, 1911) p. xxvii-xxx. The principal laws governing naturalization within New York Colony were passed by the Legislature in 1683 and 1715.

[2] Whether because the privileges thus conferred were considered superior to those granted under the British Act of 1740 or for some other reason, up to the time of the Revolution many aliens in New York Colony preferred to pay the higher fee of nineteen shillings in order to be naturalized by the Colonial Assembly under the Act of 1715. For the names of a number of persons naturalized in New York Colony between 1715 and 1773 see L. F. Bellinger's "Our Early Citizens; Names of Those Taking the Oath of Allegiance from 1715 to 1773," in Lou D. MacWethy, *The Book of Names* (St. Johnsville, N. Y., The Enterprise and News, 1933) p. 1-7. Additional names may be found in "The Oath of Abjuration, 1715-1716," *The New-York Historical Society Quarterly Bulletin* III (1919) 35-40.

[3] C. O. 324, nos. 55, 56. These are two quarto vellum-bound volumes of some two hundred and sixty pages each (of Volume II only 14 pages are filled) lettered "Names of Persons Naturalized in His Majesty's Plantations in America." These were probably the only transcriptions made, as the second volume is obviously incomplete. In many cases the original annual or cumulative lists are extant also.

[4] The Library classification for these two documents is: New York, *Colony and State.* Naturalization statistics, giving names, etc., of persons naturalized, 1740-1769; also a list giving names, etc., of immigrants, 1802-1814. 24 pp. N. Y. F°. The later list has recently been published in *The Bulletin of The New York Public Library* for April, 1963. The names of Jews contained in the Emmet list were previously extracted and published in Leon Hühner's "Naturalization of Jews in New York under the Act of 1740," *Publications of the American Jewish Historical Society* XIII (1905) 1-6.

APPENDIX

[Both articles in the Appendix fall somewhat outside of the scope of this work and for this reason they are set apart. The first article concerns passengers arriving at Boston in 1656 and was published in *NYGBR* presumably because the manuscript upon which it is based is located in a New York library—the Pierpont Morgan—there being little other apparent connection with New York. The second article, however, "A Passenger List for the Ship *William*," does indeed contain a list of passengers bound for New York, but it is a list of the post-Colonial Period. This article appeared in the number for July 1970 and was therefore not cited in the Lancour bibliography, the most recent edition of which was published in 1963.]

THE PASSENGER LIST OF THE "SPEEDWELL," 1656

From the Original Manuscript in the Pierpont Morgan Library
and Reproduced through their Courtesy

NOTES ON THE EIGHT NAMES MARKED AS QUAKERS IN THE SPEEDWELL PASSENGER LIST, 1656.

CONTRIBUTED BY JOHN COX, JR.

1656 A List of the Pasingers abord the Speedwell of London Robert Lock master bound for New England.

	Aged		aged
Richard Stratton			
John Mulfoot			
Richard Smith	43	Nathaniel Goodinough	16
Francis Brinsley	22	John Fay	08
Thomas Noyce	32	William Tayler	11
Mathew Edwards		Richard Smith	28
Joseph Boules	47	Mahahuliett Munnings	24
Q William Brand	40	Margarett Mott	12
Q John Copeland	28	Henery Reeve	08
Q Christopher Holder	25	Henery Seker	08
Q Thomas Thurston	34	John Morse	40
Q Mary Prince	21		
Q Sarah Gibbons	21	Nicholas Davison	45
Q Mary Weatherhead	26	John Baldwin	21
Q Dorothy Waugh	20	Mary Baldwin	20
Lester Smith	24	Rebeca Worster	18
Christopher Clarke	38	John Wigins	15
Edward Lane	36	John Miller	24
Tho: Richardson	19	Thomas Home	11
John Earle	17		
Thomas Barnes	20	John Crane	11
Shudrack HopGood	14	Charels Baalam	18
Thomas Goodynough	20		

The persons above named past from hence [in] the shipp above mentioned and are according to order registred heare. dated Searche^{rs} office   Gravesend   30th may   1656

Theise were Landed at Boston in   Edward Pelling ⎫
N. E. the 27th of ye 6 menes 1656   ⎬ Searchers
   JE [John Endicott, Governor]   John Philpott ⎭
(Transcription of Speedwell Passenger List, herewith reproduced).

The Pierpont Morgan Library has a single page manuscript, reproduced herewith, giving a list of the passengers on the Speedwell in 1656. This list was published in the New England Historial and Genealogical Register, Vol. 1, page 132, and was also published in S. G. Drake's "Founders of New England." The transcription of the list is not wholly accurate as heretofore published; so we reproduce the original in facsimile here, by kind permission of the Pierpont Morgan Library.

The names of the eight Quakers were probably so marked after arrival at Boston, and as soon as the offense of their preaching was known. Our popular feeling against "reds" and Bolsheviks, although akin, cannot be as strong as was the general fear of these peace-proclaiming folk, whose worship and preaching were considered acts of spiritual rebellion equally by theocratic New England, and the established Church of Old England. So it is not to be wondered at that the eight were promptly jailed till the ship should go back, and the captain ordered to take them. He stood on his right as an English captain to take passengers to any port they desired, so he too was jailed until he agreed. Samuel Gorton wrote to them while they were in jail, and the four men wrote him a lengthy reply, telling of the ship Master's dilemma (Besse). Of the eight all but two came again in 1657 in the *Woodhouse,* and two of the *Speedwell* group had each the right ear cut off in Boston in 1658 for their persistent proclaiming that the soul of man needs no intermediary to reach God. By 1659 the New England fear for their theocracy reached the point that they hanged four Quakers. By 1666 it had grown to the hysteria known as the Salem witchcraft.

The following data on the eight Quakers is digested mostly from Norman Penney's notes to the Cambridge (unexpurgated) edition of the *"Journal of George Fox,"* 1911, to which work and to Besse's "Sufferings of the Quakers" the researcher and the genealogist are directed for sources.

WILLIAM BRAND (properly spelled Brend, but written Brande in the Fox Journal). He came again in the *Woodhouse* in 1657, and again got into Boston, where they laid him "neck and heels in Irons for 16 hours," and the next day gave him "117 Stroaks with a pitcht rope." He visited Rhode Island and Barbados. In 1664 he was in Newgate prison whence he wrote some tracts, and was under sentence of banishment to Jamaica, but this was not carried out. "William Brend of the liberty of Katherines near the Tower, a minister, died the 7th of the Seventh Month (Sept.), 1676, buried at Bunhill Fields."

JOHN COPELAND, one of those who came again in the *Woodhouse,* in 1657, had his right ear cut off by order of the Boston court in 1658. Two pamphlets were written about him and John Rous, 1659, and Besse's Sufferings of the Quakers II, 178-195, tells of his cruel suffering.

CHRISTOPHER HOLDER (1631-1688), born in Gloucestershire. He was of independent fortune, educated, refined and cultured. He came again in the *Woodhouse,* went at once into Rhode Island, thence to Boston, where he and two other Quakers were jailed. From that jail they issued in 1657 the earliest written statement of Quaker belief. In 1658 Boston was again annoyed at him and by order of the court his right ear was cut off. He married in 1660 Mary Scott of Providence, who died in 1665. He married 2d, Hope Clifton of Newport, and 3d, Grace Beaton. Christopher's Hollow, in Mass., "A secluded place in the woods," was said to be so named from his holding meeting there, but was probably named from a descendant. He died in England. He is the ancestor of the Quaker Holders and of many of the Slocums of America. Holder's "Holders of Holderness," 1902, gives an account of him and his descendants.

THOMAS THURSTON was born about 1622 according to the *Speedwell* list. He too was from Gloucestershire. He came again on the *Woodhouse* and although persecuted by the Christian officials in several Colonies he received from the Indians courteous entertainment in lodging and food, they sparing their own for him when sick on the way, and when the Susquehannas heard that he was in prison in Virginia some of them came to visit him. About 1665 he "fell away" and was "lost to the Truth," although Fox on his American journey, tried to reform him. Although once expelled from Maryland (for gross conduct) he was elected to the Assembly in 1688 and excused from taking the oath.

MARY PRINCE was one of the six Quakers "who pretended to goe to convert the grand signior; but the consill at Smirna hindered them; so they are gone to Venice, pretending to convert the Jewes." (Report of the English

Consul at Marseilles, 1658.) She was one of the ninety-four who signed as witnesses the marriage certificate of George Fox and Margaret Fell, 1669. She died at Bristol, a widow, Mary Prince, in 1679, leaving daughters. (Journal of Friends Historical Society, London.)

SARAH GIBBONS, of Bristol, b. about 1635; d. 1659, came again in the *Woodhouse,* and visited New Netherland, Rhode Island, Boston and Barbados. Again arriving off Rhode Island in 1659, her death is thus related in a letter from William Robinson, one of the four Quaker martyrs, to George Fox, dated Boston Gaol 12/5th Mo (July), 1659. "She & another friend, Who is Katherine Scotts daught of a place called providence . . . did passe into a sloope to goe to Providence as they Came neare to ye shoare . . . there Came a man in a Canow to fetch y^m where into they went . . . & soon after they were in it ye Canow fylled wth wat^r & did sinke . . . S: G: was drowned & was not found untill it was low water & then found her & ye next day buried her in Rich: Scots Orchard . . . who hath left a good Savour behind her."

MARY WEATHERHEAD came again in the *Woodhouse,* and went into Rhode Island, and later further into New England. It was reported to George Fox in 1657 that she was "shott at sea by a Dutch privateere & killed" (Cambridge Journal, II, 336) but she was shipwrecked and drowned in 1658 (ibid, Penny's notes, p. 479; Jones' Quakers in the Am. Colonies, p. 47).

DOROTHY WAUGH was of Hutton, in Westmoreland. She and her sister Jane were once servants, doubtless in a Quaker family, in Preston Patrick, a village near Kendal, and still a centre of Quaker activity. She came again in the *Woodhouse.* Shortly after her return to England she married William Lotherington, of Whitby, Yorkshire, and "travelled in many parts of this nation, and Into America, where she suffered very much by whiping & imprisonment &c^t, espeshally in and about Boston in New England" (Besse).

This is the story of the eight Quakers and of the barbaric treatment of them by the American government of those days. We take pride in having become more liberal than our forbears—but, since the World War no one, believing as Quakers then did and now do, regarding war, is admitted as a citizen of this free and noble land.

Port Greenock,

An Account of Passengers going on board the <William of New york Ezikiel Purinton>Master, for

<New york>   Burthen <three hundred & thirty eight>Tons per<British measf>required by Circular

of 15th December 1773 - founded upon an order of the Lords Commissioners of the Treasury.

No.	Names.	Age	Sex	Quality, Occupation or Employment.	Former Residence.			Place whither going, or to which they have agreed to be carried.	On what Account, and for what purpose they leave the Country, and conditions on which they have been received on Board.	Other Remarks
					Place	Parish	County			
1	Ezikiel Purinton	36	male							
2	Jebediah Payne	24	"							
3	Augustus Gardiner	25	"							
4	Charles Russell	26	"							
5	John Goff	24	"							
6	James Coffee	27	"	Crew						
7	Thos. F. Goold	19	"							
8	John Roberts	21	"							
9	John Blazedell	29	"							
10	George Ellzie	15	"							
11	Frederick Landberger	24	"							
12	Bolto Bray	24	"							
13	Thos. Oaks	16	"							
14	Robert Bryson	30	"	Labourer	House of Burn[1]	Monyvair[2]	Perth	New York	to follow his business	steerage
15	Elizabeth Bryson	22	female	Spinster	do	do	do	do	to accompany her husband	"
16	Jean Bryson	2	do		do	do	do	do	to accompany her parents	"
17	James Bryson	23	male	Labourer	do	do	do	do	to follow his business	"
18	Malcolm McGregor	20	"	do	do	do	do	do	ditto	"
19	Robert Bryson	30	"	do	Chapelhill	Moneddy	do	do	ditto	"
20	Christian Bryson	24	female	Spinster	do	do	do	do	to accompany her husband	"
21	James Drummond	27	male	Labourer	Quaig[3]	Monyvair[2]	do	do	to follow his business	"
22	William Bell	28	"	do	Methven	Methven	do	do	ditto	"
23	James McQueen	22	"	do	Dulvereck[4]	Monyvair[2]	do	do	ditto	"
24	Robt. Morton	24	"	do	Glasgow	High	Lanerk[5]	do	ditto	"
25	Daniel Douglas	32	"	do	Craginfam[6]	Logierait	Perth	do	ditto	"
26	Jas. Wallace	27	"	do	do	do	do	do	ditto	"
27	Thomas Clark	45	"	Farmer	Lochwinnoch	Lochwinnoch	Renfrew	do	ditto	"
28	Andw. Frome	22	"	Merchant	Glasgow	Northwest	Lanerk[5]	do	ditto	cabin
29	Wm. Kirkwood	31	"	do	Girvan	Girvan	Ayr	do	ditto	do
30	John Fullerton	30	"	Labourer	Buttergask[7]	Cargill	Perth	do	ditto	steerage
31	James Gallitly	25	"	do	Pittensorn	Little Dunkeld	do	do	ditto	"
32	John Blank	26	"	do	Lundy	Lundy	Forfar	do	ditto	"
33	John McQuistan	40	"	Merchant	London	St. James	Middlesex	do	ditto	"
34	Jane McQuistan	40	female	Spinster	do	do	do	do	to accompany her husband	"
35	Mary McQuistan	15	"		do	do	do	do		"
36	Arabella McQuistan	13	"		do	do	do	do	with their parents	"
37	Charles McQuistan	9	male		do	do	do	do		"
38	Myrtilla McQuistan	2	female		do	do	do	do		"
39	Duncan McArdle	35	male	Labourer	Dulvereck[4]	Monyvair[2]	Perth	do	to follow his business	"
40	John Gorrie	37	"	Merchant	Perth	Moneddy	do	do	do	cabin
41	Donald Geddes	24	"	do	London	St. James	Middlesex	do	do	steerage
	Greenock;Sept 1817					HH Connochy Junr.				

Ezikiel Purinton

Custom house Greenock, 4 September 1817
These certify that the above is a true Copy of
the Crew & passenger list given to us by Ezikiel
Purinton master of the William bound for New York
William McDowell Com.   Adam Johnston Com.

---

[1]It has not been possible to locate House of Burn.

[2]Monzievaird .

[3]"Quoig. A farm 2 miles east of Comrie."

[4]"Dalvreck. A farm about 1 1/2 miles east of Comrie."

[5]Lanark.

[6]Cragganfearn. A small farm or cottage, fairly high above Ballinluig village.'

[7]"This farm must have been split up into two or three units sometine about the 1840's.
I also have a record on an earlier map of Upper Buttergask. This corresponds to West B. on the
current editon of the map."   (All quoted material in these notes was contributed by Prof. Ian A. Fraser).

A PASSENGER LIST FOR THE SHIP *WILLIAM*

By Dagoberto Molerio

Recently, while searching through the Filed Papers of the City Clerk in the Municipal Archives and Records Center of New York City, I discovered an original and hitherto unpublished passenger list for the year 1817.[1] Its publication will help to fill the gaps in this area of genealogical research, because heretofore no passenger list for ships arriving in ports of the United States has been made available for the year in question.

The list is for the ship *William* which, according to the declaration made at Port Greenock by the ship's master, Ezikiel Purinton, set sail for New York from the Scottish port on 4 September 1817 with twenty-eight passengers and a crew of twelve. However, upon the ship's arrival at New York the *Commercial Advertiser* for October 18, 1817 reported that the *William* had arrived the previous evening and that she had put to sea on September 1. The same report said that the ship had been out "thirty-six days from land with coals, dry goods etc. to T. G. Collins, of Charleston, owner" as well as for other consignees, and that in a severe storm, Charles Russell, a crew member from Germantown, Pennsylvania, had been lost from the foretop sailyard.

By November 2, 1817 the *William* had cleared the port of New York and had sailed for Wilmington, North Carolina, according to the *Commercial Advertiser* of the following day.

Charles Nelson Sinnett in his genealogy of the Purinton family in America[2] lists a Captain Ezekiel Purinton who was born February 1, 1782 and died February 25, 1841.[3] This descendant of the family of George Puddington, who before 1642[4] had established himself in Georgiana, Maine, after leaving his native England, is most probably the Ezikiel Purinton who was the master of the *William*. Although the compiler of the genealogy does not indicate the captain's place of birth, the presumption that he was born in Maine is supported by the fact that a large number of the Purinton family were natives of that state, and that the woman he married on April 7, 1810 was Isabella Wilson of Topsham, Maine.

No information could be found on T. G. Collins, the man from "Charleston" whom the *Commercial Advertiser* identified as the owner.

[1] Municipal Archives and Records Center. City Clerk—Filed Papers. Location: 2999. Folder: Board of Health, Death Records, Miscellaneous Papers, 1819-1835.

[2] The Purinton, Purington families in America. Sketch of the American ancestor, George Puddinton with his will and family. An appendix, with records of the Puddington family in England. Index to the names of parties. Compiled by Rev. Charles N. Sinnett. [Fertile, Minn. 1925] 162, 49 pp., 4°. Typewritten.

[3] *Ibid*, p. 58.

[4] *Ibid*, p. 9. He was listed as an alderman of Georgiana in that year.

However, evidence of a very close association between Collins and Captain Ezikiel Purinton may be discerned in the name given by Captain Ezikiel Purinton and his wife Isabella to their fourth child and only son born on August 26, 1826. They named him Israel Collins Purinton.

Some observations are in order about several items on the passenger list.

Passengers numbers 14 and 19 are both listed as being named Robert Bryson and both aged 30.

The "quality, occupation or employment" of three of the married women is listed as "spinster." At first sight this may seem contradictory, but a check of an unabridged dictionary will make it clear that the term was being used in its second meaning, that is, to designate "a woman who spins, a spinner," and not, as one might at first suppose, to indicate an unmarried woman.

The identification of some of the villages and farms presented some difficulty, but, thanks to Miss Joan P. S. Ferguson, Hon. Secretary of the Scottish Genealogy Society, and to Prof. Ian A. Fraser of the School of Scottish Studies, University of Edinburgh, these, with the exception of one, have been located.

INDEX OF NAMES

170

John 66
Richard 66
Read, John 69, 71
 Mabell 25
 William 25
Rebell, Jacob 87
Reber, Andreas 135
Reck, Jacob 102
Reckhart, Justus 98
Redick, Andrew 126
Reed, Jacob 142, 144
 John 71
 Sarah 66
Reeve, --- 22
 James 22
 John 81
Regel, Matthes 120
Regler, Andreas 140
Rehm, Anton 110
Reichard, Caspar 104
 Henry 105, 120
Reichardin, Anna Barba 97
Reichardt, Valentin 118
Reichman, Anne 122
Reid, Nicol 121
Reidel, George 89
Reideman, Martin 109
Reif, John Peter 108
Reigler, Jeronimus 135
Reinders, Wiggert 45
Reinhard, Henry 100
Reinhold, John Georg 96
Reischardt, Christian 115
Reisdorf, Johan 101
Reisenberger, Lorentz 99
Reiser, John Peter 88
 Michel 110
Reisper, Casper 139
Remsen, Rem Jansen Vander
 Beeck 10
 family 3
Remmy, John 139, 140
Renare, Martin 45
Rendall, Giles 66
Rendel, John Peter 93
Reneau, Jacques 45
Rennersbacher, Christian 115
Rentel, Johan Nicol 102
Resch, Adam 114
Resler, Jacob 139
Rester, Hantil 126
Reuling, Jacob 85
Reuter, Henry 121
 Ludwig 118
 Nicol 118
Reve, Henery 148, 149
Revera, Jacob Rodrigues 135
Reyerse, Adriaen 7
Reyslar, Jacob 140
Rhinehart, Valentine 141
Rhinelander, William 138
Rhinlander, Willem 136
Rhod, Jacob 111
Rhode, Johan Juste 100
 Philip 109
Richard, Peter 92
Richardson, Joseph 81
 Tho. 148, 149
Richardt, John 90
Richarvie, Pierre 45
Richter, John Andreas 93
Rickston, Richard 81
Ridder, Barent Joosten 45
Rider, Niclas 87
Ridges, John 81
Ridout, Nicholas 69
Riedell, John George 88
 see Reidel

Riegel, Christian 118
Riegeler, Leendert 136
Riegler, Jeronimus 135
Ries, J.F. 136, 137
 Jean Frideric 136
 John 144
Riesenbucher, Mattheus 93
Riesenburn, Jacob 95
Riet, Jan 45
 John George 93
Rightmeyer, Coenradt 133
Rightmier, Johan Ludowick 126
Riker, --- 7
Ringer, John Thiel 110
Rink, Melchior 115
Rinner, Hans Henrich 90
Risler, Jacob 141
 Tunis 138
Ritman, Daniel 141
 David 140, 141
 Michael 141
Ritter, Henry 138
 Michael 138
Ritweil, Fredrick 91
 Jacob 91
Ritz, John 99
Ritzema, J. 136, 137
 James 138, 140, 141
 Joan. 136
 Johanes 141
 Johannes 135, 143
 Ruds. 142
Roach, John 70
Roan, Martin 126
Rob, Christopher 127
Roberts, John 68, 152
 Roger 81
Robinson, John 81
 William 151
Robuck, Jarvis 141
Rockefeller, Christian 137
 Christn. 137
Rockefelter, Johan Peter 126
 Johannes 126
 Peter 126
Rockeln, Elizabeth 96
Roe, --- 22
 Thomas 66
Roeger, Dietrich 109
Roelofs, Boel 45
 Matthys 45
 Sophia 45
Roelofsen, Boele 45
 Jacob 45
 Jan 45
Roemer/ Roemers/ Ramaere, Jan
 75, 76, 77
 John 117
Roeters, Susanna 127
Roethgen, Nicol 108
 Peter 109
Roge, John 133
Rohn, Johan 103
Rohrbach, Christian 84
Rokhefeller, Simon 139
 Tiels 139
Rokheffeller, Johannes Petrus
 139
 Simon 139
Rokkenfelder, Christian 137
Roll, Jost 120
Romeur, Peter 127
Romeyn, Stoffel Janse 45
Roome, John L.C. 144
Roos, Lodowick 138
Roosa, Albert Heymans 10
Roose, Lodwick 138
Roosevelt/ Rozenvelt, Claes

Martensen 10
 Jno. 134
 Klaas Martensen van 3
Ropblor, Jacob 143
Rosbach, Peter 106, 115
Rose, Anna 88
 Catherine 88
 Christoph 121
 Johan Peter 142
 John Christoph 93
Rosens, Clement 45
Rosenthal, Johan 105
Rosing, Matthas 119
Rosmanin, Catherin 112
Ross, Johannes 127
Rossel, Henry 144
Roth, Andreas 121
 John 91
 John Peter 93
Rothenbuhler, F. 139, 140
 Frederick 139
Rottenflohr, John 107
Rou, L. 134
 Lewis 133
Rougeon, Peter 140
Rous, John 150
Rouse, John 127
Rowneing, Christopher 66
Roydon, Wm. 82
Rubel, Joh. Casp. 145
Ruck, Martin 134
Rudman, William 66
Rudolf, John 96
Rudolff, John 86
Rudolph, Jno. Mattw. 141
 Joh. Matth. 138
Rudyard, Tho. 82
Ruehl, John Peter 93
Rufel, John Nicol 101
Rufenacht, Benedict 93
Rufer, Peter 109
Rufner, Thomas 107
Ruger, Frederick 141
Ruhl, Daniel 111
 Jacob 101
 John Caspar 101
Rup, George 105
 Johan 100
 Margretha 113
 Peter 116
Rupert, ---, Mr. 113
Ruperti, ---, Mr. 90, 123
 George Andrew 89
Russell, Charles 152, 153
Rutgers, --- 12
 Harmen, Capt. 3
 Hermanus 134
Rutgersen, Ryckert 45
Ruytenbeeck, Annetje 45
Ruyter, Claes Jansen 46
Ryerse/ Ryersen/ Ryerson,
 Adriaen 46
 Jan 46
Ryerse 3
Rynlander, Bernard 136

-- S --

Saar, John 118
Saboriski, Albert 46
Sadler, Thomas 82
Sahlbach, Edmund 116
Salbach, John 116
Saline, John 36
Salisbury, Richard 66
Salling, Francis 120

174

INDEX OF SHIPS